Thirteen on Form:
Conversations with Poets

THIRTEEN ON FORM:
CONVERSATIONS WITH POETS

Edited by
William Baer

Measure Press
Evansville, Indiana

Copyright © 2016 by William Baer
All Rights Reserved
Printed in the United States of America
First Edition

The text of this book is composed in Baskerville.
Composition by R.G.
Manufacturing by Ingram.

No part of this book may be used or reproduced in any manner whatsoever without the prior written permission of both the publisher and author.

Baer, William
   Thirteen on Form: Conversations with Poets / by William Baer — 1st ed.

ISBN-13: 978-1-939574-17-6
ISBN-10: 1-939574-17-X
Library of Congress Control Number: 2016946888

Measure Press
526 S. Lincoln Park Dr.
Evansville, IN 47714
http://www.measurepress.com/measure/

Acknowledgements

The author wishes to thank the editors of the publications in which these interviews and chapters have appeared, sometimes in slightly different form.

The Formalist
Measure: A Review of Formal Poetry
Writing Metrical Poetry: Contemporary Lessons for Mastering Traditional Forms (Measure Press, 2015)

CONTENTS

Preface	ix
WYATT PRUNTY	1
DANA GIOIA	29
TIMOTHY STEELE	63
RACHEL HADAS	85
BRAD LEITHAUSER	107
CHARLES MARTIN	133
R.S. GWYNN	159
FREDERICK TURNER	183
MARY JO SALTER	205
DAVID MIDDLETON	227
DICK DAVIS	251
RHINA P. ESPAILLAT	277
A.E. STALLINGS	299
Appendix I: "Pound, Flint, Imagism, and *Vers Libre*"	323
Appendix II: "The Formalist Revival"	331
Index	336

Preface

In the final two decades of the last century, a group of young poets, mostly Americans from the Baby Boom generation, initiated, rather tentatively and gradually, a formalist literary revival. Given the status quo of those times, it was no small accomplishment, and the literary revival continues to this day. The interviews in this book discuss a wide range of poetic issues with many of the most significant figures in the metrical revival.

During the final decades of the last century, free verse was the dominant poetic mode in the literary journals, the poetry societies, and the proliferating creative writing programs. In 2001, in an interview with *The Kenyon Review*, Nobelist Derek Walcott expressed his concern:

> I teach classes, and most of the young writers have never had any training in meter and have been told, horribly enough, you mustn't be too musical, rhyme is dead, etc. It is horrible that there are poets, young poets, who are taught this as almost an American law.

Walcott, a native of St. Lucia in the Caribbean, had taught for many years at both Harvard and Boston University; and, as a result, he had both an "outsider's" and an "insider's" view of the American poetry scene. In an earlier interview in *The Formalist* in 1994, Walcott had an even harsher assessment:

> In truth, all you can really do at a young age is apprentice yourself to the craft. And the total absence of that apprenticeship in this country has made most of the verse unbearable.

Given such an environment, it's easy to understand why many younger metrical poets were frustrated, and this problem was compounded by the fact that there was never really any kind of "center" for a responsive counter-movement. Years later, various

Preface

individuals would claim to have "initiated" the formalist revival; but, in truth, it began in many different places, in many different parts of the country, and among many unconnected younger poets who simply wanted to incorporate rhyme and meter into their poetry, and who believed that metrical poetry was the mainstream of a literary continuum that went back to Homer, included Dante and Shakespeare, and continued into the 20th Century with such canonical poets as Yeats, Robinson, Hardy, Auden, Larkin, Bishop, Nemerov, Wilbur, and many others.

Despite the discouraging literary biases of those times, some of the Baby Boomer formalists managed to get their first books published, including Rachel Hadas, Charles Martin, Timothy Steele, and others. Very quickly, however, they came under attack by many poets in the literary establishment; and, in response, other formalist poets such as Brad Leithauser and Dana Gioia joined in the debate. In 1985, in an article published in the *AWP Newsletter* entitled "The Yuppie Poet," Ariel Dawson dubbed the young metrical poets: "The New Formalists." Although the term was meant as a pejorative, it soon caught on and became the unofficial name of the disparate formalist movement, even though there was nothing really "new" about New Formalism, except that the poets were young and considered "outside" the poetic mainstream.

In 1989, I established a small poetry journal, *The Formalist*, as an outlet for the younger formalist poets who were still having difficulties getting published in most of the mainstream literary journals. I fully expected the journal to run for an issue or two, but things turned out quite differently, and *The Formalist* lasted fifteen years. In 1993, I began conducting interviews for the journal with the senior poets most admired by the younger formalist poets. The first poet interviewed was Richard Wilbur, and that interview was followed by conversations with Derek Walcott, Maxine Kumin, Anthony Hecht, and many others. In 2004, the University Press of Mississippi collected these earlier interviews with the senior poets into a book entitled: *Fourteen on Form: Conversations with Poets*. The present book, *Thirteen on Form: Conversations with Poets*, contains the thirteen subsequent interviews with poets of the New Formalist generation: six of which were published in *The Formalist* and seven

Preface

of which were published in *Measure: A Review of Formal Poetry*. Only three of the poets included in this collection are not members of the Baby Boom generation: Frederick Turner, who was born in 1943; the influential senior poet Rhina P. Espaillat, who'd delayed her own literary career until after she'd raised her children; and A.E. Stallings, born in 1968, a recent MacArthur fellow who seems the perfect transition into subsequent generations.

I'm very grateful to all those who've helped me with the transcriptions of these interviews, especially Rob Griffith and Paul Bone, the editors of *Measure*, who initially published seven of the interviews contained in this book. I'm also very grateful to Wyatt Prunty, Director of the Sewanee Writers' Conference, where several of these interviews took place, and, similarly, to Dana Gioia, Michael Peich, and Kim Bridgford, former Directors of the Form and Narrative Poetry Conference, where several other interviews took place.

Finally, I'd like to thank the thirteen talented, thoughtful, and always pleasant poets who contributed to this book. As I wrote at the end of the preface in my previous collection of interviews, now it's time to let these fascinating poets speak for themselves!

[Note: For readers interested in a brief history of the rise of free verse in the 20th Century and a short narrative about the formalist literary revival, the publisher is including an appendix containing two reprints from my book *Writing Metrical Poetry*: "Pound, Flint, Imagism, and *Vers Libre*" (page 323) and "The Formalist Revival" (page 331). Also, the interviews in this collection have been reprinted without alteration, and there's been, for example, no updating of the poets' biographical information.]

Wyatt Prunty

*T*he *Southern Review* has called Wyatt Prunty "one of the most gifted and technically accomplished American poets of the post-World War II generation."

Born in Humbolt, Tennessee, Wyatt Prunty was raised in Athens, Georgia, where his father was a Professor of Geography at the University of Georgia. After graduating from the University of the South in 1969, he served in the U.S. Navy as a deck and gunnery officer. He later continued his education at The Johns Hopkins University (M.A. 1973) and Louisiana State University (Ph.D. 1979). After teaching at Virginia Polytechnic Institute and The Johns Hopkins University, he returned to the University of the South in 1989 as the Carlton Professor of English and Poet-in-Residence.

He is the author of six collections of poetry, all published by The Johns Hopkins University Press, including *Run of the House* (1993), *Since the Noon Mail Stopped* (1997), and *Unarmed and Dangerous: New and Selected Poems* (2000). His poetry has appeared in *The New Yorker*, *The New Republic*, *American Scholar*, *Ploughshares*, *The Yale Review*, and many other distinguished journals. In addition, he is the author of the critical study *"Fallen from the Symboled World": Precedents for the New Formalism* (Oxford, 1990); and the editor of *Sewanee Writers on Writing* (L.S.U., 2000).

Wyatt Prunty is also the Director of the Sewanee Writers' Conference and the General Editor of the Sewanee Writers' Series, which is published by the Sewanee Writers' Conference in conjunction with The Overlook Press in New York City.

This interview was conducted at the poet's home in Sewanee, Tennessee.

Did you hear much poetry growing up in Athens, Georgia? Or in west Tennessee where you spent your summers?

WYATT PRUNTY: My grandmother in Newbern, Tennessee, was quite literary, as were her two sisters. They grew up in Trenton,

WYATT PRUNTY

Tennessee, and were first cousins to Peter Taylor's father. The Taylors were all great storytellers and lovers of literature. So pretty early on, my grandmother got me interested in a couple of poets, Jonson, and especially Sir Thomas Wyatt. So I was exposed to a certain kind of poetry which I really didn't understand very well, but which I definitely admired and *wanted* to understand.

What about music?

WYATT PRUNTY: There was lots of classical music when I was a child. My earliest memories, when I was two or three, are fooling around with my father's hi-fi when I shouldn't have been. Every night, I'd listen to Mozart and Beethoven and many others, and by the time I was thirteen, I'd gotten very interested in the guitar and folk music, and I started writing folk songs which I continued right through high school. Mostly, they were pretty conventional, written in a ballad stanza. In high school, I sang with a group of older college kids who actually went to Washington, D.C., one summer and performed at The Cellar Door and The Brickskeller. This was, of course, back in the days of Dylan and Baez, and when my friends returned from D.C. that fall, they were quite a bit more polished than I was. They'd received an offer to perform for two weeks at the Bitter End in New York City but opted to return to college. We continued to work together, however, and I enjoyed it very much.

Were you writing poetry as well?

WYATT PRUNTY: I was. I had a good friend up the street who was on the swimming team with me, and we both wrote poetry and often exchanged poems. I can still remember being very excited when Frost came to Athens when I was in the sixth grade, and our teacher took the class to hear him read. It had quite an impact on me, but the songwriting still dominated. During those years, my reading of poetry was pretty eclectic and not particularly exceptional, but I did enjoy it a whole lot. Given my interest in songwriting, I read a lot of ballads, and the songs of Shakespeare and Campion and Wyatt. By my senior year in high school, I had a pretty thick stack of poems to go along with the songs.

Then you went to the University of the South.

WYATT PRUNTY: Yes, and in my sophomore year, I took that big stack of poems to Andrew Lytle who was the Editor of *The Sewanee Review* at that time, and he said, "Well, I only look at typed manuscripts." That was something I hadn't thought about before. I'd always enjoyed writing poems in longhand, and not just my own poems. I always felt that the slow, laborious task of copying, word-by-word, what someone else had written was the best way to absorb a poem and study the craft. Anyway, Lytle finally relented and said, "Okay, I'll look at them anyway," and he was very encouraging. On occasions, his good friend Alan Tate would visit Sewanee, and he was also very encouraging. Then, during my senior year, Tate actually taught at Sewanee, so I was very fortunate to be able to work with him at such a young age. By the time I graduated, Lytle had published several of my poems in *The Sewanee Review*.

Were you still writing songs?

WYATT PRUNTY: Early in my college years, I became bored with writing songs because they seemed so limited. Also, my musical range was limited. In a song, you have to do things very quickly — you have to catch the listener right away — and there's a definite limit as to how complicated you can get in a song. On the other hand, the power of the melody and the song's potential to move listeners and make them want to hear it over and over again still held a great attraction, so I wanted my poems, like my songs, to be melodic and give pleasure to the reader. I also wanted my poetry to be understandable. Maybe not fully comprehensible on the first or second reading, but eventually, if someone stayed with the poem, I wanted it to be accessible.

Who were your favorite poets at the time?

WYATT PRUNTY: I especially loved Ransom and Robinson, but

soon there were many others. My real introduction to the great tradition of poetry came while I was a student at Sewanee in its strong English department.

After finishing your undergraduate degree, you served in the U.S. Navy as a deck and gunnery officer. Did you write much poetry in the Navy?

WYATT PRUNTY: I did. As a matter of fact, I had six poems published in *The Sewanee Review* in 1972, and five of them were written in the Navy. Of course, on ship, I never let anybody know I was writing poems because I was afraid that the captain wouldn't trust me to drive the ship on the mid-watch. Years later, my mother told me that my father had said at the time, "Well, if he's kept on writing and sending out that stuff while he's in the Navy, I guess he's really meant to be a poet."

Who was your main poetry professor at Johns Hopkins when you went there after the Navy?

WYATT PRUNTY: Eliot Coleman taught the poetry workshops. He was originally known as a sonneteer and a skilled translator, but later he wrote a book called *Mockingbirds at Fort McHenry*, which was free verse. So he eventually made the transition from formal to free verse that so many other poets at that time did as well. As for me, I'd never written anything but formal poems and folk songs; and, suddenly, at Hopkins, everyone around me was writing free verse. I was also the only one in the program who'd been in the military, who had short hair, and who had a Southern accent.

But I think Hopkins did me a lot of good, especially regarding subject matter. In the past, I'd always begun writing with the form in mind — like you'd have the melody in mind for writing a song — and then I'd put down the words to fit to the form. But at Hopkins, I started writing down whatever came to mind, and then I would round everything up and put it into an appropriate form. This opened me up quite a bit — freeing my imagination — and I feel it was very beneficial. For the first time, I started to let the subject come first and drive or "choose" the form.

Did you ever abandon the meter entirely and experiment with free verse?

WYATT PRUNTY: Not entirely, because the iambic pentameter line was so natural for me. But when I went to L.S.U. for my doctorate, Donald Stanford felt my poems had become too loose. He felt that I was varying line lengths too much within the stanzas, that I wasn't rhyming enough, and that I was exaggerating some of the liberalities that I'd admired in a number of Ransom's poems. Stanford, who was co-editing *The Southern Review* with Lewis Simpson at the time, had studied with Yvor Winters who was stricter about formal practice than Ransom. Stanford saw Winters as a rationalist and classicist who preferred a more detached mode, while Ransom, in his opinion, although also a rationalist, was a bit more local and culturally engaged, despite his irony.

Stanford also felt that Ransom was a bit too willing to accommodate variation in the metric. So he and I would debate back and forth about these things, and he never minded that I tended to take the Ransom position. He was an excellent teacher, and I was very fortunate to study under him. In time, he got me involved in *The Southern Review*, and he published me in it as well. There was also a very stimulating circle of student writers at L.S.U. at the time — like John Finlay and David Middleton and others — and I benefited greatly from knowing them. I also got to know Walker Percy who was teaching down there at the time. Percy meant a great deal to me in terms of subject.

Before your first book came out, who were your early models?

WYATT PRUNTY: Yeats, of course, and Frost and Robinson and Auden. I remember doing a long seminar paper on Auden back at Hopkins. Also, when I was still in Baltimore, I started reading Howard Nemerov. I can still remember when I first read "The Blue Swallows," and "Painting a Mountain Stream," and some of his other poems about process. He wrote so marvelously well on that subject, and I'd read enough to know that "process" philosophy was crucial to what was going on in our century, so those poems were very important to me. By the time I got down to L.S.U., I was also full of Tate and Ransom, and I loved Roethke. I'd just started reading Lowell, but I knew very little about Wilbur or Justice or Bishop or Van Duyn. And all those poets quickly became very important to me.

At L.S.U., I did my dissertation on Lowell, especially on his revisions of "The Mills of the Kavanaughs." In the revised version, Lowell eliminated all his earlier allusions to the Catholic faith that had propped up the text, leaving only the melodrama of a disintegrating marriage to hold the structure together. I was, and still am, very interested in the notion of "truth claims" in poetry — in what makes us *really* believe something. In "The Mills of the Kavanaughs," it was Lowell's neo-platonic Christian view, but when he lost his faith and re-wrote "The Mills," he lost, in my opinion, what had made the poem, as it first appeared in *The Kenyon Review*, aesthetically compelling and authoritative.

You mentioned Nemerov, and your poem "Extravagant Love" talks about the "tough" poetry of "Larkin, Nemerov, and Cunningham," and how their work:

> *Takes getting used to, three foxed S-O-B's*
> *Whose best lines run across the page like scars*
> *Carved in the tree of us healing crookedly*
> *Over the dead foliage of who we are.*

Do you feel a kinship with their kind of poetry? Or just an admiration?

WYATT PRUNTY: Definitely an admiration, and I think that relates to the question of truth claims once again. Those writers used an acid bath to distill their subjects and get down to what's essential and truthful. They wanted each of their poems to hold up in the way that Howard describes in "Lion & Honeycomb" when he says:

> Just for the sake of getting something right
> Once in a while, something that could stand
> On its own flat feet to keep out windy time . . . .

Cunningham did it with an economy of wit. Howard would shock you not only with wit, but also with harsh statements, humor, and all kinds of other things, to shake up sentiment and the reader's expectations. As for Larkin, he often seems so scathing and contemptuous, but in fact, I think he's actually quite compassionate about the people he's discussing, but he's absolutely determined not to be sentimental in any way. So they're all tough guys, and they all applied a tough, intellectual rigor to their subjects that often seems a kind of harshness towards others. But I think it was a conscious aesthetic method they used to avoid sentimentality, not an indication of disdain for their subjects.

Yes, something like "The Goose Fish" is much more than just cynical. It's real and human and sadly sympathetic as well.

WYATT PRUNTY: That's right. Howard always tries to get to the truth of things by clearing away our typical normative patterns. They all did that. As Donald Justice once said in "Nostalgia of the Lakefronts," there can be "a love that masquerades as pure technique," and I would say that that description applies to all three of those poets.

After finishing at L.S.U., you taught at Virginia Tech for a while, and then you returned to Johns Hopkins. Did you enjoy coming back to Hopkins as a professor?

WYATT PRUNTY: I did. Virginia Tech was in the process of building up a huge English department, and they'd actually brought in fifty-seven assistant professors. It was social Darwinism, and it quickly backfired, and I wasn't happy with the situation. So when John Irwin called from Hopkins, I was delighted. He said, "Would you like to come up for a year and teach as a visitor?" and I said sure. Our kids were still small at the time, so off we went. Eventually, Hopkins offered me a good raise for a second year, and after teaching at Bread Loaf that summer, we moved to Baltimore permanently, it seemed. I very much enjoyed teaching there that second year since I'd recruited the in-coming class, which had such excellent young writers as Greg Williamson, Phil Stephens, and Danny Anderson.

At the same time, I was working on *"Fallen from the Symboled*

World": *Precedents for the New Formalism*. So it was a busy year of intense and enjoyable activity, seven days a week: writing poems, working on the students' poetry, recruiting, and writing the critical book. At one point, my boy Ian said to me, "Maybe by the end of the year, you'll be able to come down out of your study and see Baltimore." Then the offer came from Sewanee.

Did you always want to get back to Tennessee?

WYATT PRUNTY: Yes, but I never thought that it would be possible because there just aren't that many positions at the University of the South. I'd liked Hopkins very much, but we've felt more settled here in Tennessee. I remember when we first moved into this house, when Ian was about three-and-a-half or four-years-old, and he said, "I have a question for you." And I said, "What is it?" So he led me into his new bedroom, and he stood in front of his bed, and he folded his arms and asked, "This is it, right?" So I said, "What do you mean, Ian?" And he said, "No more moving, right?" So I said, "Okay."

Were the Carlton Chair and the Writers' Conference part of the position right from the start?

WYATT PRUNTY: The Carlton Chair was clearly specified, and they were also talking, in somewhat vague ways, about the Tennessee Williams' money, although no one knew how much it would be, or when it was coming, or exactly what would be done with it. Then, very soon after I arrived, the endowment was set up, and we began planning the writers' conference.

Years earlier, in 1982, your first book of poetry, The Times Between, *came out, and since then you've published five more collections, including* Unarmed and Dangerous: New and Selected Poems. *I'd like to ask you about a few of the specific themes that run through your work, beginning with the notion of "balancing." Your third collection was entitled* Balance as Belief *(1989), and many of your poems have dealt with this theme, like "Balloons," "Water," "Learning the Bicycle," and others. "The Kite" ends very beautifully:*

> *This craft of putting fragile things aloft,*
> *Of letting go and holding on at once.*

WYATT PRUNTY: Well, it *is* a preoccupation of mine. It has something to do with achieving a kind of equilibrium in our lives by the careful use of opposing forces. It's also, I believe, what all successful art does with experience, giving it a sense of order. One purpose for art is to celebrate what's good, but another purpose — and the one that interested me the most back then — is that it can ferret order out of experience by using modes of thought which, if they're reliable and properly crafted, reveal something that we haven't seen before, or it can, at least, show something in a new light. The fundamental meaning of trope is to give things a "turn." A writer takes an object that we've seen many times before, and he puts it in a mode of thought, and a form, that "turns" the subject enough so that the reader can discover something new.

In my opinion, the aesthetic resilience of the poem, of the art object, is crucial to the proof that it's really reliable, and all those things have to do directly with balance. Now some people might complain that that's trying to achieve a kind of wholeness or completeness that's actually illusory or arbitrary — that doesn't really match the "real" world — but I believe that the effort to bring things into balance, however temporarily, is one of the most important ways that we encourage ourselves to keep going forward. We do it in all kinds of ways. We do it with our children, and we do it with ourselves.

Your wonderful poem "Learning the Bicycle" expresses that perfectly. A father is trying to teach his wary daughter how to ride her bike, and the poem ends with a poignant sense of balance and its repercussion:

> *. . . till distance makes her small,*
> *Smaller, beyond the place I stop and know*
> *That to teach her I had to follow*
> *And when she learned I had to let her go.*

WYATT PRUNTY: I had been a Brown Foundation Fellow — a

visiting writer, essentially — and when we returned to Virginia after the fall of 1986, my daughter Heather discovered that all her friends had learned to ride their bikes while we were gone. So I did teach Heather how to ride her bike, and it made me reflect on the whole process of teaching, especially writing. How do you teach someone to do something? Either to ride a bike or to write a poem? Teaching creative writing is not like teaching students how to understand Shakespeare, where you can explicate what the poem means. In creative writing, you simply can't guide students that directly, and you certainly can't write their poems for them. You can always warn them about all the pitfalls and dead-ends you have encountered, but eventually, they'll have to move ahead on their own momentum, and they'll have to arrive at that critical moment when they truly believe that they can do it, despite their doubts. Then they have to push ahead into the unknown with as much confidence as they can muster. Momentum helps sustain balance. So it's not only a question of properly balancing things; it's also about developing a kind of faith and confidence that lets one try.

Another aspect of your work is that nature, often in the form of the weather, is never sentimentalized in your poetry. It can be an inexorable force, as in "March" and "Reading before We Read, Horoscope and Weather"; or dangerous, as in "Falling through the Ice" and "Haying"; or even terrifying, as in "New Territory," where the narrator, seeing a group of starlings attack a wounded bird, reflects:

> *. . . till she swore*
> *She'd poison the seed then take the feeders down,*
> *As she turned a different way for home.*

WYATT PRUNTY: Years ago my mother got a small place on the PGA Golf Course in West Palm Beach to be near my older sister in the winter — so my sister could be of help if needed. One day, when my mother was out walking, she saw a bunch of blackbirds attack another bird that had something wrong with it. It's something they'll do sometimes, just a factual aspect of nature. In my generation, back in the sixties, there were a lot of people who wore earth shoes, ate granola, and said they were going to try to "get back to nature." They also blew silly smoke and felt virtuous and sensitized. But I never saw nature as being that nominative. The Latin root for the word "nature" means "to be born," and I've always witnessed nature as process. We come into this world, and we go out of this world, and it's a much more threatening environment than many of my contemporaries of the sixties were usually willing to admit, even though they felt it. So they sentimentalized the world, especially nature, and as a consequence, they refused to allow it to be what it really was.

Growing up in the South, I feel that I was very aware of the dangers of this world right from the very beginning, and I believe that my poem "A Child's Christmas in Georgia, 1953" addresses that issue. It's a world where you eat and you pray that you'll not be eaten. There's always that threat of mortality. Maybe this was especially significant to me when I started writing because, at the time, I was an agnostic without really knowing it. At L.S.U., Walker Percy had introduced me to Kierkegaard, and I was also reading Kant and Heidegger and Schopenhauer. Nowadays, I think there's something rather comic about being agnostic and not knowing it — and I say that at my own expense — but a benefit of my thinking at the time was to read nature as something quite different from the "consolation" of the Romantics or the "elevation" of Emerson and the Transcendentalists. I was in a personal debate with those attitudes, and with the attitudes of my contemporaries as well.

This ties into another important theme in your work: the sense of loss, or the possibility of loss. This is clear in many of the poems like "Husband," "Oh General, Oh Spy, Oh Bureaucrat!", "Falling through the Ice," and "A Baseball Team of Unknown Navy Pilots, Pacific Theater, 1944," which ends:

> As all we know is they returned to bases,
> Went up when told, came home or not.

Then, of course, there's also "A Child's Christmas in Georgia, 1953" where there are various deceased ancestors and missing family members who are "grieved" by the child's parents.

Wyatt Prunty

WYATT PRUNTY: Yes, I wrote that poem consciously, and maybe rather rudely, as a rejoinder to Dylan Thomas's "A Child's Christmas in Wales" which seemed to me a bit too wholesome and pleasant for a man who'd eventually drink himself to death. Thomas's memories seemed to me to have a certain unreality about them, and my own childhood memories were much more mixed, both pleasant and not so pleasant. And much of the latter, I believe, ties into my southern heritage. Even as a child I was loaded up with all the Civil War stuff. I could easily see that the world can come to a bad end if you make mistakes — like the terrible suffering that came out of the wrongness of chattel slavery, the hubris of cotton, and a regionalism mistakenly taken for nationalism.

My father was a geographer, and his specialty was the South, and the whole family was steeped in southernness. I was reading *Lee's Lieutenants* when I was ten or eleven-years-old. As a little boy, I actually played with my great-grandfather's ivory-handled Colt 32 revolver that he wore all through the Civil War. I would put on his Confederate holster and walk around with the Colt dangling from my waist. And I knew all about him and his history. How he'd left Tennessee as a young man for the California Gold Rush, taking his college tuition, got rich selling supplies, came back to college, and eventually set up warehouses in West Tennessee. Then when the war started, he was elected major, fought at Shiloh and Chattanooga and other places and ended up a full colonel under Lee's command.

At the end of the war, he was the only surviving officer among thirty-two enlisted men, which indicates the kind of carnage that took place in that war. In the meantime, the troops passing through had raided his warehouses, leaving nothing but worthless currency — chits — behind. So he had to sell all his land, everything except his home, and at the age of forty-six, he married the younger sister of his deceased first wife, and started all over again. He eventually had six sons, the youngest dying at thirteen of disease, and the two oldest brothers developing debilitating drinking problems — which was a serious weakness in the family — and one of them had a breakdown of some kind.

It sounds like Faulkner.

WYATT PRUNTY: It does, and it's all true. So a sense of history and its misfortunes were crucial to my family and my upbringing. My great-grandfather took it so seriously that he taught history to his own grandsons. They were actually taken out of school for him to teach during the normal history lesson. He wouldn't let the local teachers do it, and nobody could argue with him because of his reputation and his accomplishments. He insisted on teaching his descendants that the Civil War was a mistake, and that slavery was a mistake, and that the terrible war should be called the Civil War and not the War Between the States. Tennessee was the first state to get itself back in the Union and try to get over the thing, but they'd also provided the most soldiers — the Volunteer state — and lost the most people, and most of the Tennesseans that fought in that war had absolutely no economic investment in slavery. They were regionalists who believed they were nationals.

Anyway, as you can see, I was immersed in all this stuff when I was a boy, and you could still see the signs of Jim Crow all around you, when you would be out driving in the car with your family and see the Klan marching. So I knew very early that evil begat evil, whether it was "isms" or unnecessary wars, whether it was racism or Communism or civil war or Cold War. So I guess that's a rather overlong response to your question about loss in my poems, but it's something that I was very conscious of, even as a kid, although I don't want to make it sound like I was obsessed with the grimness of such things. But it was a reality which I was very aware of, and I still am. On the other hand, members of my family, especially my grandmother and her two sisters, the Taylors, would tell stories at dinner that left us weeping with laughter.

Since we're on the subject, how do you feel about the "burdens" of being a southern writer?

WYATT PRUNTY: I think that if you've grown up with it, then you realize that the stakes are serious. The Wyatts came very early to Jamestown — one ancestor was the first clergyman there, and his older brother was the second governor. So, in my family, there's this sense of being in the South from the very beginning and knowing that something very tragic and serious went terribly wrong. When I was a kid, I would read Peter Taylor's short stories, not only aware that he was a cousin and a good friend of my mother, but often knowing the anecdotal histories that inspired the beginning of some of the stories. I was so immersed in all this stuff that by the time I got out of the service and went to Hopkins, I was actively turning against a lot of the southern mythology. I distrusted it. Maybe I'd seen too much of the southern literary industry to fully trust it. And later, when I was at L.S.U., I saw it all over again, the good and the bad.

Fortunately, at that same time, I became very good friends with Walker Percy — a friendship that I'm sure was much more important to young me than it was to older him. And Walker was in the process of working out for himself a way to deal with the same southern "problem" of using your heritage without succumbing to it. In those days, I was pretty acidic about a lot of things, especially Vietnam, and I'd observed how language had often been manipulated to create suffering. The rhetoric of the Johnson administration, like a lot of the rhetoric about the Civil War, had been used unethically. So I believe that every writer has to deal with the realities of history; but, thanks to loss, those realities are always very much on the mind of southern writers, and the issues need to be dealt with carefully.

One way to deal with the many difficulties of the world is humor and wit, which you use in a number of your poems like "Elderly Lady Crossing on Green," "The Actuarial Wife," and "A Note of Thanks." That last poem is about a thief who steals a couple's wallet, uses their credit cards, and then writes them a postcard saying, "I thought I ought to jot a note of thanks." I would suspect that these poems, despite their underlying seriousness, are a pleasure to write.

WYATT PRUNTY: Yes, I was quite gleeful when writing "A Note of Thanks," but as you indicated, I'm also quite serious about those sorts of poems as well. Humor can be another kind of acid bath for a poem — an objectifying astringent applied to the situation described — which makes the reader more complicit in what's happening. It's a device, like melody, for example, that makes us participate more fully in the poem. Humor tends to gather people together, whereas wit is a little more isolating. But either one can serve as a test for the objectivity and truthfulness of what's being said. Humor is also a way of bringing the reader into the stance of the poem because it tends, rather quickly, to engage the reader in the poem's perspective. So, it's a very useful aesthetic device, if we can use it properly.

In general, every poem is a kind of timing device that delivers information in a certain and careful manner or pattern or rhythm or speed of development that creates recognition at a critical moment. And if that recognition comes at just the right moment, then there's an element of acceptance on the part of the reader for what's been said. This is especially true of humor in a poem, and if it's done effectively, it can clear away the reader's doubts and engage him more. So I like to try using humor to clear the ground for something more serious. Humor at the beginning of a poem can work like a cold front coming through and clearing the air — or maybe even more like an electrical storm that releases a certain amount of energy as it also creates a certain kind of openness for whatever comes next. Humor can definitely set the stage for something serious. Humor can also provide closure, if a somewhat erosive closure.

Turning to another aspect of your work, Richard Wilbur has discussed the "haunting lucidity" of your poetry; and others, like Mark Strand, have praised your effective use of "plain style." Similarly, Howard Nemerov once wrote of your work, "His diction is plain, but his thoughts are not." How do you feel about the idea of "plain style"? Are you comfortable with the term?

WYATT PRUNTY: I am, and I have an article coming out in A.W.P.'s *Writer's Chronicle* about Don Justice that claims that he's a contemporary master of the plain style. I argue that the concept of plain style is at the heart of the stylistic debate in American poetry between Dickinson/Whitman and Tate/Warren and, more recently, Wilbur/Dickey, to cite a few examples. Some poets are very elaborative in their poetic style, which operates reflexively to reveal the invigorated sensibility they bring to the world. But I feel it's generally not an accurate representation of our culture, and I find the plain style much more effective.

Wyatt Prunty

The danger with the term "plain style" is that it might imply that its practitioners — like you and Don Justice and Richard Wilbur — never use powerful rhetorical passages in their poetry. But that's clearly not the case.

WYATT PRUNTY: That's right. Some people might mistakenly assume the range is limited. But, in my opinion, the rhetorical flights have far more effectiveness when they arise out of a more understated, meditative style.

Which is like Jarrell's "law of effects" — if you have too many fireworks in the line, they'll either be missed or unappreciated.

WYATT PRUNTY: Exactly. A writer like Don Justice can be so effective when he does make a rhetorical move because his poem isn't cluttered with too many effects. So it's the mutual dependence of apparent opposites. If you don't have the tightening, if you don't rein things in, then you'll lose the effect when you open up.

This ties into a related subject regarding your own work. Walker Percy once said that in your poems "familiar things and places . . . are recovered and illuminated." Donald Justice, similarly, praises this as your "exaltations of the ordinary," and many other critics have used the word "domestic." Obviously, that's not always true in your work, but you do, very often, write about subjects that seem quite ordinary — taken from the life around us — and then find significances within them.

WYATT PRUNTY: Yes, I'm very interested in the large debates that rise out of the familiar and the ordinary, and in the end, there's nothing domestic about it. I like to think that poems become dramatizations of the weird ways that the modern mind works. I've always felt that considerations of large subjects and issues — like cruelty, and charity, and goodness, and absurdities, and incongruities, and modes of violence, and so on — are much more effective if they arise out of our own personal lives, rather than if we see them portrayed on T.V. or in the newspapers. The personal experience of these things is more profound, and it's more likely to lead to serious deliberation and action.

So I believe that the best way to enter the world of ideas is through the familiar. I have to admit, I'm very distrustful of the grand scale. As Don Justice once pointed out, the really great subject for people is the ordinary because that's where we all live, even if we do find ourselves, on occasion, within the extraordinary.

I'd like to turn now to matters of craft, and the ways that you embody the objectives you've been discussing. You've written poems in a wide variety of forms, including sonnets, blank verse, quatrains, couplets, etc. And you mentioned earlier that, while at Hopkins, you began letting the subject find the form. Is that your usual approach?

WYATT PRUNTY: It is. I generally pick up the form after the poem has begun. When I was younger, I would say, "This is going to be a sonnet," and then I'd write one, but nowadays I get an idea, and I start writing about it, and at a certain point, usually after I've written a few lines, I say to myself, this seems to want to be a sonnet, or blank verse, or whatever feels most natural. So I move into the form when I sense which form seems most appropriate to what the poem is trying to become. Form is a marvelous thing. It elevates utterance, and it's the very best way for young people to learn how to write poetry. It's absolutely essential to understand the forms that are natural to our language. Over and over, I tell my students, "You've got to understand what formal verse is before you can ever comprehend what free verse is. You have to understand what you're freeing yourself from." As Allen Tate used to point out, one of the great things about writing in forms is that it usually tells you when you're failing. It's a very natural and pedagogical thing, and it's a method and an aesthetic that the young beginning poet has to master.

I believe that it's necessary for poets to understand what's been done in the tradition. Every poet needs to fully comprehend that forms exist because they make natural use of the rhythms that characterize the language. Forms came about for very practical reasons, and they take advantage of what's already there in the language — the natural alternations of stress and non-stress, the phonetic patterns, the syntactical patterns, the rhetorical patterns, and many other things as well. Form is something that is given us by the very fundamental character of our language, and we should take advantage of it.

One of your roles as a teacher has been directing the prestigious Sewanee Writers' Conference since its inception twelve years ago. How did it come about?

WYATT PRUNTY: Tennessee Williams generously left his estate to Sewanee with a few complications involving Harvard. In the end, Harvard got his manuscripts, which seemed appropriate, and we became the administrators of the Memorial Fund named in honor of Tennessee's grandfather. All this was in the works as I was being hired, and in my first or second week here at Sewanee, I was asked to make a general proposal. I suggested three things: a writers' conference, a visiting writer's program, and a publishing series. The conference seemed the most important place to start at the time, so I was given a monetary figure and asked to submit a more specific proposal, which I did. Then they raised the money amount, asked for a more ambitious proposal, and things were quickly approved. So I went to work.

I called up a number of my friends like Tim O'Brien, Bob Stone, and Charles Martin, as well as Mona Van Duyn, Tina Howe, Don Justice, and others. And I managed to get a very fine group of writers to agree to take part that summer. The first conference was very successful, and our subsequent conferences have been equally successful. In the very beginning, there was some pressure from various people in Sewanee to keep the conference more regional, but I've always resisted that, and we've continued to seek out the best writers available from anywhere in the country.

You certainly bring in a very impressive group of writers every year, including people like Arthur Miller and Derek Walcott and Horton Foote.

WYATT PRUNTY: Well, I spend a lot of my time talking to people on the phone! All in all, I've been very happy with the conference. And now, all three of the projects I originally proposed are successfully under way.

WYATT PRUNTY

For people who might be interested in attending the conference workshops, how hard is it to get accepted?

WYATT PRUNTY: This year, we accepted, on average, about one out of every 3.5 applications, although it varies a bit by genre. We have four fiction workshops, two in poetry, and one for playwriting. The fact that it's competitive to get into those workshops indicates the high quality of our students. We've always had excellent students at the conference, and that makes it a special pleasure for the faculty.

How many applications do you get?

WYATT PRUNTY: We usually get about 1400 requests for application forms, and then receive anywhere from 30 to 40 percent of that figure in terms of completed applications. As time goes by, there's been more and more of a self-selection process. We used to get applications that were not very realistic — which really didn't stand much of a chance for acceptance. But now the quality of our applications is extremely high.

How do you decide?

We have a group of readers, and we accept people on the basis of their submitted manuscripts.

I can certainly vouch for the quality of the students, many of whom we've published in The Formalist. *Since I first came down here, in your third year, it's been amazing to see how many young people who've come through the conference have gone on to publish in prestigious journals, and in many cases, to get their books published as well.*

WYATT PRUNTY: Yes, we're very proud of that. We've never tabulated exactly how many of our students have ended up with published books, but it's quite a few, and it's very gratifying.

Running the conference seems like an exhausting task. I realize that you've had excellent help over the years from Cheri Peters, and now Phil Stephens has come on full-time, but it still must be difficult.

WYATT PRUNTY: It is, and it's certainly taken up a lot of my time, but it's always been my choice, and I've enjoyed it.

How has it affected your writing?

WYATT PRUNTY: Well, I definitely get less prose done, but I don't think it's affected the poetry that much. If I get an idea for a poem, and I'm ready to write it, I make the time and do it. I never get writer's block. If I'm not writing a poem, then I'll write an essay or a review. So I never spend any time staring at a blank page. All in all, things have worked out nicely, but I do wonder if a little more distance from the conference might be helpful. This Guggenheim year that's coming up should give me a better idea about whether I'd be better off creating a little more distance from the day-to-day activities around here for the sake of my writing. But you can't be sure. You remember the story about Howard Nemerov at Yaddo? He spent the whole first day trying to decide which desk to put his typewriter on, and then he called back home that evening, and his wife was having a bridge party, and they were all having a lot of fun, and he felt like he wasn't accomplishing anything. So he said, "The heck with this," and he went home the very next day. Sometimes our daily routines, no matter how busy they are, are conducive to productivity.

More recently, you've founded the Sewanee Writers Series in association with Overlook Books in New York, and you've published a variety of books by John Irwin, Greg Williamson, and many others. What are your goals for the series?

WYATT PRUNTY: That we publish excellent work, and that we make a serious effort to promote the book and its author. With our commercial New York publisher, and with distribution by Penguin, we've been very aggressive about advertisement and exposure for the books — and we get them more exposure than any other series that I, at least, know of. We've also been receiving excellent reviews — in all the places you'd like to be reviewed — so things have been going extremely well. Our third book, for example, *Siam* by Lily Tuck, was a Pen Faulkner finalist, and a subsequent novel, *The Aerialist* by Richard Schmitt, has sold very well, has gone into paperback, and has a movie deal floating around. We also did Horton Foote's latest play, *The Last of the Thorntons*.

With all these projects going on, I wonder what courses you generally teach at The University of the South?

WYATT PRUNTY: Everybody in the English Department at Sewanee agrees to teach at least one section of the freshman course each year — which is a course in the lyric with a focus on Shakespeare. We teach at least four of Shakespeare's plays, and then we read Herbert and Herrick and Donne and take it right up into the twentieth century. After the Shakespeare, every teacher selects whomever he wants to teach.

So Shakespeare always remains the base for the course?

WYATT PRUNTY: Yes, and as a matter of fact, Shakespeare's the base for the entire major. All Sewanee English majors are required to take a full year of Shakespeare, in addition to the freshman course. When I first came here, it had been a long time since I'd taught Freshman English, but to be perfectly honest, I love teaching Shakespeare, even though I consider myself an amateur in Renaissance literature. I also teach a course in poetry writing and another course in poetry since World War II. In that class, we read mostly Americans — Lowell, Bishop, Nemerov, Van Duyn, Wilbur, Hecht, Justice, and so on. Usually, I slip in Larkin somehow, and then we look at younger contemporary poets, and I use the work of different writers at different times.

How many students do you have in the poetry workshop?

WYATT PRUNTY: The course maxes at fifteen, but I shoot for twelve. So, generally, I'm teaching around forty-five students a year.

Wyatt Prunty

And you teach two classes in the Fall and one in the Spring?

WYATT PRUNTY: That's what I've done in the past, but I may consider doing all three in the Fall semester. Because of the conference, I spend eleven and a half months a year in Sewanee, so I may think about readjusting my schedule to allow for a little more freedom to get out of town on occasion.

Over the years, you've taught a number of students who've developed into very talented poets, like Greg Williamson, Danny Anderson, Phil Stephens, Preston Merchant, and others. How do you approach the teaching of creative writing?

WYATT PRUNTY: I teach them forms, and I make them write in forms. Then I try to teach them how to open up the trap door and let all the ghosts and goblins in. I try to get them to open up, to be spontaneous, to be more imaginative. Like in the kite poem, I try to teach them how to rein it in, while, at the same time, letting it go. I want them to use their imaginations and be inventive, and I tell them over and over, "You've got to become good liars." At the end of the semester, the students have to turn in their best eight poems, and their grade is based on the quality of their work. I also have them do what I call "the good poem/bad poem exercise" where they go out and find a poem they admire and one they think is awful — both from distinguished magazines. And then they have to explain to the class why the one is good and why the other's not. In the course of doing so, they begin to articulate an aesthetic — even though they didn't realize that they *had* an aesthetic when they began. It forces them to confront their own assumptions.

Overall, our goal at Sewanee is to give our students what is often lacking at most other schools — a historically grounded, solid major in English literature. Our students take a comprehensive exam in their senior year which covers five of the seven overall periods they've studied — like Medieval, Shakespeare, the Romantics, etc. And they're also required to explicate a poem. Can they actually read a poem and truly understand what it is? So it's a rigorous English major, which is the biggest major at the college, in the biggest department. In our creative writing courses, we try to teach, at the very least, a kind of poetic literacy which students could never comprehend if they didn't try their hands at actually making something new themselves. They can learn a great deal by seeing how a poem feels when the page is still blank.

In your critical study "Fallen from the Symboled World": Precedents for the New Formalism, *you point out that "The shift that distinguishes contemporary from Modern poetry is not an exchange of Romanticism for Realism or metaphor for metonymy but the replacement of symbol and allegory with simile-like tropes." Is that something that poets should be more aware of?*

WYATT PRUNTY: I believe we should. A poem is a mode of thought, and in the last century, the general thinking grew more and more skeptical, especially after the Nazi Holocaust, the atomic bomb, revelations about the holocausts in the Soviet Union and China, and the Vietnam War. The result, I believe, has been an abandonment of symbol for simile-like tropes. In the earlier part of the century, both Yeats and Eliot, despite World War I, could still aspire to a symbolic level of meaning in their lives and their poetry. They believed that symbols — like the gyre or the cross, for example — could serve as a link between the temporal and atemporal worlds, where symbols could indicate a relationship like the one expressed in the Lord's Prayer: "on earth as it is in heaven." They still believed that symbols could link the visible world with a world beyond — or with some kind of higher order, as did Dante, Spenser, and Bunyan before them.

But our more recent skepticism has been pretty sweeping, and it includes doubts about human rationality, history, language, meaning, and the ability of language to actually apprehend the truth. People became less and less confident about making the grand leap beyond the physical world, and poets, as a result, became more apt to simply liken one thing to another, and operate in the world of similitude. This results in a constitutive poetics where poets pick up this particular thing and then another particular thing and try to reconstruct a world. We've lost the ability that Herbert or Herrick had to make the connection between our creatureness here on earth and some higher power beyond this world, and it all stems from a deep-seated skepticism about faith and truth and reason. So since poets will not make arguments about things they don't believe are true, they've fallen back on the usefulness of simile-like figures. They liken and compare and contrast, and they avoid the symbolic and allegorical.

That's very limiting.

WYATT PRUNTY: Yes, it is. It's a loss of ambition and a consequence of our loss of faith. In his poem, "The Loon's Cry," Howard Nemerov says of himself:

> . . . For I had fallen from
> The symboled world, where I in earlier days
> Found mystery of meaning, form, and fate
> Signed on the sky, and now stood but between
> A swamp of fire and a reflecting rock.

So he's left with just the realities of his situation.

But Howard was always, rather relentlessly, aspiring after those things, even if he failed to prove them to his own satisfaction.

WYATT PRUNTY: That's right, and it's one of the peculiar ironies of our present condition that it's often only the nay-sayers like Howard who keep the symboled world alive — no matter how bleak their poetry or their conclusions might be. It's like putting a negative sign in front of a positive assertion about the higher order of things.

Yes, and Howard always leaves the door open, as well. No matter how strong his skepticism and his agnosticism, he's always striving, like Melville or Dostoyevsky.

WYATT PRUNTY: That's true. In order to fully understand Howard's work, you have to recognize that his poetry is a great seeking after a higher order, even though he could never fully believe in it. He's always in dialogue with it, and he never gives up the proposition.

WYATT PRUNTY

While most other poets simply ignore the possibility.

WYATT PRUNTY: Many seem to. As I often tell my students, poets are like the canaries that miners used to take down in the mines. If they start dropping dead, you know you're in bad air. They're barometric. They tell you about what your culture is able to believe or not believe. So when you see a whole generation of poets shying away from a certain type of poetic thinking, and employing an aesthetic that's empiricist and that avoids the symbolic, then you can assume that there's been a traumatic shock to the general psyche that's so powerful that people are reluctant to assert a connection between this world and some higher possibility. I actually think this phenomenon is a more powerful marker of the poetry of our times than the rise of freer and more "experimental" verse forms.

So what do you tell your students?

WYATT PRUNTY: I tell them to learn their craft, know the tradition, and engage themselves in the history of ideas. I encourage them to be ambitious and imaginative and confident about what poetry can do. I'd like to see them break free of the empiricist and positivist assumptions of the times and help return poetry to the grander scope and a broader aesthetic.

Let's talk a bit about the New Formalism. Do you think there's anything really "new" about it? Or is it just a somewhat misleading term for a group of contemporary poets who've chosen to write metrically in the great tradition of English-language poetry?

WYATT PRUNTY: Well, I would begin by making a distinction between the more programmatic New Formalists and people of the same generation who are not so programmatic but who also write formal poetry. I would also say that the only thing that gives any permanent life to a literary movement is the quality of the writing by the poets who are part of it. We still remember the Fugitives because the poems of Ransom and Tate and Warren hold up so well.

That's right. Even Pound said that we have to judge a movement by the quality of the work it produces.

WYATT PRUNTY: Right. So I think, as I wrote in *Fallen from the Symboled World*, that the New Formalism is a little misleading because it sometimes appeared to be acting — when the term first popped up in the late eighties — as if it had risen from nowhere, with little reference to the previous generation of Nemerov, Hecht, Wilbur, and the rest of them. The younger poets were, I think, quite understandably, trying to position themselves in contrast to the magazine world where for a while you couldn't get a formal poem published, except in *The Southern Review, The Sewanee Review, Perspective, Canto, Counter-Measures, PR Review* over in England, and a few other worthy journals.

So I think the New Formalism can be looked at as a two-tiered thing: there's the apparatus that was talking about itself as a "new" movement and writing about the "New Formalism," and there was the simple fact that many people of that generation had already been writing and publishing formal poetry for years. My own formal poems were published in the late sixties, and I was hardly alone. At L.S.U., for example, I had fellow students like John Finlay and David Middleton. At the same time, Charles Martin was writing formal poetry up in New York, and Tim Steele was out in California, and Dick Davis and others were over in England.

And there were plenty of other people who were writing formal poetry but not seeking publication yet. And they were doing so, not as part of some kind of movement, but just because they preferred writing in the tradition.

WYATT PRUNTY: That's right. There was never, in this country, a complete break from what Robinson and Frost were doing at the beginning of the century. It's just that the eventual emphasis on modernism and experimentation led to a huge wave of free verse which took over the writing programs in the universities and many of the literary magazines as well. So the leaders of the New Formalism certainly had something to complain about, and they accomplished some very good things. They clearly promoted the minority point of view, and they added to the discourse, and we've all benefited by it.

I agree. But is there anything "new" about it?

WYATT PRUNTY: Not really, except in the sense that different historical times always create a different context for the poems that are written.

Which happens in every generation.

WYATT PRUNTY: Absolutely. If you're writing a sonnet in the twenty-first century, it's obviously going to be different from an Elizabethan sonnet because the issues will have shifted, along with the vocabulary and other matters. One of the dangers of "new" movements is that they often feel they have to emphasize their uniqueness to justify themselves, but very often they're just repeating arguments that have already been made in the past.

Recently, you've received a Guggenheim Foundation Award, and you'll have a year off from your teaching duties. This must be especially gratifying given that your father, a geographer, received a Guggenheim when you were a boy.

WYATT PRUNTY: It is. My father received a grant in 1957 to study sediment patterns and land utilization, and I went on a number of field trips with him when he was doing his research. It was very special, and he accomplished some good work. I know that if he were still around, he'd be very happy, and I'm certainly very glad to get the grant. As a result of my good fortune, people keep asking me, "So where are you going on your Guggenheim?" But oddly enough, I think one of the distinguishing characteristics of my application was that I didn't propose going anywhere. My proposal was pretty much to shut the world out and work right here in Sewanee. Then, a week after I heard about the Guggenheim, I got the good word from the Rockefeller Foundation about Bellagio.

So you're going to Italy?

Wyatt Prunty

WYATT PRUNTY: Yes, it's a month-long residency, but most of next year I expect to be writing right here in Sewanee — or down at the beach in South Carolina where my family has a place. Peter Taylor would often live in three different houses in the course of a year, believing that each new place created a slightly different context from which to consider the stories he was working on. He felt that it gave him a new perspective, so I'll get a chance to see, over the next year, if some distance from Sewanee is really beneficial to my work. But I definitely won't be traveling all around the world trying to do my work. It's just not the way I do things.

Well, I hope you enjoy the break from teaching. Maybe we could finish up today, as the twilight approaches, by reading the last few lines of your lovely poem "Late Fall, Late Light" which ends:

> *While overhead the round-eyed sky*
> *That never blinks but eyes us blindly on*
> *Goes on as bluely blank as ever,*
> *Till the low sun levels through the trees,*
> *Its thousand changes burning into one.*

Thanks, Wyatt.

WYATT PRUNTY: Thank you, Bill.

Dana Gioia

Dana Gioia is a distinguished poet, critic, and literary polemicist. Robert McPhillips, in *Verse* magazine, has written that Dana Gioia "has already established himself as a poet with a permanent place in the canon of American poetry."

Born in Los Angeles, California, Dana Gioia grew up in the Hawthorne area of greater Los Angeles. After graduating from Stanford University in 1973, he received a Masters in Comparative Literature from Harvard University in 1975. He then returned to Stanford University where he completed an M.B.A at the School of Business in 1977. For the next fifteen years, he worked as a corporate executive for General Foods in White Plains, New York, where he eventually became a company Vice President. In 1992, he left his position at General Foods to work full-time as an independent writer, eventually returning to California with his family to live in Santa Rosa.

He is the author of three collections of poetry, all published by Graywolf Press: *Daily Horoscope* (1986), *The Gods of Winter* (1991), and *Interrogations at Noon* (2001). He is also the author of *Can Poetry Matter?: Essays on Poetry and American Culture* (Graywolf, 1992) and *Nosferatu: An Opera Libretto* (Graywolf, 2001). Among his various editorial projects are several popular classroom texts co-edited with X.J. Kennedy for Longman: *An Introduction to Poetry*; *An Introduction to Fiction*; and *Literature: An Introduction to Fiction, Poetry, and Drama*.

Dana Gioia is also the co-director with Michael Peich of the Exploring Form and Narrative Poetry Conference held each summer at West Chester University in West Chester, Pennsylvania.

This interview was conducted at the poet's home in Santa Rosa, California.

You grew up in a working-class family in the Hawthorne section of Los Angeles. What inspired your early interest in the arts?

DANA GIOIA: Although she'd probably deny it, my mother is

primarily responsible for getting me interested in the arts. She is a woman who harbors deep suspicions of artists and intellectuals, but my earliest memories of works of art are the poems that she used to recite to me. They weren't poems that figure prominently in today's academic canon, but they made quite an impression. Some of her favorite writers were Edgar Allan Poe, Rudyard Kipling, James Whitcomb Riley, and Eugene Field, and she knew many of their poems by heart. The poem I most closely associate with those early memories of my mother's recitations is Poe's "Annabel Lee." It took me many years to understand how much of the sadness and loss that had figured in my mother's life resonated in that poem. I believe one of the primary reasons that people need poetry is to find the words to articulate certain emotions which they are either incapable of expressing or reluctant to try.

Were there many books in the Gioia home?

DANA GIOIA: Yes, we were a working-class family, but we had an exceptional library of books and records that had once belonged to my uncle, Theodore Ortiz, a merchant marine. He was an old-style, proletariat intellectual who unfortunately died in a plane crash at the age of twenty-eight when I was six years old. He was apparently a brilliant polymath who had been a member of the Communist Party, but who had eventually left the party and converted to Catholicism. So I grew up in a house filled with books in five or six different languages, musical scores, art books, and recordings. Even though my parents took no interest in these things, they kept them out of a sense of family duty. This extraordinary library had a marked influence on my life.

Did your interest in the arts start very young?

DANA GIOIA: It did. I realized, at a very early age, that many of my interests were different from those of other boys my age. I was thrilled by music, poetry, and art in a way that wasn't typical. I did everything I could, within my limited environment, to involve myself with those things. I can still remember, quite vividly, the many complicated steps I took to attend my first symphonic concert in the company of the nuns when I was around ten or eleven. That first concert was a great experience for me, comparable to the way other boys felt about sports games and athletic achievements.

You originally went to Stanford on scholarship to study music — to be a composer — but during your sophomore year-abroad in Vienna, your interest shifted to poetry. What happened?

DANA GIOIA: In Vienna, I was studying music, German, and literature. For some reason, the intense experience of speaking a foreign language drew me, ironically, to English poetry. I started reading poems every day, and writing them constantly. I remember reading a lot of Auden and Pound that year. By the time I returned from Vienna in the spring of 1971, I knew that I wanted poetry to be my life's work.

Returning to Stanford, you became the editor of the University's literary journal, Sequoia, *which you greatly improved. What was that experience like?*

DANA GIOIA: *Sequoia* allowed me to immerse myself in the literary life. At the time, *Sequoia* was on the verge of bankruptcy, but we managed to turn it into the largest "little" magazine on the West Coast. In all honesty, I feel that I learned more about both literature and business by running *Sequoia* than I did in either my literary graduate studies or business school.

In what ways?

DANA GIOIA: Well, as you know, Bill, being a literary editor forces you to develop a strong but flexible criterion for accepting poems. It also forces you to visualize a broad view of what you'd like the journal to become — and then to do whatever it takes to create that journal. When I took over at *Sequoia*, we made lots of changes. We began doing long interviews for the first time. We also began to solicit work from a wide range of writers whom I admired, and we started doing theme issues. I'm still very proud of a special translation issue that we did which featured interviews with Robert Fitzgerald and Mary de Rachewiltz, Ezra Pound's daughter, who had translated the *Cantos* into Italian. So the challenges of creating a small journal definitely helped develop my own aesthetic, and it also deepened my knowledge about how the literary world works.

You also published a lot of formalists.

DANA GIOIA: That's true. Back in the seventies, it was almost impossible to publish formal poetry except in a few places like *The Southern Review*. But *Sequoia* was different. We published many of the writers who later became known as New Formalists at the very beginnings of their careers, people like Timothy Steele, Robert Shaw, and many others.

After finishing at Stanford, you went to graduate school at Harvard where you studied under Robert Fitzgerald in the Comparative Literature program. Could you discuss Fitzgerald's impact on your thinking and your work?

DANA GIOIA: Robert Fitzgerald was, without doubt, the single most influential poetry teacher I ever had. He was an extraordinarily charismatic man — and to know him was to love him. He was also someone with a profoundly spiritual understanding of the importance of literature, which was always in evidence when he discussed his favorite poems — Homer's *Odyssey*, Virgil's *Aeneid*, and Dante's *Inferno*. I learned a great deal from having a teacher who placed human, rather than merely intellectual demands, upon poetry.

I also took a class with Fitzgerald on the history of English versification. In addition to the readings and scansions, we had to write a poem every week in whatever form we were studying at the time — beginning with classical meters and continuing all the way through the history of English poetry. In the process of writing those poems, I truly learned metrics. Before taking the class, I thought I understood poetic form, but Fitzgerald's class greatly refined my understanding. He saved me five, maybe ten years, of mistakes. Finally, Robert Fitzgerald was Catholic, and it was, in personal terms, extremely valuable to study under a great literary intelligence who professed his Catholicism. He was the first and only openly Catholic teacher that I had in my eight years of study in college and graduate school.

How about Elizabeth Bishop? You also studied with her.

DANA GIOIA: Bishop wasn't as good a teacher as Fitzgerald, but she was a delightful person. I was very fortunate to become a good friend of hers during my last year at Harvard. After most classes, in fact, we would go off for tea together. As Bishop herself admitted, she wasn't an especially good teacher, and she didn't really like to teach. Nevertheless, she did instill in me a number of very valuable lessons.

Probably the most important thing that Bishop taught me was that the surface of the poem *is* the poem — that, in other words, to understand a poem one must begin and end by paying attention to every word, image, and detail in the text. Her deliberately literal approach came as quite a shock. Initially I thought she was rather naive as a critic, but as I continued to study with her, I realized how much more I was learning about the way a poem really operates because of her relentlessly precise examination of the surface of the poem. This was quite different from my classes in the German department, for example, where we got lost in deep speculations about the philosophical implications of a poem, or the possible meanings of its subtext.

So she emphasized the craft over the interpretation.

DANA GIOIA: Yes. Elizabeth Bishop had almost no interest in interpreting poems. What she loved was *experiencing* good poems. And I gradually came to realize the great wisdom in her approach. By the time I finished her class, I was, in some sense, a changed person, in the same way that, through Robert Fitzgerald, my understanding of the harmonics of verse had altered and expanded. Both these experiences proved decisive for me as a poet. As a matter of fact, I threw away every poem I had ever written before I studied with

Dana Gioia

Fitzgerald and Bishop.

You were very lucky. It takes most people ten or fifteen years to discover that the craft is as important as the meaning. Assuming that they ever learn it.

DANA GIOIA: We tend to intellectualize too much, out of the fear of seeming naive. So it takes us time to appreciate the basic lessons of the art form. Poetry is not a conceptual kind of language. It is a uniquely different way of knowing and speaking, which is experiential and holistic. Conceptual intelligence only gets you so far in poetry.

After your M.A. at Harvard, you returned to Stanford for an M.B.A. Naturally, this seems a bit incongruous. What was your thinking at the time?

DANA GIOIA: I went to Stanford Business School to become a poet. People find that hard to comprehend, but to me the choice was fairly clear. Harvard was the best intellectual experience of my life, and I was, in many ways, sad to leave it. But Harvard was also training me to become a literary theorist. When I first entered the discipline of comparative literature, I really didn't understand what it was all about. I thought I'd be reading great literature in the original language to develop my taste and understanding. But academia was, even back then, beginning to change into what we have today with a primarily theoretical — and therefore ideological — approach to literature.

One of my teachers at Harvard, for example, was Edward Said who was then in the vanguard of the theory school. He made us read Michel Foucault in French, and, at the time, all I could think was that I had learned French to read Flaubert and Baudelaire, not Foucault. Harvard was trying to turn me into an academic trained to speak in an elaborate and complex Mandarin code. But the more efficient I became at mastering that code, the weaker my poems became. I was also aware that I had a natural propensity for theoretical discourse. After all, I had gone to Catholic schools for twelve years, and I was trained in theology. But literary theory wasn't what I wanted. It wasn't useful for my poetry, and I decided that I had to get out of it.

So my challenge, at the time, was to find a way of making a decent living while also creating some time in which to continue my writing.

Why did you choose business rather than other possible professions?

DANA GIOIA: The most respectable choice for literature students leaving graduate school was, of course, law school. But I noticed that all my literary friends who'd gone off to law school had pretty much stopped reading. For some reason, the law seemed to occupy that portion of the brain previously inhabited by poetry and literature. On the other hand, I had never noticed any M.B.A.s whose minds were particularly cluttered with conceptual thoughts. As a matter of fact, whenever I walked by the Stanford Business School, most of the students were sitting outside on the steps drinking beer. So I said to myself, "I can do that." In retrospect, I think it was a good choice. In business school, most of the skills I learned were mathematical, logistical, and practical, and they didn't, for the most part, invade the same part of my mind inhabited by the poetry.

How did you find the time?

DANA GIOIA: I made the time. When I decided to go to business school, I made a promise to myself that I would spend three hours every day either reading or writing before I did any of my business studies. While I was in business school, I published about forty essays and reviews on writers including Nabokov, Bellow, Cavafy, Pound, Montale, Burgess, and many others. I also published a great many poems and translations.

Your earliest collections of poetry were, interestingly enough, various fine press editions by well-known printers like Kim Merker, Harry Duncan, and eventually Michael Peich. For a number of years, you actually turned down publication offers from larger publishing houses. What was your thinking at the time? Most young writers would have jumped at the chance.

DANA GIOIA: I was always very aware that a writer has only one "first" book, and I felt certain that I shouldn't rush into it.

Dana Gioia

The process of discovering one's self as a poet is not an easy one, especially in recent times when there are so many influences, styles, and aesthetics. So I made up my mind to have a good sense of who I was as a poet before I brought out my first book. It's true that I did turn down several unsolicited offers from various presses, but I felt I wasn't ready yet. I waited until 1986 when Graywolf brought out *Daily Horoscope*. In the meantime, I felt that the smaller fine press books of my work allowed me to establish some sort of literary identity without going all the way to a full first book. They struck me as a very valuable intermediate step towards full publication.

You also had a serious commitment to fine press publishing.

DANA GIOIA: Yes, and I still do. I've always loved beautiful books, and it remains a great privilege and pleasure to have someone actually design a book specifically for your own poems. I was very fortunate to have some of the most distinguished literary letter-press printers in American history — people like Harry Duncan, Kim Merker, Gabriel Rummonds, and Michael Peich — do books of my work.

After Stanford, you worked for the General Foods Corporation in White Plains, New York, for fifteen years, eventually becoming a vice president. How did you have the energy to write poetry after your long days in the business world?

DANA GIOIA: I forced myself. I would come back from working ten- or twelve-hour days, and I'd make myself something to eat, and then I'd sit down and write for about two hours every night before I went to bed. Even when I was utterly exhausted, I discovered that if I could just get started, I could get a second wind and get something done. If I were writing prose, I would simply recopy by hand the last paragraph I'd written the night before, and in the process of copying it, I'd begin to revise it and gradually re-enter the argument of the piece. Usually by the end of the paragraph, I was full of ideas again. Generally, I'd set myself very small but attainable goals — like one useable paragraph if I were writing prose, or a single good line or stanza if I were writing verse. For me, the most important thing was to just keep writing *every* night, to keep the continuity of the imaginative effort flowing.

You once told a class of my students that it was like a runner's second wind.

DANA GIOIA: That's right. When I was in college, I took a curious one-credit PE class called "Conditioning." It was the class that the athletes took in the off-season, so one quarter I'd be with the football players, and then the next quarter with the basketball players, and so on. In that class, we would do various exercises, but we always ended up running four miles. Now, even though I'd been running since high school, after about two miles, I'd start feeling sick and exhausted. Everything would ache, and I wanted to quit, but I knew that if I could get around the track one more time, do another quarter-mile, then suddenly I'd get a second wind, and then I could run forever. Later, I found that the same thing was true with the writing. No matter how exhausted I was when I'd come home from work, if I could just get through that first paragraph, then I'd get that second wind. This trick, however, led to another problem a few hours later. I would often have trouble getting to sleep because my mind was so jazzed up.

Given your later success as a poet, people tend to forget that most of your early literary work was as an editor. You continued your association with Sequoia *even after you graduated from Stanford, and you were also the editor or co-editor of your first two books: a collection of Weldon Kees's short stories, and an anthology of Italian poetry with William Jay Smith. How did these experiences prove valuable?*

DANA GIOIA: During my early years in business, I was always working on poetry, but I stopped sending it out. I wanted to figure out who I was without the external pressure of publication, so for nearly seven years I wrote privately. My public literary identity was as an editor, critic, and translator. Working in the corporate world, I was hungry for literary life. Editing had the practical advantage of allowing me to meet many writers, translators, and publishers I would not otherwise have encountered. Editing has always seemed to me one of the essential literary tasks. So much of the health and vitality of literary culture depends on the people who edit the journals, anthologies, and presses.

While you were working at General Foods, you kept your "other" life as a poet secret. Why did you do that?

DANA GIOIA: I felt that it wouldn't do me any good in the business world to be known as a poet. It might turn out to be a distraction, or a curiosity, or worse. At the same time, I really didn't feel the need for some kind of outer affirmation of my vocation as a poet. In fact, I feel that this need for external approval is a mistake that I often see in younger poets. Some of them seem to need institutional validation in order for them to write. But, of course, if you're a real writer, you'll write anyway, regardless of what anyone else thinks. I've always admired Flannery O'Connor's rejoinder when someone asked her what should be done to "encourage" young writers, and she replied, "I don't think we discourage them enough." Obscurity, suffering, loneliness, and difficulty are all nourishments for a poet. They may not be pleasant, but they are the fire in which we refine our sense of mission.

In 1984, your "cover" was blown by Esquire *magazine when you were chosen for their first registry of "Men and Women Under 40 Who are Changing the Nation." Included in that group were Steven Spielberg, Julius "Dr. J" Irving, Whoopi Goldberg, and Bill Clinton. How did this affect your working situation at General Foods? Was it as bad as you expected?*

DANA GIOIA: When *Esquire* called to say that they were planning to write an article about me, I tried to discourage them. But they made it clear that my own wishes had nothing to do with it since they intended to run the article anyway. Most people at General Foods were pretty shocked, especially my boss who was an Annapolis graduate who'd been an all-American in two sports and a commanding officer in combat. He was a big, athletic, dark-haired Irishman who chomped on cigars and looked quite a bit like the old comic book hero Sgt. Fury. So when he heard the rumor that I wrote poetry, he called me into his office, and he asked me if it was true. When I reluctantly conceded that it was, his only response was, "Shit."

How did it turn out?

DANA GIOIA: By that time, I was already recognized as a valuable senior executive at General Foods, but I have to admit that being known as a poet didn't make my life any easier.

In 1986, Graywolf published your first book-length collection, Daily Horoscope, *to a wide range of diverse commentary. You've pointed out in the past that your evolving poetic aesthetic was very much influenced, in a negative way, by the Beats and the Confessionals. Could you discuss that more specifically?*

DANA GIOIA: When people talk about literary influences, they inevitably list the writers they love and admire. The familiar argument is that one imitates the writers that one most admires, or, at least, learns from them. That is certainly true, but it's only half the story. There is also a natural impulse to be consciously different from the writers you dislike. Growing up in the sixties and seventies, I didn't care for most of the contemporary poetry I read. I thought it was dull and self-indulgent. I also felt that it lacked music. So, to a considerable degree, my gradual process of self-definition as a poet consisted of consciously rejecting the contemporary fashions in poetry and trying to discover who my own true ancestors really were. That required a lot of reading and much trial and error.

Could you be more specific?

DANA GIOIA: Well, I've come to believe that poetry casts a kind of auditory spell over the reader. It creates a kind of mild hypnotic trance, which invites the listener to pay heightened attention to the poem, and which also helps the listener access his or her own deepest memories and unconscious impulses. But most of the poems that I read or heard back in the seventies lacked any kind of verbal music. They were, in general, flat and unmemorable. I also felt that the confessional poetry of that era was long-winded and self-pitying to the extreme, and that the so-called Deep-Image poetry of the time was mostly pretentious, being either simplistically symbolic or intentionally incoherent. So it seemed that on every side — be it the New York School, Deep-Image, the Confessionals, Black Mountain, or Beat — I was being offered models for various kinds of poetry that were unable to move me in any significant way. Perhaps I'm wrong, or maybe I have a blind spot for those kinds of writing, but the fact remains that I couldn't build on sources which didn't move, fascinate, or delight me. I believe that the greatest mistake a young writer can make is to fake responses. Any work that is built on inauthentic responses will create a void in the reader. My own early work was very much a reaction to what I felt were the various failures of the contemporary poetry of those times.

Who were your most important positive influences and models?

DANA GIOIA: In high school, I discovered Eliot and Auden, and they have remained among my favorite poets. In college, I became besotted with Ezra Pound. For years I tried to educate myself according to his suggestions, and I'm still very grateful for that apprenticeship because he encouraged me to learn foreign languages and to immerse myself in the history of European poetry. But by the time I was writing the poems that were included in *Daily Horoscope*, my models had definitely shifted a bit to certain writers whom I'd read in the past but whom I now came to appreciate much more, especially Robert Frost and Wallace Stevens. Also, Weldon Kees. From the first moment I read Kees, he dazzled me. He was doing brilliantly the sort of things that I was, independently, trying to do. So Kees was, to use Baudelaire's term, *mon frère*, right from the beginning. Other poets who were especially important to me were Theodore Roethke, E.E. Cummings, Elizabeth Bishop, and Philip Larkin.

The "big" one missing there is Yeats, especially since some of the delicacy and lyricism in your own work seems reflective of his poetry.

DANA GIOIA: I have always had a complicated relationship with

Yeats. I adore his music, and I've definitely been influenced by it. Under Robert Fitzgerald, I studied Yeats's extraordinary use of tetrameter, but I've always resisted Yeats in other ways. He had a lamentable capacity for talking himself into dubious philosophical assumptions which hurt his later poetry. By contrast, Auden remains a great poet without sacrificing his intelligence. The same could be said, in different ways, for Stevens, Larkin, and Bishop.

In writing your own poetry, you always took a stand against the standard "workshop poem" of the time, once dubbed the "McPoem" by Donald Hall. Could you delineate that type of poem and its failings?

DANA GIOIA: The typical workshop poem of the 1970s and 1980s was a one-page, free verse, autobiographical poem usually about childhood or young adulthood. Those were *exactly* the kinds of poems I didn't want to write. I must admit, I was always deeply suspicious of confessional poetry. Once we start to speak of ourselves in openly autobiographical terms, we lose critical distance and objectivity about both our subject matter and our tone. These are very serious problems. As a result, I have written almost no directly autobiographical poems.

I'd like to turn now to a few themes in your work that begin in Daily Horoscope *and then continue through your subsequent collections,* The Gods of Winter *(1991) and* Interrogations at Noon *(2001). One of the most consistent motifs in your work is the persistence of loneliness — often related to lost love or a nostalgia for the past — as in such poems as "Cruising with the Beach Boys," "The Memory," "Speaking of Love," "Summer Storm," and many others. "The Corner Table," for example, ends:*

> . . . *What matters most*
> *Most often can't be said. Better to trust*
> *The forms that hold our grief. We understand*
> *This last mute touch that lingers is farewell.*

How conscious have you been of that recurring motif?

Dana Gioia

DANA GIOIA: I'm not sure a poet always has the ability to recognize such things in his own work. A poet doesn't choose his poems. At least, for me, the poems either come unbidden or not at all. I discover my own thematics just as my readers do. I'm often quite surprised, as my books are taking shape, by how thematically unified they are, which was certainly not conscious or intentional on my part.

As for the specific theme of loneliness, I suppose a lot of my poetry does deal with solitude. My life, even in childhood, was often solitary. Both of my parents worked, and I had a happy, lonely childhood. It was even true in the business days because I worked in isolation. So solitude has been my natural element from childhood. I don't think that's necessarily a bad thing. I believe that most people have a profound sense of solitude in their lives. What usually breaks that up for most people is marriage and parenthood, when we bring other lives into our own, but up until that time in my life, I think solitude was very much my medium. Even today I spend most of my days working alone. I don't think it's a negative thing, so I'd prefer the word "solitude" rather than "loneliness." Many poets whose work I greatly love — like Stevens, Frost, Cavafy, and Kees — are all great poets of solitude, each in his own way.

A number of your poems, like "Insomnia," for example, go beyond either loneliness or solitude, and fall into a kind of self-recrimination for the narrative "I." For example, in your poem "Interrogations at Noon," an uncompromising voice accuses the narrator, saying "you cultivate confusion":

> And play the minor figures in the pageant,
> Extravagant and empty, that is you.

So, in some of your work, the poetry is being used to remind us, in no uncertain terms, of our potential failings.

DANA GIOIA: That's true. I like to make poems out of unresolvable arguments, and I try to avoid going for more than eight lines in a poem without some kind of dialectical shift. As I write my poems, I think of them as a statement, countered with an argument contesting that statement, and then followed by more debate. I do that because

I think that's the way we experience life. We have a thought, an experience or an emotion, and we begin, almost immediately, to qualify or challenge it. So it seems to me that poetry should mimic that particular process of the mind and heart by which we clarify our perceptions, rather than just stating a static emotion. One problem I find with a lot of the poems is that they don't go anywhere. They offer an emotion, an intellectual state, or whatever, but they never challenge or clarify it. But as Yeats pointed out, "We make out of the quarrel with others, rhetoric, but of the quarrel with ourselves, poetry." And I absolutely agree.

I also think, in response to your question, that the kind of self-recrimination you mention has something to do with being Catholic. A Catholic is trained from an early age to undertake spiritual self-examination. We not only examine our actions, but we also question our motives for those actions. For many years, I wasn't aware just how deeply Catholic my process of thinking is, but it was formed by not just twelve years of Catholic education, but by my lifelong existence within the church.

That's exactly what I was thinking of — the examination of conscience that prepares the sinner for the sacrament of penance.

DANA GIOIA: Once again, let me go back to the poetry of the sixties and the seventies. It seemed to me that a great many male poets of that era were writing what I would call "confessional" poems that were, in some sense, sexual self-advertisements of themselves as sensitive, caring lovers. I always found that distasteful and dishonest. I strongly dislike any kind of self-congratulatory, moralizing poetry in which the author advertises his own moral perfection. Yet that type of poetry is *still* quite common. It's a kind of new didacticism with a narcissistic bent. Do I sound too grumpy?

Not at all, I couldn't agree more. Now let's talk about your narrative poetry, specifically the dramatic monologues. I'd like to ask you about your exceptional tercet poem, "Counting the Children," where the narrator, a Chinese-American accountant, sees a roomful of abandoned and/or dismembered dolls, and then later, in his sleeping daughter's bedroom, observes her dolls staring at him with "contempt." But he's still moved by their future abandonment:

> *I felt like holding them tight in my arms*
> *Promising I would never let them go,*
> *But they would trust no promises of mine.*
>
> *I feared that if I touched one, it would scream.*

What was the genesis of this poem? Where did the dolls come from?

DANA GIOIA: I remember the genesis of that particular poem very well, although it was quite complicated. The poem began after I'd visited a madwoman's museum in rural Alabama. The poet Chase Twichell took me there after I'd given a reading at the University of Alabama at Tuscaloosa. The museum consisted of a series of chicken shacks full of bizarre objects, the last one being a tiny barn full of dolls, not unlike the collection I describe in the poem. I first attempted the poem as a short lyric, but I didn't feel that it communicated the extraordinarily powerful emotions that I'd experienced in that unbelievably disturbing room full of discarded dolls.

So I rewrote the poem, adding two characters who witnessed the dolls together, thinking that this would allow me to project the appropriate emotions through their experiences. But as soon as I'd done that, I realized that in order to *really* show the impact of the dolls, I need to give one of the characters a past and a present life. So I gradually created Mr. Choi as the protagonist, who is in some ways very much like me, but in other ways, quite different. The Chinese, for example, are very much like Sicilians in their family devotion.

I did an early version of the poem which I thought was almost finished. I thought I was just a few lines from the end when I wrote the passage that is now in part three:

> I felt so helpless standing by her crib,
> Watching the quiet motions of her breath
> In half-darkness of the faint night-light.

> How delicate this vessel in our care,
> This gentle soul we summoned to the world,
> A life we treasured but could not protect.

Within a few days of writing those lines, my first son died unexpectedly at four months of sudden infant death syndrome. The almost completed version of the poem was very much about the experience of fatherhood, but now that experience had taken a terrible turn. I didn't write anything for many months, but eventually I tried to finish the narrative. Almost immediately, however, I realized that what I'd previously thought was the ending of the poem was actually only a mid-point, so I drastically revised it, creating a much more complicated narrative. The poem now consists of four parts: an experience, a nightmare, a memory, and a vision. It also has a covert three-part structure based on Dante's *Comedia*. It goes from hell through purgatory to a vision of paradise. Most of the Dantean elements emerged only after the death of my son.

Was it changed to tercets with Dante in mind?

DANA GIOIA: No, the poem was always conceived in tercets, right from the beginning, but it's about twice as long now as it would have been. The poem began before my son was born; it was seemingly finished while he was still with us; and then it was completely revised and expanded after his death.

The original "dolls" aspect of that poem leads me to my next topic regarding a selection of your poetry that I'm especially fond of: your eerie, creepy poems, like "Beware of Things in Duplicate...," "Thanks for Remembering Us," "Guide to the Other Gallery," and "Time Travel." These and many others have a definite "Twilight Zone" ambiance, as in "The Letter," where people are characterized as waiting rather desperately for a possibly misplaced letter that would set "Everything straight between us and the world," and for which we eagerly wait:

> Checking the postbox with impatient faith
> Even on days when mail is never brought.

Dana Gioia

DANA GIOIA: My favorite television show as a child was *Twilight Zone*, and I grew up reading science fiction and supernatural novels. H.P. Lovecraft was an early enthusiasm of mine, and I wrote my senior essay at Stanford on Edgar Allan Poe's short stories after having researched the whole *doppelgänger* motif through German and English language literature. I've always felt that the eerie and the supernatural are a natural subject matter for poetry, and I'm surprised that there isn't more of it.

The critical commentary on your poetry tends to avoid those poems.

DANA GIOIA: You're right. I think critics are much more comfortable talking about those poems that come out of the more mainstream literary traditions. But one of the things that I'm proudest about is the variety of my poetry, even though, for many critics, that kind of diversity raises the suspicion of inauthenticity. I believe that such thinking is yet another one of the more unfortunate legacies of confessional poetry: the notion that a writer's work is simply an extension of his or her personality and should never be allowed to wander into the realm of the imagination.

Which is very limiting.

DANA GIOIA: It definitely is. In both fiction and poetry, there are two great traditions. One is the realistic tradition, and the other is the romantic tradition, which includes supernatural literature, horror literature, and science fiction. Both realms — it seems to me — are viable products of the human imagination. I wouldn't want to participate in a literary tradition that didn't offer both.

You once said that "the task of a serious poet is to master the craft without ever losing sight of the spiritual purpose." A number of your poems, like "Prayer" and "The End of the World," clearly relate to the spiritual dimension of human existence; but, in general, how do you try to approach spiritual concerns in your poetry?

DANA GIOIA: I believe that the writer's most important spiritual obligation is to be truthful. Sometimes the truth can be difficult to determine, so the writer needs to begin by refusing to lie, since we generally know when we're not saying what we truly believe. As a result, I've always been wary of what Auden called the "resonant lie."

Another aspect of the spiritual consciousness is the understanding that much of the world that the poet describes is invisible. Certainly our emotions, our thoughts, and our dreams are quite intangible, but I also have the conviction that there is another world which coexists with ours, which is invisible, but no less real — and that there's something very significant beneath the fabric of reality. Even though I don't consider myself a devotional poet, much of my work is religious.

In 1991, your essay "Can Poetry Matter?" appeared in The Atlantic Monthly, *and it created much discussion, both positive and negative — as did your subsequent collection of essays,* Can Poetry Matter? Essays on Poetry and American Culture, *published by Graywolf the following year. At the time, you became, as April Lindner has pointed out, "something of a lightning rod for criticism against Expansive poetics," meaning a poetics more open to traditional forms and poetic narratives. How did it feel to be so controversial?*

DANA GIOIA: I've never had much desire to be famous. In fact, I prefer privacy. My ambitions have been to write as well as I possibly could and to be well-known enough to have the freedom to pursue the things that interest me. So I feel very lucky right now. As a writer I'm well-enough known that, even though I have to earn a living as a writer, I can still chose the projects which sincerely fascinate me. Years ago, after *Esquire* wrote that article about me, I suddenly became "famous" as the "business-man poet." An endless stream of articles appeared about me in newspapers, magazines, and other media, saying I was the new Wallace Stevens. And no matter how much I discouraged those articles, they continued to appear.

So when "Can Poetry Matter?" appeared in 1991 and created what proved to be somewhat of a literary event, I was not unprepared for dealing with the media, but it still quickly took on a life of its own. I was on the *Charlie Rose Show*, the B.B.C., Canadian Broadcasting, and many other places, and I must confess I didn't enjoy it very much. On the other hand, I felt an intellectual obligation to appear on those shows and talk to reporters about literary ideas that I thought were important, but it soon became an extraordinary drain on my time. The truth is, if you're picked up by the media in our society, one article generates another, and another, and another, and soon you can get lost in the "fame" game. So one of the primary reasons I moved back to California six years ago was to get away from New York where I'd become a public figure in the arts. I felt that while, in some ways, my minor celebrity was fun and useful, it was very bad for me as a writer.

Because of the time?

DANA GIOIA: Yes, because of all the time it takes, but also because once you start talking and thinking in newsbites, you begin to suffer intellectual damage. About a year and a half ago, B.B.C. wanted to do a T.V. show about me, and I turned them down. They were completely dumbfounded, but I told them I was already famous enough. It's unusual for a poet to become well-known in our society, and when it happens, it's usually for extra-literary reasons. Then the media fosters some sort of stereotype, which is always a reduced version of your real personality. I guess I'm now famous as the "bad boy" of American poetry, the maverick who challenges the establishment. Well, some of that is true, I suppose, but I don't really think that it summarizes my true identity as a writer. But fame always requires a reduction of identity.

You're always identified with the formal revival of the late eighties and early nineties, often called the New Formalism, and I'd like to ask you about that. The term, unfortunately, seems to imply that the younger poets choosing to write in forms were somehow doing something different from Donald Justice, Howard Nemerov, Anthony Hecht, Richard Wilbur, Mona Van Duyn, and the other distinguished voices of the senior generation. Now I realize that the term was used by some critics as a way to lump you and Tim Steele and others together, but I've never liked the "New" business, and I'm just curious how you feel about it.

DANA GIOIA: I've always disliked the term New Formalism, but it's the term that's been adopted by the culture, so we're stuck with it for the foreseeable future. It was coined by Ariel Dawson in an attack on young writers working in forms in the AWP newsletter in 1986. She was attacking what she called "yuppie" poets, some of whom were named, and some of whom were not. I believe she specifically had in mind Brad Leithauser, Vikram Seth, and me.

But I do disagree with you in one sense. I think there is something, if not entirely new, at least meaningfully different in the use of form by the American poets of my generation. Unlike Wilbur, Justice, or Hecht, we were raised in a literary culture which had openly and conclusively rejected rhyme and meter in poetry. While it's true that the older poets were still able to get published, one forgets now how often they were attacked back then. *American Poetry Review* regularly mocked Richard Wilbur in its early issues. We grew up in a culture where rhyme and meter were forbidden techniques, and we were met from the very beginning with bitter hostility. That was not a bad thing in some ways. While it destroyed a number of young poets, it toughened up the rest of us. It made us understand that what we were doing would come at a cost to our careers, and the situation bred a certain amount of necessary courage and passion.

In such a hostile environment we found few useful models for our own work. Consequently, we looked back two generations to several poets who were then very much out of fashion — Robert Frost, E.A. Robinson, and Robinson Jeffers. They suggested enormous imaginative possibilities not offered by the current literary scene — most notably narrative poetry. This commitment to the narrative mode, to telling stories about imagined lives rather than autobiography, is one of the things that separates our generation most clearly from both the Confessional poets and the mid-century formalists. Another significant difference between us and the generation of Wilbur, Justice, Hecht, and Hollander is our comfort with a more emotionally direct and less ironic style. That also comes from Frost and Jeffers — as well as, I think, from popular culture.

So what we did, in a sense, as all new generations of poets do, was invent our ancestors. Since there was almost no one to help us within the generation of our "fathers" — because those were the very people that were teaching the creative writing classes and editing the magazines — we went back to rediscover who our "grandparents" were, and we began re-connecting with poets like Robert Frost, E.A. Robinson, and, for the narrative, Robinson Jeffers.

One of the great curiosities of American literary history was why Robert Frost, who is arguably the greatest American poet ever, had so little influence on posterity. But Frost's broad influence became apparent for the very first time in our generation. This didn't happen by some kind of group consensus. Each of us, working independently, searched through our history and saw in Frost the unrealized potentials that we could pursue. We did what all new generations do — we reinvented the tradition.

I also think that the New Formalists are post-modernist in a way that Richard Wilbur, for example, was not. By the time the New Formalists began writing, it was clear to all of us that Modernism, whatever its literary achievements, was now a dead tradition. We began to try and find a way to balance the useful elements of Modernism with the things that had been lost, especially form and narrative. That sense of Modernism being dead doesn't exist in Justice, Wilbur, or Hecht.

Though it might seem heretical, I like to think that our example both heartened and curiously influenced some of our older heroes. Hecht, Justice, Wilbur, and others of that generation eventually started writing narrative poems again. And maybe that was because we were trying to open up the possibility. As you know, I have the most profound admiration for the mid-century generation of Formalists, whom we continually honor at West Chester, but my generation still had to make its own way in a hostile literary culture.

I wouldn't disagree with most of that, although I feel that Frost had a much greater influence than you recognize — early Lowell, Wilbur, Kumin, Hall, and even Walcott, for example. But I still don't think that your points indicate that there's anything really "new" about the formalism itself. Certainly those younger poets faced a different environment than the previous generation, but that's always the case. Coleridge's environment was different from Dryden's.

DANA GIOIA: Well, I don't like the term either, but it's there, and it's interesting to speculate why it caught on. One of the crucial things that distinguished those younger formalist writers was that they were deeply nourished by the great, dead poets, and not by the contemporary workshops of the time. They came to their various practices by returning to the great tradition, rather than by conforming to the current official culture.

One more question about the New Formalism. One of the supposedly "new" aspects of the movement was a closer relationship with the popular culture — despite the fact that the senior generation of formalists had done so in the past. Richard Wilbur, for example, wrote a very clever poem about the film version of The Prisoner of Zenda *(1937) and even mentioned the film's star, Ronald Colman, in the poem. How do you feel about that?*

DANA GIOIA: I think the New Formalists' debt to popular culture is often misunderstood. People tend to think that it means writing poems about subjects drawn from the popular culture, and there was certainly a bit of that. I've written a poem that refers to the Beach Boys, and others have written poems about pop songs and movies. But years ago, when I was trying to introduce this concept into the critical discourse, I had something very different in mind. I felt that we should learn from the forms and modes of popular culture — things like the power of narrative, the pleasures of form and genre, and the intrinsic relationship between song and lyric poetry. It seemed to me, for example, that there are ways of telling stories that the cinema has developed that are also natural to poetry. I also thought we could learn from the various ways that rock music effectively projects emotions. There is a kind of direct emotionalism exhibited throughout the popular arts that the mid-century generation of poets was deeply suspicious of, but which my generation felt was very useful in creating an expressive sort of lyric poetry. It is really the methods of popular culture that we found most useful rather than the subject matter. Of course, each of those methods would have to be properly disciplined and intensified in the appropriate ways that great poetry requires.

Isn't it true that those popular culture methods were learned from earlier literary and artistic sources? And that, for example, the western film, which learned its narrative from Homer and Shakespeare, made us long for those older methodologies once again, especially since they weren't being used in contemporary poetry?

DANA GIOIA: Yes, our generation's deep familiarity with and affection for popular culture always reminded us of the viability of traditional modes of story-telling and song-making that had existed since the origins of literature, whereas late-Modernist and contemporary poetry seemed to hold itself aloof from those things. In the end, I think that we learned as much from the movies as we did from the Modernists.

One more question about pop culture. I must admit that I'm always wary of the pop culture, since, by definition, most of it will end up forgotten and its references footnoted. On the other hand, useful references to aspects of the popular culture can be made clear in the poem, even if the reader doesn't understand the specific reference. For example, a hundred years from now the Beach Boys may be totally forgotten, but in your poem which refers to the band, it's perfectly clear that they're a singing group who once sang a song in the narrator's youth that now incites a powerful nostalgia. On the other hand, the reference to the filmmaker Cecil B. DeMille in the same poem is not clarified, and will, most likely, need an explanatory footnote in the future. In other words, it seems to me that there are two ways to use the pop culture. One is to drop it in the poem without clarification, and the other is to use it in such a way that the reader will understand the allusion even without knowing the specificity of the reference.

DANA GIOIA: I absolutely agree. I've consciously crafted the poems in my last two books to exclude almost any reference that might create difficulties fifty or a hundred years from now, unless they're clarified in the context of the poem. Poems that are laden with contemporary references will be fatally damaged in the future. Even Cecil B. DeMille, that great Hollywood director, is already becoming a footnote. There is a wonderful epigraph in a poem by Edgar Bowers that is a quote from one of his students: "Who's Apollo?" When I wrote "Cruising with the Beach Boys," I did so with the conscious intention that the reader could insert any song by any group that he or she has had a similar relationship with.

Over the last ten years, I've come to the conclusion that part of the way poetry communicates is by leaving out essential details and by inviting the reader to project appropriate ones from his own life into the poem. Those projections, in fact, are a crucial part of the experience of reading a poem.

One of the ambitious goals of Expansive poetry — and the related New Formalism — was the difficult task of attempting to reclaim poetry's "lost" audience — to try and appeal beyond the universities to a more general readership. Do you feel much progress has been made?

DANA GIOIA: I do, and I would like to emphasize the positive aspects of the situation. Although we faced an open hostility by the official literary culture and were excluded from many venues, the resurgence of form has, nevertheless, not only survived, but actually thrived. Our books get published, and many sell quite well. Form is back in many of the journals again. And most importantly, from my point of view, audiences respond positively and deeply to our work. If we're not too famous, that might be a good thing. Being well-known enough to have the freedom to continue our work is all that we should really expect. Most important, over the past twenty years some extremely fine poets have emerged who have written work that will eventually become part of the canon of American poetry.

Those were all important successes, but what about the appeal to a wider audience?

DANA GIOIA: I think that over the last ten years there has been a noticeable resurgence of interest in poetry by the general public. There are now poetry readings at bookstores, libraries, museums, everywhere. There are community-based poetry festivals all around the United States. Poems are regularly quoted in movies and on television in a way that you didn't see twenty years ago. There are many poetry radio shows. Newspapers are providing more coverage of poetry than they used to. I'm not saying that all these things qualify as a renaissance, but it's certainly a resurgence. The populist instincts of New Formalism are one of the important reasons for the revival.

Dana Gioia

Let's return to your own poetry and talk about your excellent third book, Interrogations at Noon. *In what ways do you see it as different from* Daily Horoscope *and* The Gods of Winter?

DANA GIOIA: I think that *Interrogations at Noon* is meaningfully different from my earlier books. My life has become so busy with other activities — criticism, editing, and my role as a public commentator — that it took me quite a long time to bring the new book out. The poems grew very slowly, one by one, over the last decade, and when I finally began to put them together, I noticed certain changes in my work. Firstly, the poems have gotten shorter. I've developed a passion for cutting things out. A poem, almost by definition, should leave quite a bit to the imagination of the reader. Secondly, I'm now using rhymed stanzas more than I did in the past. I want to make the poems more overtly musical and song-like. Thirdly, I've begun working in non-iambic meters much more than before. Aside from the iambs, the book has anapests, trochees, dactyls, and various kinds of stress meters. I much prefer that kind of metrical diversity. I've often felt that the New Formalism could have been called the "New Iambicism" because most of the poems were written in either iambic tetrameter or iambic pentameter. Lastly, I think my newer poems are more emotionally direct. They are, I believe, much closer to Hardy than to Stevens.

Do you set aside specific times for writing your poetry?

DANA GIOIA: I have to. I now make my living as a writer, and I publish something every week — an article, a review, editorial work, or narratives for B.B.C. broadcasts. So I have to set aside time to write my poems; otherwise, they would never get done. Since I work seven days a week, it's hard to find the time during a given week, so I try to isolate a few weeks for nothing but poetry writing. Also, when I travel, I often bring along drafts of my poems, and I work on them in the airplane and in my hotel room — where the phone isn't ringing all the time. Ironically, it's been harder for me to write poems leading a "literary" life, than it was during my "business" life. In my corporate days, my two lives were entirely separate. Now they're entirely intermingled.

How do you go about crafting your poems?

DANA GIOIA: Well, let me start by saying that I'm a slave to inspiration. Poems are "given" to writers. I actually experience inspiration as a physical sensation that I feel in particular parts of my body. I get a strange feeling in my throat and a burning across my temples. Then I know I have a poem emerging.

Will this happen anywhere? As you're walking down the street?

DANA GIOIA: Yes, and if I'm walking down the street, and I don't get to some quiet place where I can write down some notes, I'll lose it. Over the years, I've lost many poems because something has interfered. The man from Porlock follows me everywhere!

Do you carry paper in your wallet?

DANA GIOIA: Whenever I travel, I always have a pen with me and usually something to write on. Often, it's just the back of an envelope or the margins of a magazine or concert program. As I'm writing, I usually go into a kind of trance for about thirty or forty-five minutes, sometimes an hour. When I emerge, I find that I've written down some notes that wouldn't make much sense to anyone else. Sometimes, it's just some lines written in a particular rhythm. I usually don't know what my poems are *really* about until they're done.

So is the original idea usually a concept or a rhythm?

DANA GIOIA: Often, it's the first line or an image — or something that I'm certain will appear within the poem, even if I'm not sure why. Most of the poems that begin in this first flush of inspiration never go beyond that sketchy set of notes. In order for me to continue with a poem, I have to determine what its form is. If it's metered verse, I need to know what the line length is, and the stanza shape, and whether it's rhymed. Sometimes it takes a long time to determine those things. It took me about seven years to figure out the form for "The Litany" which was included in *Interrogations at Noon*. I kept going back to my notes, and I'd play with the lines again, over and over, but I couldn't find the right shape. Eventually, when I finally get the form, I can proceed with the poem.

Where do the forms come from?

DANA GIOIA: I think that a poet has to listen closely to the language, and, then, determine what shape the language suggests. Form is never imposed from outside the poem. It grows naturally out of the language that is there. Only after you've recognized the shape that the language itself suggests, can you finish the poem. This is something that opponents of form have never fully understood. They think that form is a conceptual template that is imposed on the poem. But I see form as the language itself revealing the secrets of its being.

Then what happens?

DANA GIOIA: Then I try to get what I call a "first finished" draft. I always write in long-hand with a fountain pen on lined paper in a tablet. But most of the composition is done while I'm walking around mumbling to myself. I like to compose aloud. If anybody ever saw me doing this, they'd probably think I was psychotic.

Wordsworth did that, and Yeats sometimes.

DANA GIOIA: For me, at least, the physical movement is very conducive to composition. Back when we still lived in New York, there was a long country path I'd often take, mumbling things to myself and jotting them down as I went. I might say a hundred versions of a line before I write one down. For me, it is the most natural way to write.

Are you actually composing the poem as you walk along?

DANA GIOIA: Yes, I'll often do a stanza at a time, especially when I'm working in rhyme. I feel oral composition is absolutely essential when I'm going after sound. I need to recite the lines aloud. Much of the pleasure of poetry, of course, comes from hearing it and saying it. Poetry should always consist of a language that's pleasurable to recite — to wrap your tongue and larynx around. Eventually, after a few long walks, I get back to my desk and complete the "first finished" draft — which might take twenty or thirty intermediate drafts. By this point, I have a very good sense of what the finished poem is going to be like. Only at that point do I type the poem up to see what it looks like in cold print.

Then the revision begins?

DANA GIOIA: Yes, and the poem might go through another twenty or thirty drafts, cutting lines or adding new stuff as I go, but now it's easy because I've got a real sense of what the poem is all about. Finally, when I think it's done, I put it on the computer and print it out so I can, once again, look at it freshly. By that point, I'm usually just making a few tiny corrections, but it's helpful to see it "new." I do wonder if many contemporary poets aren't shortchanging themselves by working directly on the computer. They miss the new perspectives one gets by going from handwriting to typewriting to laser-printing.

You have quite an involved writing process.

DANA GIOIA: Yes, isn't it appalling? I wish I could just sit down and write a poem. That has happened a few times in my life, but usually I work in the slow, neurotic fashion I have just described.

I'd like to shift now to the very successful Exploring Form and Narrative Poetry Conference that you and Mike Peich created in 1995. How did it come about?

DANA GIOIA: Mike and I are old, dear friends, and one night at my parents' house in Sebastopol, when we were having dinner, we noted the fact that although there were, at that time, over 2,000 writers' conferences in the United States — several of which I was involved in — there was not a single place where a young writer could go to learn the traditional craft of poetry in any systematic way. Having just finished a bottle of Pinot Noir, it occurred to us it would be a wonderful thing to start such a conference. So we did, even though we had no budget, no staff, and no other visible means of support.

We drew up what we thought would be a model curriculum — classes in meter, the sonnet, the French forms, narrative poetry, etc. — and next to each subject, we put the name of the person who we thought would be the best younger poet in the country to teach that course. We felt that it was important that these techniques be taught as living traditions by younger writers who were actively using them. We also wanted to honor our elders, and so we decided to recognize, as a keynote speaker, some writer whose work we felt confident had an enduring place in the canon of American letters. We invited Richard Wilbur to be our first keynote speaker. We had no money to pay our faculty, so I called each of them up to explain why it was important that we all do this, and everyone said "yes."

Initially, we thought that the conference would probably be a one-time event, but when it was over, nobody went home. People stuck around because they'd enjoyed themselves so much, and we realized that we should do it again. Since 1995, the conference has grown and developed. Last year, for example, we had fourteen classes ranging from blank verse to dramatic monologue. We've also started critical seminars as part of a scholarly conference that runs simultaneously with the writing conference. A few years ago, we also initiated the world's first and only prosody prize, the Robert Fitzgerald Award for a lifetime contribution to the study of versification and prosody. Next year the award will be given to Paul Fussell who will attend the conference.

For those interested in attending the conference, what are the various opportunities for poets at West Chester?

DANA GIOIA: We created the conference to provide three things for the individual poet. The first is focused, informed, and practical instruction in verse craft. The second is an intellectual forum where critics and poets can talk about subjects of mutual interest. And third, and perhaps most important, we try to create a community of poets and scholars who share certain values. Probably the most important contribution that West Chester is making to American letters is the creation and fostering of a new generation of writers committed to the importance of technique, who now realize that they have both colleagues and an audience.

I can attest to the sense of community at West Chester, and it's always beneficial to meet like-minded people.

DANA GIOIA: That's right. Very few people leave West Chester without having made new friends.

Back in 1992, when you resigned your position at General Foods, you decided to earn your living entirely as a writer. Much of your time has been spent editing textbooks for universities, especially a number of widely-used texts originally established by X.J. Kennedy. Are things going well? Or is it too absorbing?

DANA GIOIA: To be honest, if I'd wanted to be just a poet, I would have stayed in business, but I wanted to be a man-of-letters in the old-fashioned sense of the term. I wanted to continue writing poems, but I also wanted to write criticism, edit books, write for the stage, and engage in the public conversation about literature and culture. Fortunately, I've been able to do all those things. It's not easy to make a living as a literary writer in our society without institutional connections. I work seven days a week and also travel constantly on the lecture and reading circuit. I've had some good financial years and some bad ones. But I've managed to maintain my independence. I have never applied for a grant or taken a full-time university job. Over the years, I've been offered a number of academic positions, some quite distinguished and lucrative, but I feel that it's important for me to stay independent from institutional life.

One of your more interesting recent projects has been the writing of Nosferatu, *an opera libretto which was set to music by Alva Henderson. This has allowed you to combine your interests in musical composition, poetry, and performance.*

Dana Gioia

DANA GIOIA: Over the last ten years, I've written quite a bit for the stage and concert hall. I translated a Latin tragedy by Seneca that was produced in SoHo, and I've collaborated with about a dozen composers on all kinds of projects, from choral pieces to song cycles. But my most fascinating endeavor was the creation of *Nosferatu* with Alva Henderson. I wanted to write a libretto that could work both as a poetic tragedy on the page and as a musical drama on stage. I believe that the libretto is one of the great unrealized poetic genres in the English language.

If you go back a few hundred years, it was taken for granted that poets could work in a wide range of genres, from hymns to epics, from ballads to verse tragedies, from satires to lyric poetry. But when I started writing poetry in the seventies, the possibilities of contemporary verse had been pretty much limited to the lyric poem and the occasional Modernist epic. While they're both fine and fascinating forms, they didn't begin to exhaust the many possibilities of poetry. As for me personally, I'd always been drawn to verse drama. I loved the plays of W.H. Auden, T.S. Eliot, W.B. Yeats, and Christopher Fry; but, unfortunately, there no longer is a living tradition of spoken verse drama in English. The only aspect of the verse drama that's still active and open to contemporary poets is opera.

Do you plan to do more?

DANA GIOIA: Absolutely. I'm already working on a second libretto — for the composer Paul Salerni. It's a long, phantasmagoric, one-act opera titled *Tony Caruso's Final Broadcast*. It contains four levels of language — prose, doggerel, Latin and Italian, and poetry — each of which is associated with a slightly different musical world. I also expect to write another opera for Alva. He and I are currently discussing the possibility of a contemporary requiem, which is an idea that I've wanted to try for many years. I would like to write a sequence of lyric poems that replicate the spiritual and liturgical journey of the Latin requiem Mass. The idea of creating a large liturgical work that would be genuinely poetic excites me. I'm not sure if I can successfully bring it off, but I plan to try.

What other projects are you working on right now? Isn't your second collection of essays, The Barrier of a Common Language, *coming out soon?*

DANA GIOIA: Hopefully. The book's been finished for quite a while, and the University of Michigan Press is ready to publish it as soon as I write the preface. It deals with contemporary British poetry. I also have several other books coming out. One is the tenth anniversary edition of *Can Poetry Matter?*, which will include a new afterword. Another is a dual volume of twentieth century American poetry and poetics that I'm co-editing with David Mason and Meg Schoerke. The last is a comprehensive anthology of California poetry from the Gold Rush to the present that I'm doing with Chryss Yost.

Any new poems?

DANA GIOIA: I've got quite a few new poems in the draft stage, but I have to admit I don't finish most of the poems I start. I also don't publish many of the poems I finish, and I don't collect all of the poems I publish. But I'm reconciled to my paltry level of production. My ambition is simply to write as well as I can, and I intend to keep writing poetry for as long as the muse is willing.

I hope so, Dana. As we finish up today, I'd like to read the lovely ending of your poem "Do Not Expect . . ." from Daily Horoscope:

> *. . . One*
> *more summer gone,*
> *and one way or another you survive,*
> *dull or regretful, never learning that*
> *nothing is hidden in the obvious*
> *changes of the world, that even the dim*
> *reflection of the sun on tall, dry grass*
> *is more than you will ever understand.*
>
> *And only briefly then*
> *you touch, you see, you press against*
> *the surface of impenetrable things.*

Dana Gioia

Thanks, Dana.

DANA GIOIA: Thank you, Bill.

Timothy Steele

Timothy Steele has distinguished himself as both an influential poet and a literary scholar. As X.J. Kennedy has written of Steele's poetry, "Whatever he has yet to do, Steele has already left his mark."

Born and raised in Burlington, Vermont, Timothy Steele graduated from Stanford University in 1970. From 1972-73, he was the Wallace Stegner Creative Writing Fellow at Stanford, where he later served as the Jones Lecturer in Poetry from 1975-77. In 1977, he completed his Ph.D. in English at Brandeis University where he had been studying with J.V. Cunningham. After visiting appointments at U.C.L.A. and the University of California, Santa Barbara, he became a professor at California State University, Los Angeles, in 1987. The recipient of a Guggenheim Fellowship (1984), he currently lives in Los Angeles with his wife, Victoria.

He is the author of three principal collections of poetry: *Uncertainties and Rest* (L.S.U., 1979); *Sapphics Against Anger and Other Poems* (Random House, 1986); and *The Color Wheel* (Johns Hopkins, 1994). His first two collections were later combined into *Sapphics and Uncertainties: Poems, 1970-1986* (Arkansas, 1995). He is also the author of *Missing Measures: Modern Poetry and the Revolt Against Meter* (Arkansas, 1990); *The Poems of J.V. Cunningham,* editor (Ohio, 1997); and *All the Fun's in How You Say a Thing: An Explanation of Meter and Versification* (Swallow, 1999).

This interview was conducted at the poet's home in Los Angeles, California.

When you were growing up in Burlington, Vermont, your dad was a teacher. Was he an English teacher?

TIMOTHY STEELE: No, my father taught political science at the University of Vermont until he and my mother divorced when I was in junior high school. His library consisted mostly of books on politics, and it included works by political novelists and essayists such as Dos Passos, Hemingway, Steinbeck, James Baldwin, and George Orwell. When I was fourteen or fifteen, George Orwell's *Homage to Catalonia* made a great impression on me, perhaps because of the fierce clarity with which he described the tragic and messy politics of the Spanish Civil War. Both my father and my mother encouraged reading, and in terms of the poetry, it was my mother who interested me in verse. When I was a child, she read *Mother Goose* to my brother, my sister, and me. She also read Robert Louis Stevenson's *A Child's Garden of Verses* — "Winter Time" and "The Land of Counterpane" were particular favorites — and Edward Lear's "The Owl and the Pussycat," and Eugene Field's "Wynken, Blynken and Nod." The Field poem about three children sailing off to the stars had a special impact since there were three children in my family. Also, my maternal grandmother, who, prior to her marriage, had taught high school, had a library in her house on Grant Street in Burlington. It had Keats and Shelley, Longfellow and Tennyson, and some of the better known modern poets like Frost and Sandburg and Eliot and Cummings. I remember, from an early age, Tennyson's "Locksley Hall," and that famous passage that seems to foretell the coming of aviation: "For I dipt into the future, far as human eye could see, / Saw the Vision of the world, and all the wonder that would be," and so on. The content of the poem was mostly beyond me, but I was stirred by its emphatic rhythms and rhymes.

Did you have a sense of Frost living in the area?

TIMOTHY STEELE: Yes, Frost lived a good part of every year down in Ripton, and we were introduced to his poems in the latter stages of elementary school. I was immediately enchanted, as I think many of my classmates were, by the magical way he could describe the landscape that we saw around us every day.

Any poems in particular?

TIMOTHY STEELE: One was "Desert Places," which we read in sixth grade, and even though I couldn't grasp the metaphysical anxiety of the poem, I was very taken by the opening lines:

> Snow falling and night falling fast, oh, fast
> In a field I looked into going past,
> And the ground almost covered smooth with snow,
> But a few weeds and stubble showing last.

This was a perfect description of what an early evening snowfall in Vermont in early winter looks like. A second poem I remember was "The Runaway," with its wonderful characterization — "miniature thunder" — of the hooves of the snow-affrighted, galloping Morgan colt. That poem was particularly meaningful because the Morgan was the official state animal of Vermont and because I'd visited the famous Morgan farm near Middlebury and had read Marguerite Henry's children's classic, *Justin Morgan Had a Horse*. A less appealing poem — and I don't know why they would inflict this on our impressionable minds, was "Out, Out —" the one about the boy who loses his hand and life to the buzz saw. That sort of killed my interest in carpentry and wood-working. I believe it was in the fourth or fifth grade that our teacher, Frances Keyes, introduced us to "Stopping by Woods on a Snowy Evening," a little before Thanksgiving that year.

Also, the University of Vermont had an excellent Shakespeare Festival each summer. The lead roles were taken by performers from Actors Equity in New York, the supporting roles by local talent and people from the University's theater department. They did three plays each summer, and I first started going to them in the seventh grade, so I saw most of Shakespeare's major plays by the time I graduated from high school. It was a wonderful experience.

Had you started writing poetry before you went away to college?

TIMOTHY STEELE: Not in any serious or regular way, but I always liked to write. When I was nine or ten, I produced my own newspaper, modestly called *The Steele Gazette*. It carried reports and illustrations on matters like our neighbor's getting a collie and our difficulties playing baseball on the slushy playground in early spring. I sold the issues, chiefly to my grandmother, for a nickel, which was a terrific bargain, considering that I did everything by hand and covered stories the mainstream media neglected.

When it was time for college, why did you choose Stanford, which was three thousand miles from home?

TIMOTHY STEELE: Between my sophomore and junior year in high school, my mother took my brother and my sister and me on a camping trip across the country. Back in the 1930s when my mother was a young girl, my grandmother had taken her and her sister on a cross-country trip, and my mother wanted us to have a similar experience. So we went to Yellowstone, and the Grand Canyon, and eventually visited some friends of my maternal grandmother out in Glendora, near Los Angeles, then drove up to Monterey and San Francisco and started back east through Yosemite. I much enjoyed California, and I hoped to return to the state at some point. Also, a friend of my parents who taught at Middlebury College had taught at Stanford, and he encouraged me to apply. So I did, and when they offered me a scholarship, that settled it.

Yvor Winters, who'd already retired from teaching, died in 1968 while you were studying at Stanford. Did you ever meet Winters?

TIMOTHY STEELE: No, by the time I arrived at the school, he had retired and was very ill with cancer; he died in January of 1968. But in the 1970s I did get to know his wife, Janet Lewis Winters, who was a wonderful person.

It's said that Winters' influence was still very strong at Stanford while you were there. Is that true?

TIMOTHY STEELE: Yes, because of him and because of the controversy his work generated, many people at Stanford — and not just those specifically involved in the English Department — were interested in modern and contemporary verse. More particularly, there were still a number of people teaching in the English Department who had been Winters' students, graduate fellows like Anne Phillips and Eugene England, and professors like Wesley

Timothy Steele

Trimpi and Kenneth Fields.

Were you able to study with Donald Davie while you were at Stanford?

TIMOTHY STEELE: I started to take a class with Donald in the spring quarter of my senior year in 1970, but, sadly, all classes came to a sudden halt after the Kent State shootings.

When you finished your B.A. at Stanford, you went to graduate school at Brandeis. Did you go there specifically to study with J. V. Cunningham?

TIMOTHY STEELE: Yes. At that point, I wasn't sure what I wanted to do — and if I really wanted to continue on to graduate studies. But I figured that it would be a great opportunity to study with Cunningham — and it was.

What was he like as a teacher?

TIMOTHY STEELE: Formidable. If you've seen pictures of him, you know that he was tall and lean and had eyes that could open an oyster at twenty paces, to use Bertie Wooster's trope. Jim didn't waste words, and sometimes his style of teaching was almost oracular. For example, he once delivered a commentary on *Othello* that consisted of three short sentences.

> There is a history of emotions, as well as of ideas.
> Envy was once a very important emotion.
> Iago's motive was perfectly clear to Shakespeare's audience.

He unsettled some students, who in those days anticipated a more user-friendly, touchy-feely approach to the pedagogical process. Jim was definitely neither of those things — to put it mildly. On the other hand, he was much more flexible than he first appeared and had all sorts of literary interests that you might not suspect from his scholarship and poetry. Whereas his distinguished seniors like Winters and Pound had very decided opinions — neither, for example, had much use for Pope or for Augustan poetry in general — Jim always found things to enjoy throughout the entire corpus of English poetry. His early, Jesuit teachers had given him a thorough education in classical literature, and he continued to study the classics all his life. But he also appreciated and had interesting observations about such works as *Huckleberry Finn,* Harriet Beecher Stowe's *Oldtown Folks,* and the cowboy novels of Eugene Manlove Rhodes.

How do you feel he influenced you?

TIMOTHY STEELE: In marked contrast to current academic and poetical careerism, Jim felt that you shouldn't publish unless you had something significant to say and were willing to make the effort to say it well. He used to say that when you read a fine poem or essay, even if it was short, you could sense that a resistance in the material had been overcome. Much poetry today seems to be quickly and haphazardly produced and, like so many things in our disposable culture, designed to be used — or read — once and tossed aside. But Jim encouraged patience and craft. I knew him for fifteen years, and knew him much better toward the end of that period, but nowhere in any of those years would I ever have dared to dash off a few poems, send them to him in the mail, and ask, "What do you think?" He was very demanding — and self-demanding — and he made you think long and hard about your own work.

Did he direct your dissertation?

TIMOTHY STEELE: Yes. The dissertation was about the history of the detective story.

Why did you chose that particular topic?

TIMOTHY STEELE: Being so interested in poetry, I wanted to do something else for my dissertation. Growing up, I'd always loved detective stories. In high school riding on the bus to football or basketball games in Barre or St. Johnsbury or Bennington, you could while away the time by reading the adventures of Nero Wolfe and Archie Goodwin or Hercule Poirot. The historical novels of

Kenneth Roberts were great bus reading, too. Also, by the time I got to graduate school, I'd studied a lot about Renaissance and modern literature, but I was weaker in the nineteenth century. Working on detective fiction forced me to read Balzac, Dickens, Poe, Wilkie Collins, Trollope, and other writers more seriously and systematically than I would ever have done otherwise.

There's something very attractive as well about detective fiction in an ethical sense. As I mentioned in another interview recently, detective stories suggest that we're all related. In *Bleak House*, a vast gulf evidently separates Lady Dedlock from Esther and from poor Jo, the crossing sweeper. But Dickens shows us that this is an illusion. This same sense of everyone's being inter-connected and interdependent informs the hardboiled novels that Raymond Chandler and Ross MacDonald wrote about Southern California; and, to mention movie detective stories, it informs John Sayles' outstanding *Lone Star*.

After you finished course work for your doctorate at Brandeis, you received a Wallace Stegner Fellowship to study and write poetry at Stanford for a year. What was that like?

TIMOTHY STEELE: It was a wonderful year. I lived in a studio apartment in San Francisco near Buena Vista Park and wrote a good many of the poems that later appeared in *Uncertainties and Rest*.

Was there a period in your younger years when you were experimenting with free verse? Did you, for example, ever publish any free verse poems?

TIMOTHY STEELE: The first group of poems I had published in *The Southern Review* included a Williamsy descriptive poem, an autumnal poem set in Vermont. There are a couple of poems in *Sapphics Against Anger* — "Snapshots for Posterity" and "Home is Here" — that are not strictly metrical, although most of the lines have two or three beats. In addition, I wrote several poems in syllabics, including "The Messenger" and "Golden Age." So I did experiment. But it became clearer and clearer that you could do so much more with meter and rhyme. You could modulate rhythm and focus feeling more subtly and memorably. And metrical structure itself can give language a sort of resistant stability. That said, I still admire the free verse of the early masters of the medium like Stevens, Williams, and D.H. Lawrence.

As you were writing the poems that eventually became your first book, who did you feel were your most important poetic influences and models?

TIMOTHY STEELE: Of the contemporaries, I'm particularly indebted to Richard Wilbur, Philip Larkin, X.J. Kennedy, Louise Bogan, Anthony Hecht, Thom Gunn, Janet Lewis, and Edgar Bowers.

And earlier poets?

TIMOTHY STEELE: Frost and Shakespeare, as we've already discussed, and also Keats, Ben Jonson, and Sidney. In terms of the modern poets, there was E.A. Robinson, the early Stevens, and W.H. Auden. There are, of course, many "different" Audens, some of them more engaging than others. Also, one of the most stimulating books I ever read about poetry and art was Auden's *A Dyer's Hand*. I should also mention Thomas Hardy, and, given my New England background, Emily Dickinson.

Your first book, Uncertainties and Rest, *was published in 1979 by L.S.U. Press, and it must have seemed like quite an anomaly at the time. Everyone else in your generation was writing free verse, and even those who weren't were still a few years away from their first books — poets like Wyatt Prunty, Brad Leithauser, Dana Gioia, and Vikram Seth. Did you feel very isolated at the time?*

TIMOTHY STEELE: I did feel a little odd, and some of the responses to the book, even in favorable reviews, made me feel even odder. I remember that Richmond Lattimore, whose translation of the *Iliad* I much admired, reviewed my book in *The Hudson Review* and he called one of the poems "desperately and delightfully unfashionable." Naturally, I thought that it was great that he found it "delightful," but it was still unsettling to appear so "desperate"!

Timothy Steele

Were you aware that there was a group of similarly-minded formalists out there?

TIMOTHY STEELE: There were definitely some stirrings in the air, but you really couldn't put your finger on it. Here and there, you'd read a poem by Dick Davis or Robert Shaw or Charles Martin or Wyatt Prunty in the periodicals, and Marilyn Hacker had included some very effective formal poems — like her trenchant and funny villanelle called "Ruptured Friendships, *or*, the High Cost of Keys" — in her first book *Presentation Piece* which came out in 1974. So there was a vague sense that things were beginning to change a little bit, but you're right, it did seem very lonely at the time. Of course, in the older generation, even though they were a distinct minority, Wilbur and Larkin and Kennedy and Bowers and Gunn — as were, to mention a few others, Turner Cassity, Henri Coulette, Charles Gullens, W.D. Snodgrass, and Helen Pinkerton — were still writing beautiful formal poems and that gave all of us who were younger and interested in form, great hope. Even if things didn't seem particularly auspicious in our own generation, we could still feel as if we were part of something that was living and vital and vibrant.

I'd like to turn to a few of the themes in your work that are present in Uncertainties and Rest *and continue with* Sapphics Against Anger and Other Poems *(1986) and* The Color Wheel *(1994). In those books, you've published many excellent love poems which effectively show how passion can be portrayed in metrical poetry without losing the passion. Some examples are "Last Night As You Slept," "An Aubade," "Eros," and "Love Poem." That last poem, dedicated to your wife Victoria, ends:*

> Awakened to your touch and voice, I see
> That evil is the formless and unspoken,
> And that peace rests in form and nomenclature,
> Which render our two natures — formerly
> Discomfited, self-conscious — second nature.

Could you discuss this concept, which seems to be a general aesthetic in your work, that "peace rests in form"?

Timothy Steele

TIMOTHY STEELE: Like many people, I have a keen sense of how chaotic and sometimes brutally discontinuous life can be, and I think we make sense of our experience by giving it form — by turning it into a narrative or some kind of measured exploration of meaning. That's one of the primary reasons that I'm drawn to form. It's often mistakenly claimed that people who write in meter believe that the universe is a nice, neat, orderly place — and thus they write in the same manner. But the truth is the opposite. I suspect that most people who write in forms feel that the obvious disorder and chaos of the world afflict us intensely, coming at us from so many internal and external sources, and that it's necessary, as a result, to be both clear and engaged — as transparent and as pure as we can — so that we can create an environment in which the things we love and value can develop and grow.

Yes, most formal poets, like William James, sense the immediacy of the world as "a humming, buzzing confusion" which can only be ordered and civilized by forms and habits and rituals. A few of your own poems respond to that chaos with a kind of desperation, like "Baker Beach at Sunset," and some of the poems offer a kind of cautious hope, like "Learning to Skate" and "1816," but most of your poems undertake a calm, almost stoical response to the situation at hand. This is especially clear in "The Messenger," and it's most memorably expressed at the end of "Sapphics Against Anger":

> For what is, after all, the good life save that
> Conducted thoughtfully, and what is passion
> If not the holiest of powers, sustaining
>   Only if mastered.

Do you feel yourself in the tradition of Marcus Aurelius?

TIMOTHY STEELE: It's probably only common sense to be at least a little bit of a stoic, though if there's a literary influence on the element of stoicism in my own verse, it probably comes more from E.A. Robinson than from either Seneca or Aurelius. I certainly agree with the idea that if one endures something, then maybe something better will happen around the corner — "the joys will return," as

I say in another poem. And even if that doesn't happen, it's still "Better to go down dignified," to use Frost's phrase, than to scream and weep and gnash your teeth and make everything miserable for the people around you.

Your individual poems are often based on a resonating incident or observation, and very often that inciting incident comes from ordinary, everyday life: a picnic, a girl working on a jigsaw puzzle, a mockingbird, shucking corn, skipping stones, etc. Do you have any conscious creative theory about how to make such ordinary things effectively resonate?

TIMOTHY STEELE: In the immediacy of the creative process, I'm usually flying by the seat of my pants and working intuitively. But I sympathize with Wordsworth's famous preface to *The Lyrical Ballads* and his aim of treating common everyday things in such a way as to bring out — I'm paraphrasing here — their indwelling magic. Later, Coleridge explained in the *Biographia* that although he preferred subjects that were rather arcane or supernatural and tried to familiarize them, Wordsworth, in contrast, was interested in taking familiar subjects and stripping away the veil of familiarity. I've always preferred Wordsworth's approach; and, even though I'm not sure how well I succeed at it, it seems a valuable aspiration because we so often dull ourselves to our own experience, and diminish life in the process. We need to be more conscious of the good things and even the wonder that surrounds us all. We need to observe it more attentively, and resist the deadening sense of fatigue and wear and tear and defeat that are inevitably a part of our human experience.

One way that you manage to enhance the common experience in your poems is by specificity, and another way is by involving a real human presence that we care about in the "action" of the poem.

TIMOTHY STEELE: I'm always trying to write poems that humanly connect with the reader. Even before I wrote *Missing Measures*, I was very conscious of Ortega y Gasset's famous opinion that much of modern literature had been "dehumanized" — sometimes intentionally in the interests of purity, sometimes simply because the literature got derailed from our common concerns. So I definitely want to try to express a humanity in my poems — one that might connect with the concerns of the reader.

In doing so, you've written in a wide variety of poetic modes — lyrics, epigrams, poetic portraits, historical poems, light verse, literary poems, etc. What would you like to do that you haven't tried yet?

TIMOTHY STEELE: I'm interested in writing poems that are more narrative and storytelling in nature. I have a poem that recently appeared in *Poetry* that attempts to deal with certain experiences in the lives of people who, like my wife, work in the culture industry — in museums and libraries and galleries — and I'd like to do more poems like that. Also, someday, I'd like to try a long poem, even though my tastes have generally been for the shorter lyric.

Given your current narrative interests, how about dramatic monologues, which is one of the poetic modes that you've generally avoided?

TIMOTHY STEELE: Although I greatly admire Browning's dramatic monologues, and the modern monologues of Robinson and Frost and the early Eliot, I've never found myself drawn to that mode. I do, however, plan to write more blank verse in the future. That's an area I'd like to develop.

Over the years, you've also written in an impressive variety of poetic forms — sapphics, couplets, sonnets, quatrains, etc. Do you have a favorite?

TIMOTHY STEELE: Not an absolute favorite, but I love the heroic couplet. It's a wonderful form with its adjacent rhymes and its pentameter lines. It allows the writer to carefully guide his meaning, and yet there's little temptation, as there is with stanzaic verse, to either clip things short or stretch things out to pad out the form — as Ben Jonson once pointed out to Drummond. With the heroic couplet, you can go on for as long as you like, and you can stop whenever you wish. But all the forms are fun. Back in the seventies, under the influence of Hardy and Herbert, I was fascinated with the idea of "inventing" new stanzas, and even though not all of the poems written from this impulse were successful, it was a pleasure to experiment with the different possibilities.

In 1990, you published your critical study Missing Measures: Modern Poetry and the Revolt Against Meter, *which is, in my opinion, one of the most important literary studies of the past fifty years. In the book you discussed how the Modernist movement, under a variety of influences, abandoned meter but then found itself unable to offer anything substantial in its place.*

TIMOTHY STEELE: Yes, one of the saddest ironies of the free verse movement is that its originators, who were initially trying to make poetry more challenging and difficult, eventually ended up like figures in a Sophoclean tragedy because their innovations produced results that were exactly the opposite of what they'd intended. Eventually, all of them admitted this fact — Pound, Eliot, and Williams.

Even before Pound and Eliot agreed to return to "Rhyme and regular strophes" in 1920, Pound knew that he'd opened up Pandora's box. But, eventually, after "Mauberley," he fell back into it again.

TIMOTHY STEELE: That's right, and I've always believed that the publication of *The Waste Land* in 1922 was the crucial moment because Eliot adopted Pound's "corrected" version of the poem rather than his original version which was much more Joycean — using various voices — and much more coherent.

The Pound version, as we can see in the Quinn manuscript, was much more fragmentary.

TIMOTHY STEELE: Yes, the Pound version was essentially incomplete, both thematically and metrically. Cunningham once called it "the edited remains of a nervous breakdown." As you know, not only were significant metrical passages in the poem entirely deleted, but in many places Pound would simply edit lines of regular pentameter by crossing out parts of a line here, or a foot over there, apparently assuming that Eliot would eventually emend the crossed-out sections. But given Eliot's mental state at that time, he apparently didn't feel capable of going back to the poem and figuring out appropriate alternatives or sutures for Pound's deletions. So the poem was printed as Pound had cut it — Eliot and Vivien made a few alterations, too — and its impact was enormous, turning things back in the direction of experimentation and fragmentation.

And this was particularly appealing, as Robert Conquest and others have pointed out, to younger professors and poets who wanted to appear fashionable.

TIMOTHY STEELE: Exactly. Pound, as you know, was an increasingly unstable and tormented man, and his instability was responsible for many of his problems. When he moved to Paris, and later when he went down to Italy, he became unhealthily isolated. He no longer had concerned people around him — like Ford Maddox Ford and Yeats and Eliot — who'd always admired his good qualities and been a moderating influence on his irrationalities and managed to keep him sane by providing a sense of community.

Pound's comments in his final years about his own poetry are particularly devastating, especially since they're so obviously sincere.

TIMOTHY STEELE: Yes, I've been told about that by several people who knew Pound, including John Espey, who wrote that wonderful book about "Mauberley." Espey, of course, visited Pound frequently at St. Elizabeth's and corresponded with him after he returned to Italy. He said that Pound was often absolutely despairing, believing that he'd made a complete "botch" of everything in his life, including poetry.

What about the subsequent and much abused notion of "organic form"? When did people begin to misinterpret the concept?

TIMOTHY STEELE: Though the idea of organic form goes back to Aristotle, it became a central tenet of poetics with the Romantics. They compared poems to plant and animal life, but like Aristotle they recognized that the natural world around us was ordered by very clear patterns. They noticed, for example, that flowers tend to take recurrent shapes, and that specific trees, like oak trees, all resemble each other. These things were not only beautiful and individual, but also their individual beauty was dependent on recurrent characteristics and was related to their cyclic and repetitive nature. Now, as I tried to explain in *Missing Measures*, various people in the modern movement took the idea of "organic form" and, in some cases appropriating ideas from the life sciences, shifted the focus from the natural but orderly object — the flower or tree — to the internal process that determined the object. And the internal process was often construed as operating dynamically and obscurely, that is, remote from easy observation. And once you get this new model of organicism in place, you find poets like D.H. Lawrence wondering if poems can be created like jets of ectoplasm or firing synapses. Or you get Mount St. Helens poetry — great emotional explosions, with ash and lava everywhere and terrified readers running for cover.

In 1999, you published a delightful introduction to meter called All the Fun's in How You Say a Thing: An Explanation of Meter and Versification. *In general, you encourage a quite strict metrical practice, condoning certain traditional substitutions at certain specific places in the iambic line. But you're generally wary of anapestic substitutions despite their rather common usage. Could you comment on that?*

TIMOTHY STEELE: There's certainly been a lot of beautiful verse written in what Frost called "loose iambic," but my feeling about anapestic substitution is that while it can produce some very nice effects in the shorter lines — tetrameters, trimeters, and dimeters — it gets a little dicey when poets start introducing anapests into the pentameter line, which is already very flexible to begin with. Even so, Frost himself uses anapests very effectively in some of his pentameter poems like "Mowing," "Willful Homing," and "On Looking Up by Chance at the Constellations." So I realize that other people feel differently about the subject than I do, and can point to excellent examples to support their position.

TIMOTHY STEELE

I'd also like to ask you about poetic diction, a subject not often discussed. How does the formal poet avoid stilted diction? And are there, in your opinion, times when it's acceptable in contemporary verse?

TIMOTHY STEELE: The poet learns these things by practice and wariness, and you can't be dogmatic about them. One of my favorite poems is Milton's *Paradise Lost*. So even though I'm certainly a child of my time in trying to make my own verse idiomatically natural, I still cringe whenever I see inversions condemned out of hand — just as I often cringe when I hear people insist that we should only write about contemporary subjects, and that it's a dodge to write about myth or history. It's wise not to be overly dependent on such things, but it's possible to become too narrow and limiting. So every time I find myself reading a contemporary poem and noticing that the syntax has been wrenched a bit for the sake of the rhyme or the meter, there's always a little voice that pops up inside of me saying, "Not so fast, Tim. Think of John Milton." And I do, and retire in critical shame.

But how about diction? And the formalist tendency to elevated language?

TIMOTHY STEELE: I think it's quite similar. You're not going to find much free verse written in Elizabethan English, but formalists, given their love for Sidney, and Spenser, and Shakespeare, and so forth, are much more likely to be lured into antiquated habits of phrasing. It's very hard, when we write a sonnet, not to hear Sidney and Shakespeare somewhere in the back of our minds. So we have to be wary. At the same time, however, the notion of "real" or "natural" speech is terribly slippery. Latinate syntax was probably very natural to Milton. The discreetly elevated diction of "Sunday Morning" and "Le Monocle de Mon Oncle" was wonderfully real to Stevens. And it would be nuts to criticize them because they failed to speak the idiom of couch potatoes addicted to Reality T.V.

When you're writing your poems, do you tend to work at specific times?

TIMOTHY STEELE: Whenever I can find the time, usually in the summers, I prefer to write poetry in the early morning, from sunup until ten or eleven. When faced with a large project like *All the Fun's in How You Say a Thing*, I forced myself, for about two full years, to work between the hours of 3:00 a.m. and 7:00 a.m. every morning.

So you were setting the alarm and losing sleep?

TIMOTHY STEELE: Yes, it was quite difficult, but I trained myself to do it. Sometimes it felt like writing that book was less an exercise in literary criticism than an experiment in sleep deprivation. But that's a rare and extreme case; mostly I write early in the mornings on the weekdays in the summer.

Do you compose in your head?

TIMOTHY STEELE: Some of my epigrams and shorter poems have been composed mentally, and sometimes I rough out various poems in my head. But most of the time, I begin with a couple of phrases or feelings in my mind — or a very general sense of a subject — and then I sit down and write in my composition notebooks. Eventually, when I get a stanza or a passage sufficiently developed, I go to the computer.

How do you find your forms?

TIMOTHY STEELE: It's very much by trial and error. I never sit down and say to myself that I'm going to write in a specific form today, like a sonnet, for example. When I began writing "The Skimming Stone" about a high school friend, I expected that it would be a much longer poem than it ended up. Originally, I intended to use numerous narrative elements about working in the factory on the Winooski River, arriving in the morning, working in the shop with my old friend Billy Knight, taking a coffee break, having lunch, and so on. But I kept coming back to skimming stones on the lunch break, and that seemed to be the heart of the poem. Eventually, I realized it would work as a sonnet. Another example would be my little poem "Janet," about going swimming with another friend from

Burlington when we were in junior high school. Originally, I wrote that poem in pentameter, but it seemed lifeless and dead. It had no "charge" to it, no impetus, no bite. So I finally decided to shorten the lines, and it worked out much better.

Do you revise heavily?

TIMOTHY STEELE: It depends on the poem. Usually when I've done enough pre-thinking and pre-writing, the poem will come relatively quickly, and I'll often leave it as it is.

Do you have many false starts?

TIMOTHY STEELE: I have many false starts! I'm sufficiently persuaded of my own ineptitudes to know that even if I have a very good subject, I can still find innumerable ways of botching it up before I get it right. In some cases, after numerous false starts, I'll give up on the poem for the time being, and then come back to it, maybe two or three years later, and make a fresh start, and then fail all over again. Sometimes, I feel like William Butler Yeats, repeatedly proposing to Maud Gonne and repeatedly being told to take a hike. But, fortunately, the Muse occasionally allows a marriage of intention and execution.

In All the Fun's, *you're wary of poets using rhyming dictionaries, but you also discuss the effectiveness of "surprising" rhymes. Aren't rhyming dictionaries good places to help young poets find the unexpected rhymes they might miss?*

TIMOTHY STEELE: Maybe so, and I suppose it depends on the poet, but if I'm stumped for a rhyme, I've always found it a better policy just to work the rhyme sound through the alphabet. That way I'm more attentive, I feel, to each possible rhyme. Even though it's a mechanical process, you're sort of discovering each rhyme and weighing it in the context of your emerging poem, which is something a rhyming dictionary can't do.

You've been teaching for nearly three decades; and, since 1986, you've been teaching at California State University, Los Angeles. How do you go about instructing young poets who, in most cases, know nothing about meter and often tend to rebel against its strictures? What's your approach to this common situation?

TIMOTHY STEELE: Most of my classes at Cal State are survey, general ed, and genre courses. I do teach creative writing, usually one class a year, and I also teach modern poetry from Hardy to W.H. Auden. In both of those classes, I teach the students about meter. We listen to tapes of Frost and Yeats and others reciting their work, and we do various scansion exercises so they can start to understand what poets are doing. In the creative writing classes, I try to convince my students that even if they want to write free verse, they should know about meter, and that it will help develop their ear for all kinds of writing. In the literature courses, I try to stress the fact that learning something about metrical structure will enable them to more fully and richly appreciate every major poet from Chaucer to Wilbur. I also try to explain to the writing students that meter, rhyme, and stanza can be instruments of discovery and that working with them can enlarge you as a writer and a person. It encourages you to look at words — and ultimately at ideas and experiences — from all sorts of angles and perspectives that you probably wouldn't have if you were just freely recording thoughts and feelings as they come to you.

Unfortunately, most literature courses only focus on meaning and thus deprive the student of fully understanding what the poem is actually doing.

TIMOTHY STEELE: That's right, and so much of the feeling in a sonnet by Shakespeare or Keats or a passage from *Paradise Lost* is inextricably connected with the metrical structure. Most of my students at Cal State have been pretty good-natured about learning metrics, and more than a few have been kind enough to say later that learning meter enriched their appreciation of the poetry they read in their other classes.

In Missing Measures, *you said that "versification, as it has been understood for millennia, is for the majority of contemporary poets an irrelevant matter." Do you think much progress has been made since you published that book in 1990?*

Timothy Steele

TIMOTHY STEELE: Things have changed. While there's still a great deal of suspicion and even hostility in the general literary community towards meter and traditional versification, at least people are talking about it now, and that certainly wasn't the case fifteen or twenty years ago. The very fact that certain people who don't approve of meter and traditional versification are actually writing essays against it — and complaining about its revival — is indicative of the change. A more positive aspect of the present situation is the emergence of a number of good, young, metrical poets, along with a real sense of community among those younger writers.

Your poetry and your scholarly work have had an enormous influence on the poets of the formalist revival. What do you find most gratifying about the contemporary scene?

TIMOTHY STEELE: I'm especially delighted that people who were formerly so isolated now have places where they can get together, like the Sewanee Writers' Conference which Wyatt directs, and the West Chester Conference run by Mike Peich and Dana. Also, the emergence of the younger generation has been very cheering. Richmond Lattimore's comment, which I mentioned earlier, that there seemed to be something "desperate" about what I was doing back in 1979, did make me wonder if I'd end up being comparable — if anybody cared — to the last surviving member of the Bull Moose Party, or something like that. But now there's been a true revival, not only among writers of my generation, but also in the younger generation, and that sense of continuity is marvelous.

What do you find most disconcerting?

TIMOTHY STEELE: Naturally, I'd like to hope that the revival of traditional versification will eventually be integrated back into the mainstream of American verse; and, I suppose, that's happened to some extent. But there's no doubt that it's still regarded with suspicion, and as something very much "on the outside" of things, by many poets and critics in the universities and the creative writing programs.

Do you think it's feasible that traditional verse could ever be brought back into mainstream academia?

TIMOTHY STEELE: I think so, and I hope so, but of course academia — or English Studies — has always favored experimental modernism. From the time when I.A. Richards and others established English as a university discipline, writers like Eliot and Joyce have been favored and writers like Robinson and Frank O'Connor haven't. Also, as you know, there were several waves of free verse poetry, and the wave that made free verse endemic in American literary culture occurred in the late fifties and early sixties. Unfortunately, that wave coincided with the sudden expansion of the creative writing programs, which brought poets into the universities in a way that had never occurred in previous generations. So the apparatus of academia — one part of it at least — became inextricably involved with free verse poets. Now I'm not suggesting that there's some vast conspiracy going on, but there are powerful cartels that have a natural, vested interest in ignoring or squelching the metrical revival. Free verse as "official" art is arguably more entrenched than any official poetic art of the past. It's a worrisome situation, and we can only hope that, to use William James's term, we'll be able to live with a "healthy pluralism," and that at least there'll be opportunities for all kinds of voices to be heard in American poetry, including the metrical voice.

Let's hope so, Tim. Are you almost ready for a new collection of poetry?

TIMOTHY STEELE: I'm about two-thirds of the way into my next book, and I'm hoping to finish it this summer. I love writing verse, and even though I was happy to work on *Missing Measures* and *All the Fun's*, I would definitely prefer, at least for the next few years, to devote whatever free time I have to writing verse.

So you'll be taking a hiatus from the critical projects?

Timothy Steele

TIMOTHY STEELE: Yes. I do have some miscellaneous essays on various poets that I've published here and there over the last fifteen years, and I'd like, at some point, to sit down and edit those pieces and maybe write a few more, but I have no large, critical projects planned for the near future.

As we finish up today, on this lovely California afternoon, I'd like to read the ending of your excellent poem "Old Letters" from Sapphics Against Anger and Other Poems*:*

> And is well to envy
> Those who refuse to hunger for event
> And who accept the wisely unbegun,
> Just wishing decently to get through life
> And trying not to injure anyone.

Thank you, Tim.

TIMOTHY STEELE: Thank you, Bill.

Rachel Hadas

Rachel Hadas is a distinguished American poet, translator, and essayist. She is generally regarded as one of the finest poets of her generation, and her verse, as Grace Schulman describes it, is a "remarkable achievement" which consistently "finds in ordinary human acts 'what never was and what is eternal.'"

Born and raised in Manhattan, Rachel Hadas received her B.A. in Classics from Harvard University in 1969, an M.A. from the Writing Seminars at Johns Hopkins University in 1977, and a Ph.D. in Comparative Literature from Princeton University in 1982. Since 1982, she has taught at Rutgers University in Newark, New Jersey, where she is currently a Professor of English. On other occasions she has also taught at Columbia University and Princeton University. The recipient of a Guggenheim Fellowship (1988), she currently lives in Manhattan with her husband, George Edwards, a Professor of Music at Columbia University.

She is the author of numerous collections of poetry including *The Empty Bed* (Wesleyan, 1995); *Halfway Down the Hall: New and Selected Poems* (Wesleyan, 1995); and *Incredible* (Wesleyan, 2001). She is also the author of *Other Worlds Than This: Translations* (Rutgers, 1994), and her translation of Euripides' *Helen* was included in *Euripides, 2: Hippolytus, Suppliant Women, Helen, Electra, Cyclops* (Pennsylvania, 1997). Her most recent collection of essays, *Merrill, Cavafy, Poems, and Dreams*, was published by the University of Michigan Press in 2000.

This interview was conducted at the Exploring Form and Narrative Poetry Conference at West Chester University in West Chester, Pennsylvania.

When you were a young girl, your father, Moses Hadas, one of the most distinguished classicists in the world, was a professor at Columbia University.

RACHEL HADAS: Yes, I still have vivid memories of the Columbia campus back then, and I also have vivid memories of looking at my father's translations. But, ironically, the "bookishness" that I've been fortunate to have throughout my life really came more from my mother, who was also a very intellectual person. Like so many other men of his generation, my father as always very busy with his work, and he didn't spend that much time with his younger children. So although my father was enormously important to me, in some ways, he became even more important after his death when I was seventeen.

How much exposure did you have to the New York intellectual life that revolved around Columbia in those days?

RACHEL HADAS: Not that much. My mother was quite shy, my father was always working, and second marriages were not that common at the time, so they were never really part of the "social swim." The big exceptions were the summers when my father taught at the Bread Loaf School of English — not to be confused with the Bread Loaf Writers' Conference, which was then considered "that bunch of drunken hooligans." So those summers were extremely important to me. I met Robert Frost when I was ten years old, and I got to rub shoulders with poets like William Meredith and John Frederick Nims. I actually sat in on one of John's classes and learned how to write a sonnet.

How old were you then?

RACHEL HADAS: Probably eleven or twelve. I always loved the friendly atmosphere up there, and so did my mother. I remember when I was eleven telling people that I was starting to write a novel! So the bookishness of the place was very, very, appealing, and my parents valued reading above everything else. They were not people with interests in sports, or bridge, or any other pastimes. For them, and for me as well, books were what it was all about.

Did you hear Frost read?

RACHEL HADAS: Yes. Frost, of course, had started the nearby Bread Loaf Writers' Conference, and whenever he came to give a reading, everyone in the audience would stand up to honor him. This would have been a few years before his death, and it was very exciting. He once wrote out in longhand one of his later poems called "Away" just for my mother, and I have it framed now, and he also signed one of his books — a children's collection of his poems with illustrations — for me: "From her new friend, Robert Frost."

As a young girl, you also knew John Hollander.

RACHEL HADAS: Yes, another entrée into the world of poetry for me was the fact that people like John Hollander and Richard Howard had been my father's students at Columbia. Although they weren't around our New York apartment that much, I knew who they were, and they would send us their books. I remember just loving John Hollander's second book, *Movie-Going*, because it was about our neighborhood, and that was a pretty sophisticated book for a young girl of thirteen to be reading. So, in many ways, I did have a very intellectually privileged and book-soaked childhood.

Despite the influence of your father, you once wrote, as you just alluded to, that "my mother did the shaping. She was a wonderful mother, and my love of poetry — of all literature, really — has everything to do with the feast she set before me." Could you describe that "feast"?

RACHEL HADAS: Books were everywhere, although, to be honest, I'm not really sure who my mother's favorite writers were. I do remember that one of the first books I ever read on my own was George MacDonald's Victorian fairy tale, *The Princess and the Goblin*. I also clearly remember that the summer when I was ten, my mother read *Pride and Prejudice* to us in the evenings — not that we couldn't read ourselves, but she always enjoyed reading aloud. Much earlier, I have memories of my mother's mother, who died when I was only five or six, reading us Lear poems like "The Owl and the Pussycat." I can barely remember my grandmother, but I can still recall her voice reading the poetry.

Given your father's classical studies, what was your youthful conception of Greece?

Rachel Hadas

RACHEL HADAS: I think it says a lot about my family that much of our access to the outside world came through books. Even though my father had been in the O.S.S. during World War II, doing intelligence work in Greece, he never really talked about it when we were growing up. Nor did he take sabbaticals in Greece — as nice as that would have been for the family. Mostly, he stayed in his study and worked, so Greece for me was a very "literary" place — not really a physical place. As a child, I didn't have a very visual imagination, and I still don't, so Greece was a kind of intellectual construct that's probably common for most readers of the classics in translation. Tolkien's world, for example, was much more vivid in my imagination than Greece.

Do you remember when you first started writing poetry?

RACHEL HADAS: When I was very young, I wrote a few very imitative ballad-like poems in an embarrassing Scottish dialect — I must have been reading Robert Burns — and I remember showing them to my father. I was certainly the kind of kid who wasn't afraid to say, "Well, I've written a poem," and my father was proud of the fact that I liked to write. By the time I was in seventh or eighth grade, I really enjoyed it, and later in high school, when I started to encounter new poets like E.E. Cummings and T.S. Eliot, I wanted to write like them. It was all very exciting.

Eventually, you went to Radcliffe and Harvard to study classics in the late sixties. While you were there, you took a poetry writing class with the well-known poet and translator Robert Fitzgerald, who also taught, at various times, Brad Leithauser, Mary Jo Salter, Dana Gioia, and Robert B. Shaw. What was Fitzgerald like?

RACHEL HADAS: He had a very light touch as a teacher, almost literally. He had a quiet voice and an inward manner, and if you turned in a poem he might write, "NTB" or "NTG" — meaning "Not Too Bad" or "Not Too Good" — in pencil in the margin. Unlike many people back then, like Robert Lowell, for example, Fitzgerald was still interested in teaching form. His assignments were generally unambitious, and I don't mean that in a negative way. He'd say, for example, "Write a rhymed quatrain." Or "Write a poem which uses all of the following words in it." So his assignments seemed almost whimsical, but they always paid a great deal of attention to technique, and I always found his gentle touch very attractive. Lowell, on the other hand, actually scared me — nothing about Lowell seemed to be "light" at all.

Did you take Lowell's class?

RACHEL HADAS: No, I didn't. You had to compete to get into either class, and though some students managed to study with both poets, most of us took one or the other. In many ways, maybe I was too young and unsure of myself to deal with Lowell, finding him too intimidating, too much of a heavy hitter. I also feared that I might never escape his influence because he had such a powerful influence on his students — many of whom started talking and gesturing and even having nervous breakdowns, à la Lowell. I think Lowell was too rich for my blood. I found Fitzgerald to be a wonderful teacher. I liked the way he ran his workshop, and he gave us all the tools we needed to go forward and do whatever we were going to do.

After graduating from Harvard, you went to Greece. How did that happen?

RACHEL HADAS: I received a tiny, little grant called the Isobel M. Briggs Traveling Fellowship, which was a meager $1,000. When I'd finished college, I honestly didn't know what to do with myself. I was just drifting, and I really didn't have enough sense of a "professional trajectory" to take time off to write. So I decided to go away somewhere, and Greece seemed like a great place to go. At the time, I was also having some emotional difficulties related to my father's death a few years earlier, so I took off for Greece.

Where you married Stavros Kondylis, met James Merrill, and ended up staying four years.

RACHEL HADAS: That's right. Just before I left for Greece, John Hollander said, "When you're in Athens, make sure you look up Jimmy Merrill. I'll write you a letter of introduction." So I did as he suggested, and I immediately realized that Merrill was an extraordinary education — reading his poetry, talking to him, showing him my own work, and becoming his friend. It was enormously productive in countless ways.

Before we leave Greece, can you discuss the arson charge?

My first husband and I had bought an olive press which had a couple of mysterious fires, and we were accused of arson — setting the fires for the insurance. It was a very frightening episode in my life, and I was still terribly young and naive. This was also during the seven-year period when the Colonels were still in control of Greece, and looking back at it now, it might as well have been the nineteenth century. There weren't even any typewriters, and even our indictments were written out by hand. It was a terrible experience, and it taught me that even the most beautiful Greek island isn't necessarily a paradise. It also made me realize that you really have to know what you're doing in this world. You can't just go barging in somewhere and expect things to work out like you want them to. Life isn't that simple. On the other hand, the experience made many other things in life seem much easier. When I was defending my dissertation, although I was naturally nervous, I knew it was a whole lot easier than being on trial in a foreign country.

Eventually, you were acquitted...

RACHEL HADAS: We were acquitted, and we came back to the States; but, at that point, our marriage was crumbling. Yet despite all those difficulties, my whole experience in Greece was like what Eric Erikson refers to as a "moratorium" — a time of pause and preparation for what's coming next. It was a very strange period, but I learned a lot, and I was reinvigorated — ever since then, I've had a better perspective on life and a lot more energy.

One final question about the arson. Did you ever learn who did it?

RACHEL HADAS: No, and I know it probably seems odd, but I don't really care anymore. It probably had something to do with the fact that my Greek husband had grown up quite poor in the neighborhood, and some people were jealous. We also thought it was political in some way, but we never learned the truth.

In 1975, Godine published a chapbook of your poems, Starting from Troy. *These poems had many Aegean themes and subjects; and, although certainly a bit more diffuse than your later style, they introduced a number of important themes that you would return to over the years. Most of them were also written in metrical verse at a time when that mode of poetry was very much out of fashion. Were you conscious that you were bucking the trend at the time?*

RACHEL HADAS: Not completely. Back then, I was living on a Greek island and then in Athens, and I was definitely out of touch. I was obviously aware that Merrill and Hollander wrote in one way, and that somebody like Allen Ginsberg wrote in another way, and there wasn't any doubt in my mind about the kind of poetry I wanted to write. But I don't think I thought about it very much. Literary politics has always made me very uncomfortable, and most of the poems published in *Starting from Troy* came from my Harvard days — and one, I blush to admit, was actually a high school poem. So, it was really my juvenilia, and I was very much isolated from the American literary scene.

Returning to the States, you went to the Writing Seminars at Johns Hopkins. Who was your primary teacher there?

RACHEL HADAS: Cynthia MacDonald.

How was the workshop?

RACHEL HADAS: Very good. Despite having been in Robert Fitzgerald's class, I didn't know much about contemporary "workshopping" because a lot of things had changed in the culture while I was abroad. My Hopkins workshop included a very impressive group of students — like Molly Peacock and Phyllis Levin — and I learned a lot from them. Hopkins was a very good and valuable year.

After Hopkins, you went to Princeton for your Ph.D. in Comparative Literature, graduating with special distinction in 1982. The next year, your second book, Slow Transparency, *was published by Wesleyan. Reviewing the book in the* Times Literary Supplement, *Anne Stevenson remarked that those early poems were "too long under the shadow of Wallace Stevens." Did you realize that Stevens was such an influence on your work?*

RACHEL HADAS: I didn't actually encounter Stevens' work until I was in graduate school. I took a wonderful seminar with a scholar of Russian, Clarence Brown, who also had an intense interest in Stevens. So we spent the whole semester on Stevens, and I was knocked over. I'd never read anything like Stevens before. At the same time, I took a wonderful course in Rilke and Valéry, and I felt very fortunate to be able to read so much inspiring poetry and so little theory. So I do think in retrospect that my first full-length book, *Slow Transparency,* was indeed still too much under the shadow of influences like Stevens. It was really, in my opinion, a young person's book.

You've already mentioned the influence of James Merrill on your poetry — and your life as well — and you've dedicated a number of poems to Merrill, including "Water and Fire" and "The Blue Bead." How do you think his work has affected your own?

RACHEL HADAS: Merrill, as well as being a great writer, had a genius for friendship, and I was fortunate to be one of his many friends. As a writer, he was like an inspirational beacon because he always seemed to be writing, and writing so beautifully, and continually developing in his art. Yet he always had time for friendships, and he was very generous. He never seemed to be burdened by life, and that was, of course, partly because he had the financial means to live without putting his nose to the grindstone, but it was also because of the very unusual human being that Jimmy was. As a writer, I think he made me very conscious that style — and the way you use language — is more important than what you write about. Jimmy could write about absolutely anything and still make it beautiful, and that's what mattered. I also loved the way he used Greece in his life and poetry, and the way he seemed to value poetry more than anything else. But even though poetry was always such an intense reality for Jimmy, he could also be perfectly content to go shopping, or have dinner, or just gossip with his friends. I found him perfectly fascinating.

There's so many things one can say about Merrill's work, but he's certainly very precise about diction, and I wonder if that consciously affected you, because I feel the same way about your poetry.

RACHEL HADAS: I hope so, and I certainly take it as a compliment. It seems to me that if we're not constantly working at diction, then maybe we're in the wrong business. Poetry is made of words, and we have to get to know them. Otherwise, it's like saying, "He wants to be a painter, but he's color-blind."

Who are some of your favorite poets from the tradition?

RACHEL HADAS: I don't have a single favorite "dead" poet, but the ones who are still the most important to me are the ones I read growing up — back when I had such a terrific memory. When I was thirteen or fourteen, I could read a Shakespeare sonnet a couple of times, and I'd remember it, and have it! So, some of my favorites are still Shakespeare, Keats, Tennyson, Hopkins, Frost, and Eliot.

Not Yeats?

RACHEL HADAS: Not as much. I love Yeats, of course, but I didn't have that same early exposure. The same is true of Hardy and Dickinson. Since I never majored in English, my reading is rather spotty, although I did have a wonderful class in the Romantics at Harvard. Naturally, the Greeks and Cavafy are also very important to me, and I've never regretted majoring in classics.

You mentioned Tennyson, and unfortunately many students don't read him anymore.

Rachel Hadas

RACHEL HADAS: I know. Whenever I read my own poem "Island Noons" from *Slow Transparency* about swimming in the Aegean, I suddenly hear lines from *Idylls of the King* bubbling up in my mind. That's what my youthful memory did for me. All of those wonderful poems have been permanently imprinted on me. Like Wordsworth. I remember when I was in Greece, and I was wandering around this Greek village with a copy of Wordsworth under my arm, and somebody said — because I really did speak Greek quite well back then — "You must be forgetting English now." And I would think, "God forbid!" Or, "Little do you know that I'm reading *The Prelude* whenever I can. I'm not forgetting English, no, never!"

From 1987 to the present, you published five collections of poetry, all of which have developed certain crucial themes, and I'd like to discuss a few. One is motherhood. In 1984, you and your husband, George Edwards, a Columbia University music professor and composer, had a son Jonathan, and starting with your 1987 collection A Son from Sleep, *you began a serious poetic exploration of the miracle, joys, and trials of motherhood. Emily Grosholz, in* The Oxford Companion to Twentieth-Century Poetry, *writes that your "poems on bearing and nursing a child, reading to him, and watching him begin to speak, are touching but unsentimental, inventive and yet steeped in literary and family tradition." Emily's certainly right, and avoiding excessive sentimentality is the primary challenge when you're writing about such a subject. So how did you approach it?*

RACHEL HADAS: Well, there was never any conscious strategy before the fact. I'm a very seat-of-the-pants and intuitive writer going into the poetic process, but coming out of the process, I'm a severe enough critic of my own work to eliminate or alter anything that might seem excessively sentimental.

One of your most popular poems is "The Red Hat" in which concerned parents track their child as he walks "alone" to school.

> *The mornings we turn back to are no more*
> *than forty minutes longer than before,*
> *but they feel vastly different — flimsy, strange,*

> *wavering in the eddies of this change,*
> *empty, unanchored, perilously light*
> *since the red hat vanished from our sight.*

How did that one come about?

RACHEL HADAS: When Jonathan was about nine or ten, he was almost ready to start walking to school alone, and, as described in the poem, George or I would walk across the street so we could keep an eye on him. It was scary to let him walk off alone. Originally, the poem had the very uninspiring title "Walking to School II," so there must have been a "Walking to School I," which I don't remember. Then I sent the poem off to *The New Yorker*, and Alice Quinn liked it, but she said, "That title could use a little work," and somehow I immediately pounced on "The Red Hat."

Did Jonathan have a red hat?

RACHEL HADAS: He did wear a red hat sometimes, but it was more like a ski cap.

It's interesting that our generation is very concerned with the concept of parenting and feels impelled to write poems about it.

RACHEL HADAS: Yes, it is very interesting. I think that many people in our generation rebelled against their parents and then had an extended adolescence. Speaking for myself, I married too young, and I was a very immature person for many years, and motherhood was the crucial experience in my life. It's the first time that another person matters to you in that special way, and there's nothing else like it. It's an all-consuming love that, in time, will have to learn how to "let go" in various ways. So it's both very beautiful and inherently tragic.

Many of your poems are about a longing for the past — "the vast / vague, forgiving vista of the past" — and what's been lost. You once said in an interview with Gloria Glickstein Brame that you're "hopelessly nostalgic for what cannot return." This is one of the great, universal themes in poetry, but the challenge is to find new ways to express it.*

RACHEL HADAS: Fortunately, poetry gives us a way of rerunning the tape of our experience. Sometimes when you've had a fight with someone you love, or you've failed to pay attention to something beautiful because you've been so preoccupied, you feel like saying, "Let's play that scene over again." And poetry not only *lets* you do it, it *forces* you to do it. Given my own temperament, I don't think I'm particularly good at exuberantly enjoying the present. I love teaching and family and other things, but often in my immediate life, I feel sort of wistful — as if I'm missing out on something. The present is such a tiny, little fraction of our experience, and living entirely in the present can make us oblivious to our feelings. But poetry allows us to express our feelings. Poetry is all about interiority, and most of those feelings come from memories and dreams and regrets and various kinds of nostalgias. Another way to look at this — in my own case — is to realize that in most ways I had a very happy and sheltered childhood, and I often look back to that time with great fondness and longing.

Part of this sense of loss in your poems has been caused by the deaths of your parents and friends, such as James Merrill and Charles Barber. In "Roadblock," the narrator asks herself:

> *Am I a noisy bird of evil omen*
> *or just a person, apprehensive, human,*
> *moving ahead, kid sister into woman,*
>
> *stonewalled by death each time she rounds a bend?*

Do you think poetry helps you deal with the loss of your loved ones?

RACHEL HADAS: Undoubtedly. Definitely. Wallace Stevens wrote in "Sunday Morning" that "Death is the mother of beauty." And I never used to understand that line because it seems so paradoxical. Doesn't he really mean that "beauty" is the mother of something?

How can death be the "mother of beauty"? In Stevens' poem, he speculated what it would be like if there were no change or death in paradise, where the fruit could be ripe and never fall. Well, the death of my father when I was seventeen plummeted me out of my childhood. Maybe I even regressed, as I tried to face the fact that a person I'd loved so much could suddenly be taken away like that. And I think that difficult experience made me a poet, and later it helped me understand Stevens. I also think that one of the crucial impulses in poetry, and certainly in mine, is elegy. We write poetry because we want to speak to and for the dead. It's akin to prayer. Sometimes in my life, like when I ran the AIDS workshop, I felt the need to befriend people who were on the narrow edge between life and death. For me, poetry and elegy and the processing of personal grief are all part of the same thing.

Sometimes, as you discuss in "In the Grove," the dead seem far more real than the living who often appear like those undeveloped "flat" characters which E.M. Forster discusses in Aspects of the Novel.

RACHEL HADAS: I'm sure I'm not the only one in this hurried world of ours — and maybe living in New York makes it even worse — to realize that we seldom get to know the people who are scurrying past us all the time. In our busy lives we encounter so many people, but how many of them do we really have the time to pay attention to? We don't even know those closest to us as well as we'd like, so when one of them dies, and we realize that we're not going to get that crucial relationship back, we start replaying it and finding new ways to make it meaningful. If you've been fortunate enough to have a really wonderful mother as I did, or a friend like James Merrill — I'm not mentioning my father because I was only seventeen when he died — then you feel impelled to have mental conversations with them. What would she have said about that? Or how would so-and-so advise me now? It seems to me that one of the challenges of getting older, as we move steadily towards our own deaths, is to deal with losing people all the time. Do you try to ignore it? Or do you start worrying about your own mortality? Or do you try to deal with it in some fruitful way? That's one of the essential challenges of being human, and poetry offers us an effective means of dealing with it.

Related to these themes we've been discussing — motherhood, longing for the past, and missing the deceased — are your many poems about the interrelationship of the generations. This is a very specific motif in your collection Pass It On *(Princeton, 1989), but it constantly recurs in your other books as well. A perfect example is "Moments of Summer" where the narrator, while "reading to my son" recalls "reading with my father."*

RACHEL HADAS: I think I've become very aware of how *much* we can give to each other, and how *little* we can give to each other. I also realize that we may not always be aware at the time exactly what we are giving to each other. I didn't have much time alone with my father, but when I was fifteen or so, we would translate Cicero together. He was usually very tired at the end of a long day, so he would lie down as we worked together. Then years later, lying in a hammock with my son in Vermont reminded me of those times with my father. Who would have thought way back then that I would now cherish those times with my father so much? I know that Alicia Stallings still has wonderful memories of her father teaching her to fish when she was a little girl. We really don't know what we're going to get from others — what will be full of meaning for the rest of our lives. In my own case, this is reinforced by the fact that I really don't have a large family. I have one sibling, and she has no children, and Jonathan is an only child. So much of my family is now in the background, in the past, and the older you get, the more you start to see yourself in the middle of the generations. There's the people who came before you, and there's your children — and even your students.

Finally, there's New York City itself, specifically Manhattan, where you're now living just a few blocks from where you grew up. A sense of place has always been important in your poems, and Emily Grosholz describes the transition that occurred after your first two books, when "the scope of the Aegean spiraled back into glints on a Manhattan window-pane." You clearly have a lifelong love of the city, and it comes through in the background of many of your poems.

RACHEL HADAS: Yes, I do wonder what would have happened if I'd stayed in Greece, or if I'd come back to the States and moved into a big house in the country. It's hard to say how that would have affected my poetry. In my early work, when Stevens was very important to my writing, I was living in the gorgeous Aegean seascape, and I kept trying to paint word pictures with my poems. I was also doing watercolors back then, but I really don't think that's what poetry is best at. And that's why the Imagist poets were so extraordinarily limited. As Frost once said, they just wrote poems for the eye, and not for the ear. So since I've been back in New York, living in an apartment in Manhattan again, I gave up trying to evoke the gorgeous Greek landscapes, and I've tried to focus more on the human in my poetry. I do adore New York City. It's valiant, beautiful, and ever-lively, but I never try to be idolatrous about it, and there are certainly other poets who have written about the city with more specificity and intensity.

Yes, it's usually in the background of your poems, but sometimes it's specifically there, like "Benefit Night, New York City Ballet" or "The Red Hat."

RACHEL HADAS: That's true. In "The Red Hat," I specifically mentioned Straus Park, and the people who know the neighborhood know exactly where it is. I often get e-mails from students asking me what the poem means, how old my son was, and where Straus Park is.

I'd now like to ask you a few questions about how you compose. Do you write at pre-scheduled times?

RACHEL HADAS: I often tell students that there are two extremes for poets. One is what Auden often did, probably on uppers or downers. He'd sit at his desk, and then write much of the day. I can't do that. I just don't have the concentration. The other extreme is to wait for the "lightning" to strike. So I'm somewhere in between. I find that if I don't work for too many days in a row, I start to get crabby, and I'll try to do something. But given my teaching schedule, I find that I do the bulk of my writing over the Christmas and summer vacations. I also do quite well if I'm on a bus or a train — in some kind of enclosed space.

I know you're a morning person. Is that your best time?

RACHEL HADAS: Morning is good, but since my husband tends to go to bed earlier than I do — and certainly when Jonathan was young — I was often the only person awake at night, so I would use the time to write.

You once said that you "work fast" in the beginning.

RACHEL HADAS: Usually, when I'm working well, I'm also working fast.

Do you focus on one poem at a time?

RACHEL HADAS: I often start working on several poems at once until one of them takes over. Over the last few years, I do a lot more paring away than I used to. I'll get myself to an incredibly sloppy draft, and then I'll start cutting it down in numerous drafts. It's not that I never add anything new, but above all, I shape and cut and discard. I recently had a poem in *The American Scholar* called "The Compact" about the little case that women use to powder their noses, but it's also a "compact" little poem. When I first wrote it, it was four stanzas long, but then I chopped it down into two separate poems. Whether we like it or not, it's an undeniable fact that everyone's concentration is shrinking. Mine certainly is, and we all know that even our best students have short attention spans, and they're much more likely to read a short lyric poem than *The Prelude.*

How do you find your forms?

RACHEL HADAS: I'll have a poetic idea or a theme, or maybe a few lines I'm playing around with, and then I'll start to think, maybe this would work best as quatrains or something like that. Merrill, somewhere in the trilogy, has a moment where he's examining one of his ideas, and he says, "It might draw well / In the glass chimney of the villanelle," and that's how it works for me too. Sometimes I'll be writing a poem, and I'll think, "This poem seems to break in the middle," and then, lo and behold, the two halves of it turn out to be thirteen or fifteen lines, and I'll think, "We're in sonnet territory." I rarely sit down with the intention of writing a sonnet; I try instead to find the form that the poem needs.

You've written in a wide variety of poetic forms. What would you like to try — or do more of?

RACHEL HADAS: I'm more cautious these days about sestinas, canzones, and even villanelles. Last summer when I was in Greece with Alicia Stallings, I wrote a number of triolets, and that was great fun. But I guess the form that works the best for me — even when I get a little weary of it — is heroic couplets. I find it a very congenial form because it can be any length I want, and because I find myself wanting to do more and more of that. Recently, I started working on a poem about being on the subway near a little boy in a stroller and noticing that his mother wasn't doing her job very well. At first, I sort of sketched out the poem, and then it started turning itself into rhymed couplets.

One of your stylistic traits is the truncated line. You do this to highlight short passages and rhythmically vary the line lengths. But you don't do them in any discernible patterns, so maybe it's intuitive. Are you conscious of these occasional variations when you're writing?

RACHEL HADAS: No, I'm not aware of it as a regular trait. Could you give me an example?

In one of my favorites, "Alternatives," which consists of two blank verse cinquains, you truncate the second line in the first stanza and the penultimate line in the second stanza.

RACHEL HADAS: I suppose it's a natural effort for variety and emphasis. Some of the so-called "New Formalists" were criticized for having an overly straight-arrow approach to form, which runs the risk of being dull — the "rocking-horse" problem that Keats complained about. So maybe we need to play against the reader's expectation a bit and vary the pace. Maybe in my own work it's also because I often have a dragonfly-like zigzag train of thought! Since I don't tend to think in a straight line, maybe those variations represent my actual thought process.

You're in good company. Shakespeare certainly did it.

RACHEL HADAS: And Frost. In poems like "Home Burial" and "The Death of the Hired Man."

You're often considered one of the more prolific poets of your generation. Are you comfortable with that?

RACHEL HADAS: It's true that I've written a lot in the past. In general, there are two kinds of poets: the ones who write very slowly, gradually adding things until they finally finish a poem, and those who write a lot and then discard what they're not satisfied with. I'm definitely in the latter group, although, over the past few years, I'm writing less and publishing less.

You're also a very talented translator and seem to enjoy the "serendipity and surrender" of translating. How do you think it affects your other work?

RACHEL HADAS: I don't really separate the two in my mind. I feel that translating is my own work because exactly the same verbal fluency and compositional facility is taking place. Where it does affect my original poetry is the way in which it forces me to take an extremely close look at another writer's poem, say one of Horace's odes, for example. That's always educational — and great fun as well. It gives me pleasure to translate and to think about my translations. At their best, they hold up to my personal standards of what a poem should sound like, although there's always the risk that Tibullus and Baudelaire will wind up sounding strangely alike! I also like solving the natural problems of translation. I think it's laziness to say, "Oh, well, this rhyme just won't come into English, so I'll do it without it." The best translators, people like Louis Simpson and Charles Martin, have been able to rhyme beautifully, and I also like to take up the challenge. In my own case, translating has generally been rather serendipitous because I've only undertaken projects when specifically asked to do so by an editor. But it's something that I love doing, and I hope to do more translating in the future.

You've been teaching at Rutgers University in Newark since 1981, and you've received a number of distinguished teaching awards. Do you teach creative writing?

RACHEL HADAS: Yes, but it's only about one-third of the teaching I do at Rutgers. I love teaching literature, and I'm not sure that I'm as good a teacher of writing as I'd like to be. In my literature classes, I have a very seat-of-the-pants approach. When one of my colleagues once asked me, "So what's your theory of literature?", I said, "I don't have one." I feel it's too limiting to look at literature through a single lens.

In your poetry classes, how do you try to interest your students in metrics?

RACHEL HADAS: I'm not really as much of a martinet as maybe I should be when it comes to meter. I use *Rhyme's Reason* and Perrine's wonderful *Sound and Sense*. Last fall, I had a very lively, engaged graduate class, and they wrote villanelles and sonnets and other things, but I find that meter is tremendously hard for about half of them. They just can't hear it, and I'm really not sure what to do. But at the very least, they can learn to recognize it in what they read. I'm always amazed how little is done about such things in literature classes, like undergraduate Shakespeare classes. Apparently, mention is seldom made of the fact that Shakespeare was a poet and craftsman! They talk about themes and plot and some imagery, but the students hardly realize that it's carefully crafted poetry.

Yes, it's sad; and, unfortunately, it's very common in present-day academia. Now, earlier, we talked about your literary isolation in Greece, so when did you first become aware that a formalist revival was gradually developing?

Rachel Hadas

RACHEL HADAS: When I was living on the island of Samos, I had no idea about the "deep image" thing that was going on back in the United States in the seventies. I was very cut off from the literary scene. Then after I came back home, I happened to meet both Dana Gioia and Emily Grosholz in 1986. I can't even remember how it happened, but by the time I'd met them, I was definitely aware of the so-called "New Formalists," and I can remember being on some conference panel in Washington, D.C., in the late eighties and criticizing some of the things the more enthusiastic new formalists were claiming, and saying, "Wait a minute! Is this really all that new?" So even though I was naturally glad to see the revival of interest, I was a little bit skeptical about some of the claims being made.

There was nothing new about it.

RACHEL HADAS: No, there was nothing new about the "new formalism."

Given your natural skepticism and practicality, you also seem to have a very healthy attitude about the importance of poetry in our lives. I think of your poem, "Flying Home," in which the narrator humorously thinks about a potential plane crash and concludes:

> *will a notebook ambered back to front with words*
>
> *rescue me from oblivion?*
> *Syrup of skittish travelers, fame. I yawn.*

Do you think that sometimes contemporary poets or aspiring poets become too obsessed with the "immortality" potential of poetry and damage their own lives and work in the process?

RACHEL HADAS: Yes, although I think it's much more likely to hurt their lives than their work, especially if they become embittered. Fortunately, most poets don't get too megalomaniacal. I think it's important to remember that the world really doesn't need anyone's poetry, and I figured that out a long time ago. As you know, my husband George is a composer; and, in my opinion, that's a much harder field. The world is much more hostile to new music than it is to new poetry. So I've learned a lot from George because he's very stoic and patient, and he only composes when he feels he's ready, and he sets very high standards for himself. I also think that getting older teaches us the same lessons — and the vocation of teaching does as well. You're not the only apple on the tree. Variety and diversity are necessary in this world, and eventually Time will come along and sift and sort through everybody's work, including my own. I understand that, and I don't have any problem with it.

I'd like to finish up today by reading the ending of your lovely poem "Water and Fire," dedicated to James Merrill, which ends with the narrator finding inspiration in the poet's work:

> *So that this seeker of eternity,*
> *finally forced to shut her eyes to the*
> *beauties whose icons prove ephemeral,*
> *turns, sighing, to your inexhaustible*
> *books, which englobe lost worlds in every word.*

Thank you, Rachel.

RACHEL HADAS: Thank you, Bill.

Brad Leithauser

Brad Leithauser is a renowned American poet, novelist, and essayist. Described by John Gross in the *New York Times* as "one of the most gifted American poets to have come over the horizon in years," he's been aptly characterized by John Updike as "A rhyming family man, amateur cosmologist, and addict of intricate stanzas, [who] warms the past and present with his lovingly intense scrutiny and powerfully compressed phrases."

Born and raised in Detroit, Michigan, Brad Leithauser received his B.A. from Harvard University in 1975 and later completed his J.D. at Harvard in 1980. After his marriage to the poet Mary Jo Salter in 1980, he was a research fellow at the Kyoto Comparative Law Center in Kyoto, Japan, for three years. He subsequently taught at Amherst College, was a Fulbright Fellow at the University of Iceland, and currently is Emily Dickinson Senior Lecturer in the Humanities at Mount Holyoke College. In 1982 Leithauser received a Guggenheim Fellowship, and the following year he was awarded a MacArthur Foundation Grant.

He is the author of five books of poetry, all published by Knopf, including *Hundreds of Fireflies* (1982); *The Last Odd Thing She Did* (1998); and the book-length poem, *Darlington's Fall: A Novel in Verse* (2002). His novels, also from Knopf, include *Equal Distance* (1985), *Seaward* (1993), and *The Friends of Freeland* (1997). His collection of essays, *Penchants & Places*, was published by Knopf in 1995.

This interview was conducted at the Sewanee Writers' Conference at the University of the South in Sewanee, Tennessee.

Given your intense interest in the natural world, I've wondered if you grew up in an urban area of Detroit?

BRAD LEITHAUSER: Actually, we lived in a suburb of Detroit, but one of the nicest things about growing up in Michigan was that the "north" never seemed very far away. About sixty or seventy miles north of Detroit, up past Flint, everything seemed to open up, and we spent a lot of time in the northern part of the Lower Peninsula. Everything seemed different and rougher up there — even the trees — and there was always a wonderful freshness and rejuvenation about that part of the country. So a sense of "heading north" made a very strong impression on me as a child, and I think my yearly trips as an adult to Iceland have become a northern pilgrimage connected to my youthful trips into northern Michigan.

Were they day trips or vacations?

BRAD LEITHAUSER: Vacations. Eventually, my father bought a quarter-share on a cabin about thirty miles south of the Mackinaw Bridge, and we would go up there in both the summer and the winter. I can still remember wading in the little Pigeon River that ran outside our cabin, and walking through the snow on the banks of the river with the water rushing by. It was very exciting and very inspiring.

Back then, your mom was both a professor and an author. What was her field?

BRAD LEITHAUSER: Originally, my mother was a scientist working at the Cancer Institute in Detroit, but in her forties, she went back to school and got her Ph.D. Her specialty was Bertrand Russell, but Russell the literary figure rather than the philosopher. So she ended up teaching English literature and composition. She also — with a writing partner — wrote poems for children and published a juvenile novel, *The Dinosaur Dilemma*. So it's almost embarrassingly obvious how I've tried to mix and match the interests of my parents in my own life. I became an attorney like my father, and I'm a creative writer with a real interest in science like my mother.

And the latter's quite unusual.

BRAD LEITHAUSER: I feel fortunate that my mother's interest made me generally curious about what was happening in science. If one could step back far enough and then look at American literature, I think our lack of interest in the sciences would seem quite odd. If someone came down here from Mars — or from some other planet — it would be obvious that one of the most interesting things about our world is how much it's being transformed or transmogrified by science, and, oddly, how little science permeates our writing, even our fiction. Even in many of the writers I love best, there's little hint of what's really going on in our world. We're living in an amazing age of spacecrafts and super-computers, and it's generally ignored.

Back in the '30s, Auden and the Pylon poets made an unsuccessful effort to encourage poets to write about such things.

BRAD LEITHAUSER: Yes, and it's still one of the things that's most striking about Auden's work at the time. I remember Edward Mendelson once saying that when you go from Yeats to Auden you move into a completely different world, even though their lives coincided long enough for Auden to write his elegy for Yeats. But for all Yeats' great poetic achievement, he never really considered the fact that his world was being transformed by science and literally metamorphosing right in front of his eyes. Maybe it's because of our natural tendency as poets to write within our personal cocoons, and maybe it's also because the scientific transformation around us is so complicated and overwhelming.

At what age did you start writing poetry?

BRAD LEITHAUSER: My mother reports that I was about six. Back then she would encourage my interest by giving me a penny a line to recite poems, and I remember making six cents with my first memorized poem, Tennyson's "The Eagle." "He clasps the crag with crooked hands" — there's one cent! "Close to the sun in lonely lands, / Ringed with the azure world, he stands." And there's three cents! So I learned lots of popular verses, like "Casey at the Bat," and I started writing my own poems. Even today, I make myself quite unpopular with my college students by requiring them to memorize poetry, but I think memorization is invaluable. As for the fiction writing, that started in high school when I began writing a number of short stories. I feel very fortunate that, in my own career, I've been able to write both poetry and fiction, but if I could write only one, I'd definitely choose poetry, since it seems to me a higher calling, a richer calling, a nobler calling. If someone ever asks me, "What do you do?" I never have any trouble identifying myself as "a novelist," but I've always avoided calling myself "a poet." It almost sounds arrogant somehow. Milton's my idea of "a poet," so I hesitate to apply the term to myself — which is not some kind of false modesty. It's just related to how much I value the notion of being a poet.

In the first part of your autobiographical poem "Two Summer Jobs," you reveal that before you went to Harvard, your "most private wish" was to be a writer. Then while you were at Harvard, you won four poetry awards. Were you an English major?

BRAD LEITHAUSER: I was an English major who, because of a new program, was allowed to do a creative writing thesis. I began as a poet, and Robert Fitzgerald was my tutor in my junior year, but when he wasn't available in my senior year, a very helpful professor named Monroe Engle agreed to oversee my thesis. Since he was a fiction writer, I ended up doing a thesis of five short stories, but I was still writing a lot of poetry; and, in retrospect, it's really amazing that my poetry teachers were Elizabeth Bishop, Robert Fitzgerald, Anthony Hecht, and Robert Lowell.

Let's start with Bishop.

BRAD LEITHAUSER: At the time, Elizabeth Bishop was the one I knew best. I felt very comfortable with her, and we had many conferences. I didn't, of course, know her intimately, but I knew her as a twenty-year-old student might know his teacher. As you might expect, she was extremely helpful with the small, specific details of my poems. She'd often say, "This isn't quite right," and then get very specific about the problem. I remember, for example, that once I'd referred to something as "pond-shaped," and she said, "Well, ponds have all sorts of shapes. Don't you really mean pond-sized?" And of course, she was right. Some of her comments, like the ones about punctuation, might have seemed persnickety to some students, but I never felt that way. She made me aware of the extreme importance of minute matters. She would even say, "You should know the etymologies of every single word you use, and especially the words you use in a poem." And even though I certainly didn't always know the etymologies of all my words, I knew she was right.

What was she like in the classroom?

BRAD LEITHAUSER: She was always a rather uncomfortable teacher. It was quite clear that she didn't really want to be teaching. Bishop, of course, had her own personal problems, and she'd often come into class unprepared, without having thought things through. It might seem hard to believe nowadays, but back then Bishop was really a sort of peripheral figure, whereas Lowell was always surrounded by students and clearly liked having a large retinue. He was very impressive. He seemed to represent a kind of "vastness," and whenever Lowell would make a remark, everyone would write it down and feel that it might somehow be useful — that it might even help to advance your career. But with Bishop, we tended to see her as a sweet old lady who preferred to be left alone, although she was glad to talk to the students she liked. In the end, I learned much more from Elizabeth Bishop than from Robert Lowell.

And Fitzgerald?

BRAD LEITHAUSER: He's been much in my mind recently since I've been listening to a tape of his translation of *The Aeneid* while driving around in the car. Unfortunately, Fitzgerald himself doesn't read the translation, but I'm still enjoying it. He was a great classicist, and I always felt he was trying to give me a broader perspective. When he was my tutor, I once told him how much I liked Yeats, so he said, "Then let's do Swift. Let's go back a couple of hundred years." So we did, and I learned a lot. I also remember his remarkable honesty. One time I asked him a question about something, and he looked out the window. He stared out the window so hard, and for so long, that I thought he'd forgotten I was still there. Not knowing what to do, I just sat there and waited. Finally, he turned back to me and said, "I don't know." And that was it. And that's the way Fitzgerald was — if you don't know something, it's best not to say anything. He believed that every line of poetry should snap like a whip — with nothing extraneous — and that's what he tried to do in his translations, most successfully, in my opinion, in *The Odyssey*, where the lines are so tight and clean. So Fitzgerald clearly represented for me the great classical heritage, and he challenged us all to be Spartan in our use of the language, whether it was simply answering a question or writing a line of poetry.

Then you also studied with Anthony Hecht at Harvard.

BRAD LEITHAUSER: Yes, he was a visiting professor for one semester in my sophomore year, and he's become a very good friend — and certainly the most important of my early mentors. As you know, he's a man of extraordinary generosity; and, over the years, he's given me extensive commentary on my work. Sometimes he'd honestly disapprove of what I was doing, and he'd tell me why in his responses. He was generous in so many ways that were clearly of no benefit to himself, other than kindness for its own sake.

When you were studying with Anthony Hecht, did you know the work of many contemporary poets?

BRAD LEITHAUSER: Oddly enough, although not terribly well read, I did know the work of quite a few contemporary poets, because back in high school I'd had an English teacher named Robert Steele who loved *The New Yorker* and introduced me to a number of contemporary poets. I remember that he was particularly fond of Richard Wilbur, May Swenson, and a poet named Ted Walker, who's now been forgotten, although I liked him quite a bit as well. I can also remember enjoying some Justice and Nemerov and Snodgrass's captivating *Heart's Needle*. Under my teacher's influence, I started browsing around my little, local library, where I found David Wagoner's first book, *Dry Sun, Dry Wind*, which I liked a great deal, and that led me to Roethke, for obvious reasons. Wagoner was and still is a true nature poet, and I was quite taken with his work.

Later in college, I fell under the spell of Berryman's *Dream Songs* and Elizabeth Bishop's poetry. But I didn't really know Tony's work before he became my teacher, and I also came to Merrill's poetry a bit later too. So those were the poets I found exciting back then; and, for whatever mysterious reasons, most of them were born in the 1920s.

After graduation you went to Harvard Law School. As you mentioned earlier, your dad was a lawyer, so were you thinking about law school all along?

BRAD LEITHAUSER: I really didn't know what I was going to do, and I believe that, like many in my generation, I just went off to law school rather unthinkingly. I always tell my students to try to figure out what they don't want to have happen to them, and to be very clear about it, because that's probably what will occur anyway. I never wanted to be a teacher, and, of course, now I'm a half-time teacher, and that's how I make my living. Part of my hesitancy was the feeling that, since so many of our poets are teachers these days, maybe it would be best to be something else. Another part of my thinking was a definite uneasiness about actually "teaching" creative writing, and that wariness still nags at me, although I do feel that it's easier and maybe even more honest to teach poetry writing than fiction writing. At least with the poetry, I can guarantee that my students will learn a certain amount of useful technical material, like prosodic terms, poetic forms, etc. But with fiction, I think that you have to encourage your students to develop a "deeper soul" and become "a more interesting person," and that's a very hard thing to foster in anyone. Anyway, when I was younger, I had all these various misgivings about teaching, so I decided to study law. Another factor was that since I'd always hoped to write, I wanted a field where I could work part-time, and I naively thought that if I had certain legal skills, and if I was pretty good at them, then I could make a living by working twenty hours a week.

Did you enjoy law school?

BRAD LEITHAUSER: I really did. Despite my misgivings about

being a teacher, I always loved being a student. I loved the idea of walking into a classroom with an empty notebook and saying to the teacher, "Entertain me. Enrich me." So unlike many classmates, I was never miserable in law school. I actually enjoyed sitting there trying to figure out how I felt about important things like the insanity defense, or punitive vs. corrective punishment. It seemed to me, even then, that these are the same kinds of larger questions you have to ask yourself when you're writing, especially fiction.

After law school you ended up clerking with a big law firm in New York City. In the second section of "Two Summer Jobs," you describe a young law clerk in New York who's struggling to find the time "to write, / or to try," and who realizes by the end of the poem that "I'll be ready to leave. Or nearly so." This implies that you were already preparing to give up law as a career even before you spent three years as a research fellow at the Kyoto Comparative Law Center in Japan?

BRAD LEITHAUSER: At the time, I felt that I was getting very close to having a completed manuscript of poems, and then suddenly, within a few weeks in July and early August of 1980, a lot happened. I took the Bar exam, I got married, and we moved to Japan. As I mentioned earlier, I'd always had these optimistic notions of finding some kind of part-time legal work so I could have time to write, and that's exactly what happened in Kyoto, and I loved it. My official job was to edit legal articles written by Japanese professors that had been translated into English, usually by one of the professor's students. So I would often work with that student, trying to put the article into sensible English. Part of this was simply editing the English in the same way you'd edit any student paper, but the other part was making sure it made legal and logical sense. So I not only enjoyed the work, but I was delighted by the fact that the Law Center opened at ten o'clock every morning. Being an early riser, I'd often get to the office at six or six-thirty, drink green tea, look over the Kyoto skyline, and work on my writing — both poems and a novel. So it was a very happy and productive period.

In 1982, while you were still in Japan, Knopf published your first poetry collection, Hundreds of Fireflies, *which was very well received. In the book, you established a number of themes and stylistic traits that carried through your subsequent three collections, and I'd like to discuss a few. The first is your careful specificity, especially regarding the natural world — what Bruce Bennett in* The New York Times Book Review *called your "meticulous examination of particulars," and your natural attraction to the peculiarities of nature — like bats, fireflies, a giant tortoise, and even mosquitoes and the Venus flytrap.*

BRAD LEITHAUSER: When I first learned that 99.99% of the species that have existed on the planet have already become extinct, I was very struck by the fact, and it made me very aware that every single creature out there is truly odd and peculiar. How did some of these creatures survive when others didn't? Especially ones that seem so dumb and slow and clumsy? I remember going to the zoo in Kyoto and finding, among all these "exotic animals," a typical North American raccoon, which had never seemed very exotic to me when they used to sneak into our attic back in Michigan. But in Kyoto I saw them anew, and they *are* very peculiar. On the other hand, there were wild monkeys in the trees of Kyoto, which certainly seemed very odd to me but was perfectly commonplace for the Japanese. So that kind of new awareness of the natural world interests me very much — as one finds in Elizabeth Bishop's poem "The Moose."

Helen Vendler, in praising Hundreds of Fireflies *in* The New York Review of Books, *discussed your "telling use of modesty of voice." Years later, you wrote of your own admiration of the "comely humility" in the essays of Randall Jarrell. Are you conscious of such a tone in your poetry?*

BRAD LEITHAUSER: It's probably something that I subconsciously aspire to. As you know, I write a lot of reviews and criticism, and I'm always wary of critics who speak with too much confidence. I certainly have my own strong feelings to express sometimes, but there's a kind of literary arrogance that I find very off-putting in both poetry and criticism. Temperamentally, I also don't fully understand it. How is it possible to walk into a library — and I don't mean the Library of Congress or the New York Public Library, I mean one's little, local library — without feeling immediately humble? It's staggering how much we haven't read and don't know a single thing about, and to my mind, that feeling is salutary. It puts us in touch with the reality of what it is to be a human being, which is to say, an individual who knows almost nothing about anything. Look at math, for example. Back in the nineteenth century, a well-educated person might know all the math developed up to that time, but in today's world, even brilliant mathematicians can only know a fraction of their field. On the other hand, there's also a dangerous kind of modesty that can seem a bit too self-congratulatory. I'm a great lover of the poetry of Philip Larkin, but sometimes his modesty can sound a bit overly self-conscious, and I feel that I need to be wary of that temptation myself.

In your second collection, Cats of the Temple *(1986), your appreciation of the natural world extended itself into foreign locations like Japan, and this would continue over the course of your subsequent writings as a number of grants — an Amy Lowell, a Guggenheim, a MacArthur, and a Fulbright — allowed you to live in various places like Italy, England, Iceland, and France.*

BRAD LEITHAUSER: Travel really does open up your eyes — *mine*, anyway. After spending a year in England, I came back home and noticed all kinds of differences, like how big our cars are. Even growing up in Detroit, the "Motor City," I wasn't really aware of such an obvious thing until I'd been abroad.

Aside from your many natural subjects, the specifically human element is also clearly present in your first book in such poems as "Two Summer Jobs" and "Old Hat," in which a left-behind hat incites:

> The slow, spiraling loss of love and pain
> that turns you, day by day, into a stranger.

But such subjects are even more common in your third and fourth books, The Mail from Anywhere *(1990) and* The Last Odd Thing She Did *(1998). Although you received some criticism for branching out further into this area, Robert Darling correctly praised the conscious "humanity" that clearly increased in the last two books, especially in your poems about family and your poems about love and loss.*

BRAD LEITHAUSER: It's true that I like writing both kinds of poems, and I'm currently organizing my next collection into two parts: poems about people, and poems about the unpeopled world.

Which you did to a certain extent in The Mail from Anywhere *where section three is called "A Peopled World."*

BRAD LEITHAUSER: Yes, and in my next collection, I want the poems to get gradually "colder" as the manuscript progresses. The second-to-last poem is about the miles of ice and rocks that I saw while hiking one day in Iceland. So I want the human element to slowly vaporize out of the book, to "ghostify," to coin a word. But there are still many human poems in the book. I'm particularly drawn to poems about family, and although I sometimes write autobiographically, most of the people in my poems are made-up.

Maybe that's your novelist instinct. The family poems tend to have a very autobiographical feel to them.

BRAD LEITHAUSER: I suppose every writer is uneasy about how to deal with the actual events of his own life. Some people clearly write about their lives and then try to disguise the fact for various reasons, but I tend to do the opposite. I generally write about characters and events that are not part of my life, but I try to write about them in such a way that they seem autobiographical. I'm very interested in the notion of trying to create poetic narratives for characters, and sometimes this has led me to longer poems like *Darlington's Fall* and the more recent "A Science Fiction Writer of the Fifties." The newer poem is about a man who writes bad pulp novels in the fifties, and I started getting very interested in the character, and the poem ended up seven or eight pages long. I find it very pleasurable to smuggle into poetry, when appropriate, many of the materials that are traditionally used in fiction. One of the things I enjoyed about writing *Darlington's Fall* was the opportunity to use so many dates and events and place names. I also greatly enjoyed the research. For example, when the main character goes off to college, it's a made-up college, but I based it on the University of Michigan during that period. So I read through the microfilm of Michigan's college newspaper for the years 1906 to 1910 in order to get a feeling for the campus back then — hoping that I could incorporate that sense of specific place into the long poem.

The narrative element in poetry has a long but sometimes overlooked tradition in our poetic heritage —

BRAD LEITHAUSER: Yes, it does, and I think that occasionally poets get the feeling that not enough stories are getting into the poetry, so they try to write more narrative poems. Byron definitely felt that way when writing *Don Juan*, and more recently, two poets who died not too long ago — L.E. Sissman and James Merrill — were both eager to incorporate narrative elements into some of their poems. The danger, of course, is that the writing might move away from poetry and start sounding like prose, but that rarely happened with either Sissman or Merrill.

Your increasing interest in poetic narrative is clear in your last two books. The powerful title poem of The Last Odd Thing She Did, *for example, is about a young woman who commits suicide in a car which she intentionally leaves sitting on the edge of a cliff with the engine running and the headlights on — as a kind of tragic marker of her death. The poem ends:*

> *... Come what may,*
> *The night will be lovely, as she foresaw,*
> *The first stars easing through the blue,*
> *Engine and ocean breathing together.*

BRAD LEITHAUSER: That poem had the oddest origins of anything I've ever written. I first got the idea when reading a novel by the Polish science fiction writer Stanislaw Lem. I don't remember which one. There was a vehicle on some distant planet in the extremely cold outer reaches of space, and the vehicle died, and the person in it died, but the light on the vehicle stayed on — like a little star, like a little glimmer of light in the middle of nowhere. In the novel, of course, that lonely light represented not only death but the remoteness of death, and the image lingered in my mind, and I eventually started imagining a car on the edge of a cliff with its headlights on. Then I started imagining that someone in the car had committed suicide. So, gradually, the poem created itself backwards from the image of the distant headlights.

Now, if we could, I'd like to shift from your more narrative and dramatic poems to your shorter, witty poems, specifically the two series of humorous poems called "Minims" which appeared in your first two volumes. "Trauma," for example, is a short quatrain of two couplets:

> *You will carry this suture*
>   *Into the future.*
> *The past never passes.*
>   *It simply amasses.*

But, unfortunately, your "Minims" stopped after the first two collections. Why was that?

BRAD LEITHAUSER: I still have a few left, and I really do enjoy writing them, but I haven't had enough of them to make a full series. The wonderful thing about writing those little poems is that, unlike other poems, they usually happen very quickly — maybe twenty minutes or so, if things go right. So if I write one at nine in the morning, I've already got four or six lines that will appear in an upcoming book, and I feel way ahead of the game for the rest of the day. It's a great feeling, especially since my other poems, with one exception, never seem to come quite so quickly.

What was the exception, and how did it happen?

BRAD LEITHAUSER: "Old Bachelor Brother." I was on the way to visit a friend one time, traveling on a night train from London to Edinburgh. When I got on the train, I had no idea about the poem; when I got off, in Edinburgh, it was done. That never happens to me, but I'm a bit of an insomniac, especially on trains, and I couldn't sleep, and I'd start drifting off, and then I'd wake up and think of the next stanza.

We touched on this earlier, but many readers, reading a poem like that, would assume that you're referring to someone you know, someone in your family, and that it relates to an actual wedding.

BRAD LEITHAUSER: I know, but it's nothing like that. To be honest, I'm not sure where the original idea came from. It just came to me on the train, and I went with it, and it was a very lovely feeling. It seemed as though that's how poetry should *really* be written; but, alas, for me, it rarely happens that easily.

Maybe this relates to part of the reason, but your poetry is always justly praised for its meticulous use of formal elements — John Updike once described you as an "addict of intricate stanzas." Within those stanzas, however, you tend to use a lot of variation involving enjambments, varying line lengths, and indentations. I wonder if you could discuss the latter, which are generally avoided by contemporary formalists.

BRAD LEITHAUSER: It's a good question, and perhaps connected to my early interest in Marianne Moore. Indentations in English poetry have generally indicated line-lengths, so if we look at a poem by George Herbert, we may easily tell the number of iambs in a line by the pattern of its indentations. But Marianne Moore turned that convention on its ear by using indentations, in many cases, to indicate her subtle rhyming patterns, which tended to be fairly well-concealed, often using off-rhymes that could easily be overlooked. So regardless of her syllabics, the real organizing principle of Moore's poetry was her rhyme.

Which would be especially true with the long lines where the syllabics fall apart and become rhythmically meaningless.

BRAD LEITHAUSER: Yes, Moore's syllabics are frequently irrelevant. In my opinion, the power of prosody is precisely related to the power it can evoke or engender when it's broken, but if Moore breaks up her syllabics in a 17-syllable line, no one will notice unless they count the syllables later, which has nothing to do with the visceral act of reading a poem. On the other hand, say in Longfellow's trochaics, if he tries to vary the meter in *Hiawatha*, it's much too disruptive and awkward, so he's unable to vary his meter much at all.

Yes, because as soon as you break a falling rhythm, the reader tends to go back to the more natural rising iambs.

BRAD LEITHAUSER: Which is why trochaic prosody in English doesn't work very well. It's too hard to vary; it's too inflexible. So getting back to indentations, I like the feeling that a poem can be free at both ends of the line. All poets accept the idea of freedom at the right-hand margin, and I've tried to experiment with being more free at the left-hand margin. It's an attempt, maybe an overly artificial one, to make the poem airborne.

In 2002, you published your ambitious 5,708-line verse-novel, Darlington's Fall, *about the life of a fictional early 20th-Century naturalist, Russel Darlington. The poem consists of a sequence of ten-line stanzas in which all of the end words are rhymed but in varying patterns. Many are solid rhymes, some are off-rhymes, and there are even a few sight rhymes. How did you decide on such a format?*

BRAD LEITHAUSER: For me personally, the common difficulty in writing a poem is not in finding something that interests me — many things do — nor in figuring out what I want to say. The real challenge is finding a form that's right for the poem. Originally, as the ideas began to germinate for *Darlington's Fall*, I considered writing the poem in *abab* quatrains, which, given the tight rhyme scheme, would have necessitated a lot of off-rhymes. But even with the off-rhymes, it still seemed like too much of a straitjacket for my overall intentions. I wanted more freedom, and I wanted to write the poem in longer units, so I started toying with a ten-line stanza. Given how I was envisioning the narrative and descriptive elements in the poem,

I felt that each stanza should be long enough to be self-contained. Of course, some of the stanzas flow into each other, but most are like blocks in the narrative, almost like paragraphs.

And the varying rhymes?

BRAD LEITHAUSER: Well, I wanted the rhymes to seem as though they were falling catch as catch can, and I also wanted most of them to disappear — or to be only vaguely there, like distant music — although I still wanted the option of ending some of the stanzas with a rather clangorous couplet. So the varying rhyme scheme gave me the freedom to use the rhymes like church bells off in the distance, and, at other times, to make them sound as if the bells were ringing overhead. I should add that I'm fascinated by and obsessed with the sonnet, and even though I didn't feel that the poem should be a sonnet sequence, I did envision the ten-line stanza as a kind of truncated sonnet, usually in a four/six pattern — a quatrain and a sestet. The book actually opens with a rather ragged prefatory sonnet, and it closes with one that's very tight, and that's how I saw the narrative progression of the main character's life, from chaos and tragedy to a final sense of order. In my mind, the poem is about the personal journey of a man who, after a retreat from the difficulties of his life, eventually falls in love and re-enters the world. So I wanted the structure of the poem to reflect that as well — to be a prosodic journey toward order, clarity, and discipline.

Since 1985, you've also published a series of widely varied prose novels, Equal Distance *(1985),* Hence *(1989),* Seaward *(1993),* The Friends of Freeland *(1997), and* A Few Corrections *(2001). How do you think the novel writing has affected your poetry?*

BRAD LEITHAUSER: I often point out to my students that we writers tend to miss over 99% of what's poetically rich and interesting in our daily lives. We're all fallible in that way, and we just don't recognize all the useful things around us. So as poets, we have to force ourselves to recognize the poetic potentials that are always unfolding all around us — just as the novelist has to pay attention to the stories. For me, one of the great pleasures of writing in both formats is that it not only forces me to pay close attention to things, but it also gives me a variety of ways to write about whatever I do tend to notice.

Does one format ever evolve into the other? Do you ever, for example, hit on something in a novel that you decide should be dealt with in a poem?

BRAD LEITHAUSER: Occasionally I've spun a poem out of the fiction. There's a poem in *Cats in the Temple*, for example, called "At Greg's" derived from a character in my novel *Equal Distance*. It can also happen the other way. I've been considering writing a novella that would take off from a moment in *Darlington's Fall* when a butterfly that has no business being in Indiana suddenly appears and initiates a whole chain of events that leads ultimately to both tragedy and redemption. So I've started envisioning a novella about a creature who suddenly appears, like the butterfly, in a place he doesn't belong, and then initiates a whole series of events.

I'd like to shift now to your writing methods. Given your various travels, you must write in many different places, but do you tend to write your poetry at certain specific times?

BRAD LEITHAUSER: I seem to work best in the mornings, but that isn't always true. Last summer, I started writing at night in a gazebo in back of our house. I worked by a little kerosene lamp I once bought in Iceland. The gazebo is tightly screened, which is a good thing as there are a million mosquitoes flying around out there, and I very much enjoyed writing in the glow of that lamp with all those frustrated mosquitoes flying nearby in the dark.

Earlier, you mentioned that you wrote "Old Bachelor Brother" on a train. Do you often write on trains and planes?

BRAD LEITHAUSER: Yes, especially if I'm traveling alone. It's one of the reasons I enjoy writing in so many different genres — poems, novels, and criticism. If the poems get stuck, or I get so sick of the current novel that I can't even stand to think about it, I can try something else, wherever I am. Since I like to work every day, I always have a number of projects going on to create some variety. Novels, of course, do take long blocks of time, and I find it harder to put them down and then start them up again than I do with the poems. It's also harder to get started with fiction. With poetry, I can always carry around a little sheaf of poems under my arm, and if I get fifteen minutes — in the laundromat or anywhere else — I have no problem getting to work.

Do you keep a list of ideas for potential poems?

BRAD LEITHAUSER: Yes, I've been keeping journals since 1971 when I first went off to college. It's not a diary, and I don't write in it every single day. As a matter of fact, it's often a bad sign if I'm writing too much in my journals because, normally, as soon as an idea starts getting interesting, I'll move from the journal and start on the manuscript.

Do you reread your older journals looking for ideas?

BRAD LEITHAUSER: Fairly often, and maybe I should do it more. I'll start looking through my old notes, searching for an interesting idea, asking myself how I could make use of this or that. Unfortunately, as I explain to my students, who seem discouraged by the idea, most poems are never finished. I'll get an idea, start the poem, and eventually realize that it isn't working. Sometimes I'll assume that the form isn't right, but then I'll try something else, and that won't work either. So many of my poems get "dead stuck," and I'll put them aside for a year and try them again, and they still won't work. But occasionally when I'll go back to one of those unfinished poems, I'll suddenly make a tiny change, often in the form, and everything will suddenly fall into place — which relates to my convictions about the "freeing" aspect of form. I must admit that I get very tired of the old cliché that form and content are the same. Well, maybe in heaven they're the same, but not down here on earth. It's much more like a dance in which the poet tries to bring the form and the content as close as possible, so they can work together.

Which creates a healthy tension.

BRAD LEITHAUSER: Yes, in heaven it's all beautifully interlocked, but in the sublunary world that we live in, form and content are always knocking up against each other, and we have to find a way to make them respond to each other in a kind of dance. Which is, it seems to me, what so much of the "search" for a poem is really all about.

Given that you're married to another distinguished poet, Mary Jo Salter, do you ever show her your work-in-progress?

BRAD LEITHAUSER: I do, but I don't like to show her anything at a very early stage. She often kids me that by the time she sees anything, it's already locked into place, and her opinions are extraneous, and maybe there's some truth to that. I guess I'm always wary of being overly influenced by comments, especially early on. It's very difficult to clear our minds once people have suggested new ideas. So I prefer to hear critical responses later in the game.

As we've been discussing, you've written in many poetic forms and modes over the years. What would you like to try — or do more of?

BRAD LEITHAUSER: Even though I usually try to find my forms *after* I've begun writing, not before, I've had a recent floating desire to work in five-line stanzas and to try to do something a bit different with them — although I'm not sure exactly what that will be. I very much enjoy playing with prosody, and I'd like to think that in most of my poems there's something a bit odd or interesting or unusual about the prosody — even if it's just a little twist or turn or playfulness.

Back in 1983, you published an essay in The New Criterion *called "Metrical Illiteracy." This was a powerful indictment of contemporary verse and its disregard of its rhythmic traditions. I personally believe that "Metrical Illiteracy" is one of the most important essays of recent times and a seminal document in the*

Brad Leithauser

formalist revival. Now that twenty years have passed, do you think the situation has improved?

BRAD LEITHAUSER: I'm not really sure. Maybe it has. But I do get tired of the two more extreme positions relating to form. Even though most of the poets I like best are formalists, I've always been wary of a certain smugness in the so-called New Formalism — the sense that its proponents were somehow "saving" the culture. Personally, I don't think there's anything intrinsically valuable about writing a poem in form, and nothing necessarily good about a poem written in form. Zero. It's a matter of what you do with it. On the other hand, there's the even more irritating notion that free verse is somehow inherently avant-garde — when in fact for a long time now it has been the reigning conventional mode. And I also get quite tired of the contemporary cliché that formalism is conservative, and free verse somehow liberal and liberating. In my opinion, even though it's very hard to do, I feel that the poetic future lies in new and variant forms — that is, playing with and against the older formats.

Which the tradition has done all along.

BRAD LEITHAUSER: That's my point. So much of what was truly exciting in the twentieth century, like Wilfred Owen's rhyming, for example, was the result of variations on the old modes of formalism.

We tend to forget, but Frost himself was considered very radical in his time.

BRAD LEITHAUSER: Exactly. So any sense that formalism is something which is "locked up" and untouchable seems deadening to me. I think the challenge and the burden of forms is to find new and different ways to move and charm our readers. The biggest problem facing free verse is that its methods have become familiar, and there's nothing inherently exciting about it anymore.

I'd certainly agree with that, but let me press you a little about the idea that forms don't have inherent value. I believe, for example, that the sonnet is one of man's greatest creations and accomplishments. And by that, I mean specifically the form.

BRAD LEITHAUSER

It's one of those magical structures, like a snowflake or a baseball diamond, that's both beautiful and good in itself. Borges once wrote a sonnet claiming that the form was actually given to the first Italian sonneteer by Apollo himself, and I feel the same way about a number of the forms, like terza rima, for example, which have an incredible, inherent power in their structure.

BRAD LEITHAUSER: I would definitely agree with that. A few years ago when I did a review of *The Oxford Book of Sonnets* for *The New York Review of Books*, I said something quite similar. I pointed out that when I was working for *Time* magazine, and they did a millennium piece about the greatest inventions in the last 1,000 years, I was very disappointed that they didn't ask my opinion, because I would have said the sonnet. So I would certainly agree the form itself can be naturally beautiful and good. Auden always felt that the key to the sonnet was its crucial mathematical ratio of four to three, which is also, of course, the basis of the typical ballad.

And ballads are a perfect example of the power of forms, especially in its traditional four/three/four/three stanza, with the occasional anapest dropped in. It creates a rhythm in the mind that's unforgettable for all human beings. So there's a definite magic in certain poetic forms, although, as you point out, that doesn't mean that anyone who uses them is necessarily going to release the magic. You can walk on the diamond and still play a lousy game of baseball.

BRAD LEITHAUSER: Exactly. We haven't accomplished anything by simply writing a sonnet unless we've somehow, in some sort of vast, Borgesian calculus, advanced or enriched the form itself.

Just out of curiosity, why didn't you include either "Metrical Illiteracy" or your subsequent and related essay "The Confinement of Free Verse" in Penchants & Places, *your 1995 collection of essays published by Knopf?*

BRAD LEITHAUSER: I've been saving my essays on poetry for a future book. The various references to poetry in *Penchants & Places* are mostly tangential. So that's another project I'm working on.

In 1999, you edited No Other Book, *the selected essays of Randall Jarrell whom you believe to be the best American critic since T.S. Eliot. Do you think that American criticism can ever return to such a respectful, erudite, and passionate engagement with the literary arts?*

BRAD LEITHAUSER: In one of those essays, Jarrell, who was always very generous, mentioned how many good critics there were writing about poetry back in those days. But in our times, I feel that we're in a very weak period for poetry criticism. There are a few exceptions, and there are a number of people who write wonderful criticism — like Richard Wilbur and Tony Hecht — who for various reasons don't wish to spend the time reviewing the contemporary scene. With too many contemporary reviews, I have the feeling that something hidden's going on, rather than an honest encounter with the literature. One thing I always enjoyed about Jarrell was that, even when he was reviewing the work of one of his close friends, like Robert Lowell, I felt I could trust his responses. I never had the feeling that something covert was going on. A related problem, of course, is that reviewing involves so much work and so little financial return. At any rate, I may not be certain about my judgments regarding the overall state of contemporary poetry, but I have no doubts about the unfortunate state of contemporary poetry criticism.

Despite your various travels, you've taught at a number of colleges over the years, and with your wife, Mary Jo Salter, you currently share the Emily Dickinson Lectureship in the Humanities at Mount Holyoke College in South Hadley, Massachusetts. I know that you teach a course called Modern Alternatives to Realism, but I wonder if you also teach poetry writing?

BRAD LEITHAUSER: I'm always happy to teach either fiction writing or poetry writing, but since the college generally needs a fiction writer, I usually do that. But occasionally I'm called in to teach a class in poetry writing.

In those classes, how do you attempt to interest young students in metrics?

BRAD LEITHAUSER: I give a lot of formal assignments, but I also allow them to avoid the ones they're most wary about. So if I give thirteen assignments over the course of the semester, I might require them to do ten of their choosing. I don't want them telling me, "I couldn't do that form," and then ending up hating the assignment. So I give them a little leeway. Also, since I'm very interested in song lyrics, I'll often bring examples into class — and play some Cole Porter or Sondheim, for example — which often engages their interest in form and structure. I also find children's poetry very helpful for illustrating certain things, especially those that are already in their heads, like rhyme. I also use advertisements, and I'll say, "Name a product that uses rhyme in its ads." Eventually, they come to understand that there's a very good reason why an advertiser use rhymes — because they're powerful and they get into our heads.

What advice or suggestions do you give to aspiring poets?

BRAD LEITHAUSER: As a teacher of creative writing, you always have a sense of futility about what you're doing. You often feel incapable of conveying what's most important, and the problem is compounded by their ages. The habits of perception of a twenty-year-old are generally in a wild and confusing flux. So each semester, I invariably end up making a speech to remind them that the most valuable thing they can learn as a young writer is to understand, in a completely unobnoxious and unarrogant way, how all-encompassing is the task of being a "writer."

To have an awareness of all the poetic possibilities?

BRAD LEITHAUSER: Yes, to train themselves to be perceptive about all the useful things going on around them. To keep their antennae up. To take notice of all the interesting details and facts and stories, and then ask themselves, "Can I do something with that?" It might be something very small, maybe just something intriguing or irregular, or maybe even just a slip of the tongue. So they need, given that they're twenty years old, to train themselves in the habits of perception which are crucial for any writer, especially a poet.

In 1994, you edited The Norton Book of Ghost Stories, *and in* Penchants

& Places, you pointed out that in your childhood, your parents tried to protect you and your "highly impressionable" brothers from things like ghost stories and Rod Serling's The Twilight Zone. *Yet you've still maintained a life-long interest in such things and have even written poems like "The Ghost of a Ghost" and your novel,* Seaward, *where the main character encounters the ghost of his dead wife. In* Penchants & Places, *you write that, "In truth, I fail to see how any serious artist, whether middling or a major talent, can avoid becoming something of a mystic." Could you discuss that a bit?*

BRAD LEITHAUSER: Although I'm usually a quite skeptical person, I think that all writers have to believe in some other kind of realm not very far removed from our own — maybe it's even part of our own — where absolutes exist. Which is to say, if you're writing a poem, you have to believe that *this* particular word is better than some other word that might offer itself. It's definitely not a relative matter, and it's not a matter of taste. Those questions can be raised after the fact, but in the actual process of writing, you have to feel that *this* word or *this* metaphor or *this* pattern is better than all the other choices. You have to have the sense that the poem you're seeking after is out there somewhere. It's almost as if the poem already exists in that other realm, and you're simply trying to uncover it. So the writer, in my opinion, is always seeking after that other realm, which is why we *know* that the twelve previous drafts are wrong, or that a certain metaphor isn't just right, or that the poem's form isn't quite apt yet. It's also how we know, with confidence, when we *do* get it right, because we've tapped into that other realm and uncovered what we're striving for — whether it's a poem about a monarch butterfly, or a seahorse, or a stormy day in Amsterdam.

So as soon as you start saying "better" or "right," then you're pressing up against the metaphysical?

BRAD LEITHAUSER: Yes, because you're insisting, no matter how skeptical you might be about other things, that at some level, there's a domain of absolutes, and that, as a poet, you're actively pursuing it.

Given that pursuit, it might be appropriate to finish up today by reading the ending of your excellent poem "An Eighteenth-Century Microscope":

> *Beyond the narrow mete and bound*
> *Of the surveyor's grounded measurements —*
> *Always the kingdom deeper, richer*
> *Than any bare, unprivileged eye could see.*

Thank you, Brad.

BRAD LEITHAUSER: Thank you, Bill.

Charles Martin

Charles Martin is a distinguished American poet and classical translator. He was once described by Dick Allen as "one of the finest younger poets of our time," and more recently, X.J. Kennedy has called him "a poet of masterly command."

Born and raised in the Bronx, New York, Charles Martin received his B.A. from Fordham University in 1964 and did graduate work in English at the State University of New York at Buffalo from 1965 to 1968. He then taught for two years at Notre Dame College of Staten Island, New York, before taking a position at Queensborough College where he still teaches. Over the years he has also taught in the Writing Seminars at Johns Hopkins University and conducted workshops at the Poetry Center at New York's 92nd Street Y.

His first collection of poetry, *Room for Error* (1978), was published by the University of Georgia Press. His next two books, *Steal the Bacon* (1987) and *What the Darkness Proposes* (1996), were published by the Johns Hopkins University Press, and both books were finalists for the Pulitzer Prize. His most recent collection, *Starting from Sleep: New and Selected Poems* (2002), was published in the Sewanee Writers' Series by the Overlook Press. He is also the author of *The Poems of Catullus* (Abattoir, 1979; revised edition, Johns Hopkins University Press, 1990); *Catullus* (Yale University Press, 1992); and *Ovid: Metamorphoses* (W.W. Norton, 2003).

This interview was conducted during the Association of Writing Programs' Conference at the Palmer House in Chicago, Illinois.

You were born and raised in the Bronx. Which part?

CHARLES MARTIN: I grew up in Parkchester, a community that was created in 1941, the year before I was born. It was built by Metropolitan Life Insurance, and it consisted of seven- and twelve-story buildings that enclosed a central park called Metropolitan Oval. It was a very attractive community, and I enjoyed growing up there. It seemed like a protected haven; there were lots of trees, grass, sidewalks, and plenty of kids to play with.

Was there an ethnic mix?

CHARLES MARTIN: At the time Parkchester was built, it was described by *The New Republic* as a liberal and progressive community, meaning that Italians, Irish, and Jews all lived together in the same apartment buildings. Back then, most of the Bronx was divided into separate ethnic neighborhoods, so Parkchester must have seemed pretty unusual.

Did the different groups get along?

CHARLES MARTIN: Yes, I grew up playing with Jewish kids and Catholic kids, and it was a nice mix. It wasn't until much later that I realized that we were, of course, just as racially segregated as any southern community. Eventually, there were gradual efforts to integrate, but by the time my parents moved to Yonkers, when I was about eighteen, the neighborhood was still mostly white. Since those days, from what I understand, the area has been successfully integrated.

Your dad was a salesman. What did he sell?

CHARLES MARTIN: He was in the woolen goods business, which was a declining industry at the time, and we were always worried about it. The woolen market didn't completely collapse until he was in his early sixties, but when I was growing up, we were always terrified of the prospect of synthetics taking over and driving wool into the ground.

Did he commute downtown to the garment district?

CHARLES MARTIN: Yes, every day. He was located right in the center of the district.

Where did you go to high school?

CHARLES MARTIN: I went to a Catholic High School called St. Helena's, which was off the Hutchinson Highway near the Whitestone Bridge. St. Helena's was a little red-brick school, the outgrowth of the parish elementary school, and it was said at the time that the students had one of two choices: either you could become a policeman, or you could become somebody that the policeman chased after. That was probably not the case, but we flattered ourselves that it was.

When did you first get interested in poetry?

CHARLES MARTIN: I was about sixteen or seventeen when I first started reading poetry, and I got very interested. Most of what I read was modern poetry, especially from Untermeyer's anthology of modern verse, which led me to people like Cummings, Pound, and Eliot. Fortunately, the local public library had a surprisingly good collection of modern poetry.

So your interest developed on its own, rather than at home or at school?

CHARLES MARTIN: That's right, although in my senior year of high school, there was a librarian, Mrs. Kelly, who was the wife of the poet Robert Kelly, and she had a significant influence on my reading. She'd say, "You ought to try this poet," or, "Try that one." So I did. Mostly, it was modern, contemporary poetry.

Which seems rather unusual.

CHARLES MARTIN: Maybe it was. But I remember reading that Yvor Winters, for example, did the same thing when he lived in Chicago. He started reading all the poetry of the period, and he later felt that he had a very weak background in pre-modern English poetry.

So when did you actually start writing?

CHARLES MARTIN: Around the same time, when I was sixteen

or seventeen.

Who were your early models?

CHARLES MARTIN: I went through a very big Cummings phase!

Even the lower case letters?

CHARLES MARTIN: Everything *but* the lower case letters. I was always quite astonished when somebody would read one of my poems and said, "Oh, yeah, E.E. Cummings," because I thought I'd concealed it so well.

What about Eliot?

CHARLES MARTIN: Well, I'd read *The Waste Land* and "Prufrock," but, of course, I really didn't understand them at the time. But I think that what you initially get from reading poetry is the rhythm, the sound, much more than the content. So when you're writing, you're trying to imitate what you've enjoyed hearing — the poetic rhythms.

Eventually, you went to the Jesuit-run Fordham University in the Bronx. Was there anyone at Fordham who was especially helpful?

CHARLES MARTIN: There were some very helpful professors at Fordham, especially my freshman English teacher. If it hadn't been for Charles Donahue, I don't think I would have become a poet. He was a very scholarly man, and his specialty was Indo-European languages. He knew at least fifteen languages, and he made us realize that the acquisition of knowledge was a lifetime occupation. Naturally, I felt horribly backward and intimidated, but at the same time, it felt quite comforting to now be involved in that kind of long-term process.

Did he read your poetry?

CHARLES MARTIN: Just a few poems. I was rather shy about pushing my poems on other people. I did allow the Fordham literary magazine to publish a few, and I'd sometimes leave the journals open on tables where they'd be seen, but in general, I was very shy about it. I also had a very good Latin professor at Fordham. William Grimaldi was a Jesuit who encouraged my interest in translating Latin poetry — and in reading both Horace and Catullus.

Did you major in English or Classics?

CHARLES MARTIN: I was an English major.

Did you take a fair number of classics courses?

CHARLES MARTIN: In my freshman and sophomore year, I took Latin each semester, and I took a very good course in Latin poetry with Grimaldi. I also took introductory Greek, but I didn't stick with it, although I started taking French, and I enjoyed it very much. The curriculum at Fordham was intended to produce the kind of Catholic gentleman that Cardinal Newman would have approved of, but actually, if you had to design a curriculum for poets, you'd be hard pressed to come up with a better one. We had lots of languages, and literature, and some philosophy.

Were you writing metrically back then?

CHARLES MARTIN: As an undergraduate, I wrote in both free verse and meter, never doing one exclusively. Then I went off to graduate school at Buffalo, and I got caught up in the academics and the dissertation, and I pretty much stopped writing poetry for a while.

What was Buffalo like in those days?

CHARLES MARTIN: It was a very good place for poetry. Unlike Fordham, which didn't have poets of the "living" kind, Buffalo had many practicing poets on the faculty. They also had a weekly reading series, and most of the well-known poets came through eventually.

Who was teaching there at the time?

CHARLES MARTIN: One of the poets at Buffalo during my first year was Charles Olson.

Did you study with Olson?

CHARLES MARTIN: Well, I signed up for one of his classes, and then I decided after a session or so that it wasn't for me. It seemed that Olson was more interested in attracting disciples than anything else, and I didn't plan to become one.

That would have been a very different Charles Martin!

CHARLES MARTIN: Yes, it certainly would have. But I must admit that some of the people who actually stayed with Olson got a lot out of the experience. He was a teacher who pushed his students in very interesting directions, and he was certainly a charismatic and influential individual. But Buffalo had many other poets as well — like Mac Hammond, Irving Feldman, Robert Creeley, and John Logan, who also had a group of young poets around him.

When did you start writing again?

CHARLES MARTIN: During my last year at Buffalo, I became friends with Robert Hass, and we started showing each other our poems, and that helped me to start writing again after the long, dry spell.

Did you continue writing at Notre Dame College on Staten Island, where you taught for two years before moving to Queensborough College?

CHARLES MARTIN: Yes, and now that I was writing again, I discovered that I was writing mostly metrical poetry. It seemed to me that the possibilities of metrical poetry were far more interesting than free verse, and it fully absorbed my attention.

Did you know any other poets who were writing metrical verse back then?

CHARLES MARTIN: Just a couple. It was very clear to me and everyone else that this was not the way things were moving.

Did you feel isolated?

CHARLES MARTIN: Yes, I did. I think that most young poets feel isolated and underappreciated, but there was definitely the sense that if you were writing in rhyme and meter you were heading for the boneyard!

And of your own volition! Like driving off a cliff.

CHARLES MARTIN: Exactly, so I had very little expectation that anything would happen with my work. But in 1968 I sent a bunch of poems to *Poetry* magazine when Daryl Hine took over as the new editor, and amazingly, he took seven pages of poetry and ran them all in a single issue. So I thought, "Okay, maybe this wasn't such a bad decision after all."

In 1978, the University of Georgia Press published your first book, Room for Error. *Later, you published* Steal the Bacon *(1987) and* What the Darkness Proposes *(1996), both of which were Pulitzer finalists. More recently, you published* Starting from Sleep: New and Selected Poems *(2002). Most of the poems in these collections are highly meditative, yet they express themselves in many different modes and employ a wide range of subjects. I'd like to start with the poems marked with wit and irony, especially the epigrams. John Hollander has written that your "epigrams are the finest of those by a living writer." One of my favorites is "Deconstructing the Zebra":*

> *"Watch out for flailing hooves," hyenas swarm,*
> *Whose one rule is, "Dig in while it's still warm."*

How do you decide whether an idea should be a short epigram or the germ of a

Charles Martin

more extended poem?

CHARLES MARTIN: That's a good question, and I'm not sure I know the answer. Most of my epigrams come to me as problems requiring short, concise answers. Occasionally, though, I'll start thinking, "Maybe it could be a little longer." So I'll try to develop the poem, and if it won't develop, I'll finally admit that it's best to leave it alone.

Do any of them come short and stay short?

CHARLES MARTIN: Yes, with a number of them, you realize right away that you can't develop them any further than they already are.

Given your classical background, have you translated much Martial?

CHARLES MARTIN: Just a bit. The truth is, I usually prefer almost anybody's English versions to Martial's originals!

So the translators are making him better than he really is?

CHARLES MARTIN: I think that's the case.

But, as you admit, some of them come out very well in the English.

CHARLES MARTIN: Yes, I think Martial offers some very useful material for English poets to snap at, and they do, often successfully. And rhyme gives English translators of Martial an advantage over the Latin version.

Another poetic mode that you like to use on occasion is parody, sometimes mixed with homage. "Four for Theodore Roethke" obviously relates to Roethke's "Four for Sir John Davies," "Just a Smack at Larkin" comes from Empson's "Just a Smack at Auden," and the epigram "Prufrock Balena" speaks for itself:

> *In the cool depths the lissome females tarry,*
> *Squawking of Calimari.*

CHARLES MARTIN

Why do you think there's so little parody done these days? We live in an age when everybody's poking fun at everybody else, so why isn't there more poetic parody?

CHARLES MARTIN: I think that part of the answer is that verse has fewer literary uses now than it had in the past, when, say, it was even used sometimes in drama. I was just talking to someone who edits a magazine about contemporary drama, and when I asked him if there were any verse plays these days, he said, "Nope, not a one."

But there was lots of poetic parody back in the thirties and forties.

CHARLES MARTIN: Yes, but I think back in those decades, there were many people who'd grown up with the kind of metrical education that allowed them to do such things. Nowadays, as you know, that kind of education has largely disappeared. Also back then, there was a large body of well-known popular poetry which naturally lent itself to parody, like "Casey at the Bat," for example, but such universally-known popular poems have also disappeared. It's unfortunate, especially since metrical poetry naturally allows for a fair amount of humor and comedy. Much more so, I believe, than free verse does.

Returning to another aspect of your poetry, a number of your poems have Biblical, classical, or literary themes, such as "Complaint of the Watchman" about the Tower of Babel, "At Home with Psyche and Eros," "A Night at the Opera" about Aeneas and Dido, and "Passages from Friday" relating to Robinson Crusoe. *Writing about such subjects allows you to not only develop the character beyond the original, but it also allows you to make grand conjectures about larger themes. In "A Night at the Opera," for example, the poem shows Aeneas sailing away from Dido and planning the city he will eventually build — one that will be strong because it will be pitiless:*

> "No fundament of stone
> Is safe to build upon;
> My city will be made
> Of Law, my laws obeyed;
> In my earth-wracking city

CHARLES MARTIN

Will be no room for pity
Or weakness of any kind . . ."

CHARLES MARTIN: I think you're right about both of those things. Using such subjects provides a kind of protection for the writer, allowing him to speak in a voice that's different from his own, and allowing him to speculate more comfortably about larger issues. Maybe, in my own case, it also comes from my Catholic education, which has a tendency, I believe, to get one to think about things in a way that's often somewhat otherworldly.

Although many of your poems deal with memorable specifics — like sharks, Dracula, the rape of the Sabine women, a snapping turtle, and Mandelstam — you're also unafraid of using abstractions, and you find some very interesting ways to make them come to life. "Even as We Sleep," for example, humorously personifies a number of human conditions while still making serious points about human "Shame," "Deceit," and "Guilt." "Death Will Do Nothing" discusses the disinterest of "Death" in a moody and very effective villanelle. These are inventive ways of using form and mode to overcome Pound's generally judicious warning, "Beware of abstractions."

CHARLES MARTIN: I think it's fun to have allegorical figures running around making their points, and it's quite challenging to find ways to overcome the rather common attitude that says, "No, you can't do that. You can never use abstractions in poetry. You've got to keep your nose to the pavement." I also much enjoy using forms in ways that might seem to go against our expectations for that particular form. When Oscar Wilde wrote the first villanelle in English, his "Theocritus," it was an artificial thing, shopworn in its sentiments. Back in the late 1800s, nobody in his right mind would have used the villanelle for anything serious, but thirty or forty years after Wilde did it, you had Empson and Auden. The villanelle has become a form used by poets for serious work, and it's occurred to me that other forms might be susceptible to such upgrading. Recently, for example, I've been thinking a lot about the triolet, a form generally considered very trivial, and I'm even writing a little article about triolets for *Iambs and Trochees*.

You also include contemporary, personal relationships among your poetic themes. My favorite is the excellent "The Two of Them" about a couple's disintegrating relationship during a trip to California. It's a very sad poem, keyed by the first line, "But no, it isn't over for them yet," and it has a very curious intrusion by an "I" late in the poem who describes the man and woman:

> Who sit where I have put them and think about
> The way it goes from certainty to doubt
>   And back again . . .

The insertion of the "I" is very effective, but it's also rather risky.

CHARLES MARTIN: I was hoping that by allowing the "I" to speak at that point, it would engage the reader more intimately.

Does that mean that the reader should associate the "I" with one of the two people in the poem?

CHARLES MARTIN: I suspect that most readers will make that association, but I suppose it could also read as a kind of sapphic triad involving three people: Sappho observing the man and the woman together. Sappho's poem is about desire, though, and this one deals with regret.

When the poem first appeared in The Formalist *in 1992, it had the title, "What the Dark Proposes," but when you published your subsequent collection, you changed the poem's title to "The Two of Them," and then used a variant of the original title for the entire collection,* What the Darkness Proposes *(Hopkins, 1996). The original version of the poem also had a footnote, "Which may be those the dark itself proposes." Do you remember these alterations?*

CHARLES MARTIN: I do. I'm always fiddling with my poems, especially when they move from journals into books, and this is particularly true with titles. I also wanted the book to include the long poem, "A Walk in the Hills above the Artists' House," which ends:

> And bless the darkness that extends
> Beyond us and proposes what
> We will all come to, no doubt but.

So the similarity between these lines and the shorter poem's original title was another reason for the change.

I never realized you were such a fiddler.

CHARLES MARTIN: Yes, I'm continually revising things. When I prepared my *New and Selected* a few years ago, I did a fair amount of rewriting lines and stanzas that I'd become dissatisfied with over the years. I came to realize that when you are writing in meter it actually takes very little to achieve useful effects — it doesn't take a great big tug at the string, just a little tug, to get the effects you want. When you're working within a metrical system, changing even one or two syllables can be just as effective as doing something more extravagant. So some of my earlier effects I no longer found interesting, and I changed them.

Returning again to your various themes, I particularly enjoy your creepy poems, like the previously mentioned "Death Will Do Nothing" and my favorite, "After," a poem which seems to take place "after" some kind of societal breakdown, maybe anarchy or totalitarianism or a catastrophic event. But you leave it ambiguous.

CHARLES MARTIN: Yes, something's definitely happening in the poem, and it has to do with some kind of societal breakdown, which is left unclear. But I must admit I'm starting to question my own sense of humor. I've recently published a poem in *The Southwest Review* called "Poison," and whenever I read it at poetry readings, I always tell the audience, "I think this is a very funny poem," but when I read it, everybody sits there stone-faced.

Well, I hope you didn't find "After" funny?

CHARLES MARTIN: No, but I've always thought that "Death Will Do Nothing" is rather humorous.

CHARLES MARTIN

I'd like to turn now to your narrative poems, some of which are dramatic monologues, like "Lot's Wife Looks Back" and your long poem "Passages from Friday" which effectively tells the Crusoe story and its aftermath from Friday's point of view in a rather broken 18th-Century English. Where did that idea come from?

CHARLES MARTIN: I was reading Elizabeth Bishop's "Robinson Crusoe," and I started thinking that it might be interesting if Friday had a chance to speak. At the same time, I was also teaching English as a second language, and I was very intrigued by the various problems of expression that people have when they try to learn another language as adults. I was fascinated by their frustrating attempts to try and transform the new language into an expression from their native tongue — or how, sometimes, they'll say things without any awareness that they're not really expressing what they're trying to say. It also seemed to me that there's a lot of self-repression involved with using a second language.

In what way?

CHARLES MARTIN: My students, given their uncertainty with the language, would often be hesitant to try and express certain things, especially personal things, in the new language. They had a natural expectation about a certain kind of formality and politeness in a language, but in their new language, because they no longer felt in control, they tended to repress things. I was continually faced with this problem in my writing classes, and I put a lot of these difficulties into Friday, who was also learning English — Defoe's English — as a second language. I wanted Friday to tell his story using the English that he'd learned from living with Crusoe and also from reading Crusoe's account. This, of course, meant that his language had to be fairly basic and prosy, so I decided to used rhymed quatrains as a way of holding it all together. It needed some kind of overall poetic formality, or it would have fallen into prose.

Yet despite his inarticulateness, Friday manages to reveal himself.

Charles Martin

CHARLES MARTIN: I'm grateful that some of that comes through in the poem.

You've also written a number of poems about — or dedicated to — various literary figures, and I'd like to ask you about two. The first is the previously-mentioned satire, "Just a Smack at Larkin," which ends, "Get over it, Phil — get a life!" How much of that poem is just literary fun, and how much of it is an irritation with Larkin's capacity for self-absorption?

CHARLES MARTIN: I'd say half and half. I've always admired Larkin's memorable little poem, "This Be the Verse," about how parents can mess up their kids, but it always seemed to me that it's equally true to flip it around. While I certainly recognize a lot of psychic temperature-taking in Larkin, on the whole, I feel he usually manages to invest it with a certain dignity, as in, for example, his poem "Aubade."

Your poem "Reflections after a Dry Spell" is dedicated to another significant poet of the last century, Howard Nemerov. Did you know Nemerov? And do you feel he's influenced your work?

CHARLES MARTIN: I knew him very briefly, in the last year of his life, when he came down to the Sewanee Writers' Conference. At that point in my life, I was going through a dry spell, and I asked him about it. He was very kind and amusing about it, so I dedicated the poem to him. As for influence, I suspect that later in one's career, it's harder to identify such things. When I was younger, the Cummings influence was pretty obvious, and later in college, I discovered Auden, who had a very conscious influence, especially as an urban poet. Auden was somebody who was writing about New York and city life in general, and when you grow up in the Bronx, you realize that you can't be another Wordsworth — it's not really an option.

In 1979, you published The Poems of Catullus *(Abattoir; revised edition, Johns Hopkins, 1990). These new translations of the much-translated Latin poet were highly praised, and Richard Moore rightly referred to your book as "the most memorable Catullus of [our] generation." Earlier you mentioned that Fr.*

CHARLES MARTIN

Grimaldi introduced you to Catullus at Fordham.

CHARLES MARTIN: Although I'd had four years of Latin at St. Helena's, I didn't encounter Catullus until my freshman year at Fordham. We had a complete collection of Catullus for the class, and a number of students knew right where the dirty ones were located, but I enjoyed all his work. Later, at Buffalo, I took a graduate seminar in Catullus with Charles Garton, an English classicist, and I read some of the translations that were available back then. I felt that they didn't really capture the originals that well, and that was the impetus for my own versions. In those days, there was the general feeling that Latin poetry was entirely quantitative and that accents were absolutely insignificant. But as I was reading Catullus, I became convinced that this wasn't really the case. There seemed to be a true stress component that I could clearly hear in the original Latin, but my teachers would always say, "No, it's really not there." But I could, nevertheless, still hear it in the poems, so I kept trying to imitate the original sound in my translations. In his sapphic ode, for example, the Latin goes, "IL-le mi par ES-se DE-o vi-DE-tur." One time, I read it to Robert Hass, and he said, "Oh, that sounds like Cowper." He'd been teaching a course in lyric poetry, and he pulled out Cowper's "HA-tred and VEN-geance, MY e-TER-nal POR-tion," which Cowper had written in English sapphics. And I thought, "Yes, I'm right! There *is* a stress element in the Latin!"

How do the Latin stresses work with the quantitative meter? Do they work hand in hand, or are they creating two different lines of sound?

CHARLES MARTIN: In most cases, it seems to me, it's two different lines of sound. In the dactylic hexameters, for example, the stresses and the quantities are quite different, and that's also true in the sapphics.

In your translations from Catullus you tried to be "as strict with my forms as I was able to, since Catullus worked within strict forms." In your "Introduction" to the book, you also expressed a disdain for the "inertial received wisdom which holds that such matters are unimportant." Do you feel that such attitudes still dominate classical translation, or has it improved since then?

CHARLES MARTIN: It's definitely improved. There are many more formal attempts at translating classical poetry, and not just classical poetry. After all, it's very difficult to imagine how you could translate a sonnet into something other than a sonnet!

Yes, but we've certainly seen plenty of it!

CHARLES MARTIN: Yes, alas, but I think things are changing for the better.

Since you always attempt to translate Catullus' various formats into an appropriate English correspondent, I wonder if you considered rendering #51, Catullus' translation from Sappho, into sapphics?

CHARLES MARTIN: I ended up taking a slightly casual approach to that poem because it seemed to work its way, rather naturally, into a comfortable blank verse with a few extra syllables — like the extra unaccented syllable at the end. It seems to me that that's about as close as you can get to the sense of the original since a very strict English sapphic would create a strait-jacket effect and not give a true sense of the poem.

I've always felt that English sapphics can only be effective in very short poems since the metrical effect is so odd that it becomes rather distracting and self-defeating. It's like some of those Longfellow poems which are quite admirable in intention but are just too sonically awkward to sustain themselves.

CHARLES MARTIN: That's right. Sometimes you have to make appropriate adjustments in the English.

More recently, you've published an ambitious and excellent version of Ovid's Metamorphoses *(Norton, 2004), generally rendering the poet's dactylic hexameters into blank verse. I was surprised to read in your prefatory "Note" that you first attempted to use English hexameters. For example, the first line of Book III:*

Charles Martin

> *Iamque deus posita fallacis imagine tauri*

was originally:

> *And now, no longer misrepresenting himself as a bull,*

before it became the much tighter pentameter:

> *And now, his taurine imitation ended . . .*

Was your initial impulse just a sense of loyalty to the original hexameters, or was it a concern that the English pentameter couldn't carry all the information?

CHARLES MARTIN: It was a combination of both those things along with a few other considerations. At first, I just wanted to see how the hexameter would carry over into English — to see if it would work. But I felt that it didn't; it sounded way too lumbering. The six-beat line simply wasn't dancing enough, especially to catch the wonderful pace in Ovid. It also seemed inappropriate for all the comedy in the poem. So I gradually shortened the line to a flexible blank verse. As a result, it was very hard to "unpack," as they say, the dactylic hexameter into the five-beat English line. It simply requires more space, so I would often end up doing, say, fourteen lines of blank verse for every ten in the original.

Your doctoral dissertation for Buffalo was about the influence of Catullus on Ezra Pound. Pound, of course, used both Catullus and Sappho as Imagist models in 1912, and he clearly made allusions to Catullus in a variety of his own poems including "The Shop Girl," "Hugh Selwyn Mauberley," and a number of the Cantos, especially "Canto V." What was your overall contention in the dissertation?

CHARLES MARTIN: I was actually looking at two different things. One was the influence of Catullus on Pound, and the other was the influence of Pound on Catullus — how he affected various modern translations of the Latin poet. Horace Gregory's translations, for example, were very much influenced by what Pound had done with

Charles Martin

"Propertius." Peter Whigham, who did the Penguin Catullus, was a post-World War II Poundian, as was Louis Zukofsky, whose dizzying version of Catullus started off translating for the sense, but ended up translating for the sound. The result was that Zukofsky's translation of Catullus needs another "translation" to make any sense of the poems.

Is it fair to say that Pound revived the Twentieth Century interest in Catullus?

CHARLES MARTIN: I think that he did. And the same is true for Sappho. But their influences hadn't completely died out. George Steiner makes the point that much of Pound's taste in the literature that he translated was very Victorian. The excellent Victorian critic, J.W.H. Mackail, for example, writes about Catullus in very much the same terms as Pound. So Pound picked up on these earlier ideas, and then he promoted them in his own century.

Do you think Catullus has affected your own work? You've certainly spent a lot of time with him!

CHARLES MARTIN: Yes, I think my interest in Catullus could charitably be described as an obsession, but I'm not sure about the influence. The only effect that I'm conscious of is a certain kind of rhythmic influence, and maybe also a predilection for conversational poetry. But maybe I've always had that tendency.

The extant Catullus has a surprising variety of tone and form, from the humorous poems to the marvelous elegiacs like his famous tribute to his brother. How much of his work has been lost?

CHARLES MARTIN: A great deal, I think. I suspect that there were once many more love poems since Catullus was especially famous for those kinds of poems. But it seems likely that we've also lost a lot of the satirical stuff.

You seem especially suited to handle Catullus's variety. Anthony Hecht has called your own work "a poetry of technical mastery," and Carolyn Kizer has suggested that, *"Less accomplished poets could learn their craft by studying him." In your own poetry, you've used a wide variety of forms, even including accentual meter in your poem "The Fissure." Is there something new that you'd like to try — or do more of?*

CHARLES MARTIN: That's a good question, and one I think about quite a bit. Currently, I'm working on a terza rima poem for the first time, and I'm also thinking about writing some poems in rhymed couplets. I'm fascinated with the couplet poems of Chaucer, Dryden, Goldsmith, and Pope. I definitely agree with Auden when he said that he needed two things to get going. One was something that seemed urgent to write about, and the other was a technical problem to solve. That's exactly how I feel. I need both of those motivations. I've always needed to have some kind of metrical challenge. Recently, I've been thinking about longer poems again. In the past, I've only done two, "Passages from Friday" and "A Walk in the Hills," but now I'm thinking about a possible book-length poem, possibly in the meditative style of "A Walk in the Hills."

That's quite ambitious.

CHARLES MARTIN: I know, and whether I'll ever get to do it, I can't be sure. But I'd certainly like to try.

Where do your poetic ideas come from?

CHARLES MARTIN: That's another good question. From a variety of sources, I guess. Sometimes they might be a response to something in a newspaper. "Easter Sunday, 1985," for example, began that way. Or a response to a poem. Or they might come from real life, like the turtle poem. Or maybe from a conversation, or even a single line in a conversation that sticks with me. Sometimes they come from dreams. Sometimes they come from other people's dreams.

Do you keep a list of ideas?

CHARLES MARTIN: I do make notebook jottings, and I do make

lists of the various kinds of poems that I'd like to write — or themes that I'd like to explore. But, oddly enough, I usually find that the specific things that I write down in my notebooks don't often lead to new poems. But I do tend to start drafts of poems, often in the same notebook. I think this has something to do with traveling. When I was teaching at Johns Hopkins, I spent a lot of time on the train, and I always carried my notebook with me. Soon I discovered that I could work on drafts of poems quite easily that way. So I started working with a pencil since it was easy to erase.

Once you're under way, do you write quickly or slowly?

CHARLES MARTIN: That depends. When I was working on a longer poem like "A Walk in the Hills," I'd go to my notebook every day and try to do a single eight-line stanza. Then the next day I'd do another one and so on. If I did eight lines each day, I was very pleased. Then, of course, I'd go back later and fiddle continually with the stanzas — never letting them rest in peace. But, initially, I needed to get them down at a fairly steady pace. This was especially true when I was translating Ovid's *Metamorphosis*. I found it extremely difficult to get back to Ovid after even a single day off. But if I could just get a little bit done each day, things went along much more smoothly.

How do you decide which forms to use?

CHARLES MARTIN: I don't have a general approach. When I did the turtle poem, for example, I did a lot of fiddling around with the idea, and I didn't even realize until the poem was finished that I'd written it in the Burns stanza. If I'd been aware of it earlier, I might have felt a bit self-conscious and constricted.

What about sonnets?

CHARLES MARTIN: Sometimes an idea will come to me and clearly present itself as material for a sonnet.

Charles Martin

Before you've started writing?

CHARLES MARTIN: Yes. Generally, when I write a sonnet, I try to get a draft of it done right away, and then I can sit and work with it. But for anything longer than a sonnet, I tend to write in bits and pieces, as I described earlier. Sometimes just the "idea" of a form can actually start to pull a poem out. I'm fascinated by the Spenserian sonnet, and I've recently had an idea for a variation on the form, so I'm just sort of waiting for something to happen. Like ice fishing.

Do you prefer to write at a certain time of day?

CHARLES MARTIN: I try to work in the mornings, but I don't have any particular ritual. I just keep a little cup full of sharpened pencils, and I write in a notebook before I eventually transfer the poems to the computer.

The dedication to Starting from Sleep: New and Selected Poems *(Sewanee/Overlook, 2002) reads, "For Johanna, closest of readers." Do you always show your wife, the poet Johanna Keller, your work-in-progress?*

CHARLES MARTIN: Occasionally I'll show her a poem-in-progress, but usually I wait until I'm finished. As a teacher of creative writing, I require my students to bring in their early drafts for discussion, but I didn't learn to write that way. So generally, I'm showing Johanna the final product or, at least, something very close to it. Then she might say something that will make me go back and make a change. This was especially true of a poem I did that was based on one of her dreams. She'd told me the dream, and I said, "That's very interesting. Can I have it?" And she said, "Well, it must mean more to you than it does to me!"

So even if the poem seems "finished," if she or anybody else says something about a poem that you feel is a good idea, then you might go back and do some rewriting?

CHARLES MARTIN: Yes. As a matter of fact, since you've just

shown me that earlier version of "The Two of Them," I'm starting to think that I should put that footnoted line back into the poem!

Earlier, I cited your epigram, "Deconstructing the Zebra," which effectively characterizes the devastating literary fad of deconstructionism, and another epigram, "To a Reviewer," speaks for itself:

> The rays that journey to us from the sun
> Illuminate the kneeling congregants
> Of Notre Dame and also fall upon
> The donkey's rump, where fleas in transport dance.

In this era of so much silly "theory" and self-important reviewers, who are your favorite writers about poetry and literature?

CHARLES MARTIN: The recently deceased critic, Hugh Kenner, was always one of my favorites. I think he was quite brilliant.

Kenner was my teacher at Hopkins. He certainly knew his Pound, but he didn't care much for the formalists.

CHARLES MARTIN: That's true. I once heard him dismiss Philip Larkin by saying, "Oh, all of those little thoughts in their little boxes." But he was an excellent commentator on the whole range of Modernist poetry. I also enjoy Guy Davenport's work and Anthony Hecht's marvelous essays. John Hollander's also a very illuminating critic, and Richard Wilbur's criticism is always useful. Unfortunately, there's so much bad stuff out there that young people are inclined to think, "Oh, it's all theory, and it's all nonsense." But it isn't. There are still some excellent poet-critics like Hollander and Wilbur and Hecht.

You've been teaching for many years at Queensborough College, and you've also taught in the Writing Seminars at Johns Hopkins. How do you introduce metrics to your young students?

CHARLES MARTIN: At Queensborough I don't actually teach

poetry, and I don't have access to graduate students there, so I'm not sure what the situation is. But over the past seven or eight years, I've been doing a lot of teaching — of more mature students — at the 92nd Street Y in Manhattan. I've discovered that more and more people are coming in with an interest in metrics, and as a result, I'm now introducing it much earlier in my classes. I used to hold off on the formal assignment — writing a sonnet — but I quickly realized, as did the students, that the sonnets were generally the best poems we saw in the course of the class. So now I actually begin the class with a formal assignment, most recently using triolets. They had a lot of fun doing them, and I had a lot of fun reading them.

What advice do you give to aspiring poets?

CHARLES MARTIN: When I was teaching at Hopkins and working with younger people, I encouraged them to do a lot of imitation — to pick a poet they enjoyed, preferably their favorite poet, and try to imitate that poet's style. I would challenge them to write a poem that could comfortably fit into the collected poems of the poet they were imitating, say, Elizabeth Bishop or Philip Larkin or whomever. Since I believe that imitation is part of a process that all young poets go through, they might as well go through it as consciously and as intelligently as they can.

Having completed Catullus and The Metamorphoses, *do you have any other large critical or translation projects in the works?*

CHARLES MARTIN: I'm planning a book about the political nature of Ovid's *Metamorphoses*, and I've also started translating some of the poems of the Italian G.G. Belli, a nineteenth century Roman poet, whose sonnets are, I think, the great undiscovered masterwork of the nineteenth century.

Didn't Dana Gioia and William Jay Smith include some of Belli's work in their anthology of Italian poets?

CHARLES MARTIN: They did, and that was the first time I

155

ever heard of Belli. Then Dana also told me about the Burgess translations.

Anthony Burgess?

CHARLES MARTIN: Yes, Burgess wrote a short novel called *Abba Abba*, in which Belli meets Keats in Rome during the English poet's last days, and Burgess also did about a dozen rather brilliant translations of some of Belli's poems. When I read them, I thought, "Wow, I'd like to try that!"

How many are there?

CHARLES MARTIN: We're talking Merrill Moore kinds of numbers. There are over twenty-seven hundred sonnets, and all of them are about the people of Rome, all written in different voices. Naturally, James Joyce was a great fan of Belli's work. It's a kind of polyphonic symphony of sonnets about Rome and the people of Rome. But he's not easy to translate since he wrote in a Roman dialect.

It sounds very exciting. Now I thought we could finish up today with a reading of the poignant ending of your excellent poem "A Burial at Shanidar." The poem describes the Shanidar archaeological site, and then it imagines the final scene at the Neanderthal burial where flowers — "Cornflowers, hollyhock, grape-hyacinth" — are tossed into the grave.

CHARLES MARTIN: I'll be glad to read it:

> They stood around the figure in the grave
> And mumbled what might have meant, *Take these,*
> *Which we have gathered at no little risk*
> *In the wild places far beyond the cave.*
> *We thought to honor you.* The reasons why
> Would perish with the last of them to die.

Thanks, Charles.

CHARLES MARTIN: Thank you, Bill.

R.S. Gwynn

R.S. Gwynn has distinguished himself as a poet, critic, editor, anthologist, and translator. Dana Gioia has described him as "one of the truly talented and original poets of my generation," and Richard Wilbur has called him "one of our best."

Born in Leaksville, North Carolina, R.S. (Sam) Gwynn received his B.A. from Davidson College in 1969 and received both an M.A. (1972) and an M.F.A. (1973) from the University of Arkansas. After teaching for three years at Southwest Texas State University in San Marcos, Texas (1973-1976), he took a teaching position at Lamar University in Beaumont, Texas, where he is currently University Professor of English. In 2004, he received the Michael Braude Award for verse from the American Academy of Arts and Letters.

His first two chapbooks, *Bearing and Distance* (Cedar Rock, 1977) and *The Narcissiad* (Cedar Rock, 1981), were followed by his first full-length collection, *The Drive-in*, which won the 1986 Breakthrough Award and was published by the University of Missouri Press. In 2001, Story Line Press published *No Word of Farewell: Selected Poems, 1970-2000*. His numerous anthologies include *Poetry: A Pocket Anthology* (Penguin, 2005); *The Advocates of Poetry: A Reader of American Poet-Critics of the Modern Era* (Arkansas, 1996); *New Expansive Poetry: Theory, Criticism, History* (Story Line, 1999); and, with April Lindner, *Contemporary American Poetry* (Penguin, 2005).

This interview was conducted at the Exploring Form and Narrative Poetry Conference at West Chester University in West Chester, Pennsylvania.

You were born in Leaksville, North Carolina, north of Greensboro near the Virginia border. Did you grow up there?

R.S. GWYNN: I did, right through college. In 1969 I finally left North Carolina to go to graduate school, but in one sense, I've lived there right up until last week, when I finally closed down my mother's house because she's moving into an assisted living facility.

R.S. Gwynn

Back in the late '60s, my mother and father divorced, and she's lived alone since my younger brother went off to college in 1975. For several years, she taught in a private kindergarten, but she was a housewife for a good part of the half century she lived in that house. Although moving away was hard, she seems to be doing well in her new situation. So I'm officially homeless whenever I go back home.

Was Leaksville rural when you were a kid?

R.S. GWYNN: Yes, Rockingham county was mostly tobacco back then, a lot of small farms. Reidsville, the other large town in the county, is where the American Tobacco Company had its plants, and there were also textile mills, but most of them have shut down over the years.

Your father was a sales manager. What was he selling?

R.S. GWYNN: In 1955 he started working for a company called Industries for the Blind in Greensboro, and they made and sold household items like brooms and mops. He had three main outlets for his sales: one was the Army commissaries; another was the small independent grocery stores; and the last was a lot of fundraising sales through the Lions Clubs. Just the other day I stopped at a store in Black Mountain that had a Lions Club booth, and they were selling products which had exactly the same labels that I remember from my youth.

How did the drive-in fit in?

R.S. GWYNN: That was earlier, and that was the romance of my childhood! In the late forties, Daddy got involved in the theater business with a couple of partners. He was the active partner, and they owned four drive-ins. The first one, The Eden, opened the day after I was born, May 14, 1948, and the picture on the cover of my book *The Drive-In* was taken that day. But eventually, when television came in, the drive-in business folded badly, so he sold out and went into sales. He was a natural salesman, and he did quite well.

R.S. Gwynn

Your poem "Randolph Field, 1938" is about a young man who's training to be a military pilot, but he gets sick and loses his chance. The penultimate stanza in the poem ends:

> It's hard to think of what he must go back to.
> He banked on everything but going back.

Wasn't the poem a tribute to your father?

R.S. GWYNN: It was indeed, but at the time I wrote it, I wasn't really certain what his feelings were back then, so I did a little bit of invention in that stanza. I later learned that he was actually eager to get back home. He was feeling homesick in San Antonio, and he was engaged to my mother, so he was very pleased to get back to North Carolina, and they were married the next year in 1939. But in Texas, he'd been walking a "punishment tour" in the Texas sun when he had a heat stroke and ended up in the hospital. When he got out of the infirmary, he was so far behind the rest of the class that they gave him the option of starting over or taking an honorable discharge. So he came back home, which was good for me. If he'd shipped out with his class, I probably wouldn't have been born!

One of your more recent sonnets is "Dogwatch," about a man on a ship in an Allied convoy in the North Atlantic in 1944. The poem ends:

> And, far behind, a home, a son, a wife,
> And, waiting with them to be lived, a life.

Is that one also about your father?

R.S. GWYNN: That one's based, rather loosely, on my dad's experiences in the Merchant Marine. In late '41 or early '42, he went down to Wilmington to work in the shipyards, and he liked the job, and he was pretty well paid. But in '43, after my older brother had been born in January, he enlisted in the Merchant Marine, and he served throughout '44. We have some diaries that he kept back then, and we've learned that he first heard about V-E Day as he was sailing back home from Salerno or Naples. When he was serving in the Merchant Marine, it was still a dangerous occupation, but it wasn't as bad as it had been in early '42, when the Germans were having their "happy time," ranging up and down the Atlantic Seaboard, sinking hundreds of merchant ships, primarily because no one had figured out that if the people living on the coast shut off their towns' lights, it would help conceal the ships. Anyway, my dad was a warrant officer in the Merchant Marine, and he actually did witness other convoy ships getting hit in the ocean.

Did your love of hunting begin with your father?

R.S. GWYNN: That was mostly with my friends. When we were thirteen-year-old kids, my friends and I — I shudder to think of it now — got our first .22s. We rode around the town on our bicycles, with our rifles slung over our shoulders, and we'd often go over to the town dump and shoot at the rats. But even in town itself, we'd walk right into the stores with our weapons. The thought of this happening nowadays is preposterous, and if my children had ever asked for a .22, and I'd consented, my wife probably would have killed me! But in those days it wasn't odd at all. As for real hunting, my step-grandfather, who took me out a few times, was a great hunter. He raised great bird dogs, and he hunted into his 70s.

When did you first get interested in poetry?

R.S. GWYNN: I was interested in writing pretty early on, but not poetry. In high school, like so many other people, I wasn't taught much poetry. We read "The Charge of the Light Brigade," and "The Raven," and some Shakespeare, but it never seemed like something that someone would actually do in contemporary times. At the time, Carl Sandburg was living in North Carolina, where he was regularly lionized, but I still never thought of poetry as a reasonable thing to do. Instead, I wrote for the high school newspaper. In truth, my first ambition was to be a film critic. I was still a movie nut from the family's drive-in years. All through high school, I read countless film books, and somewhere around '63 or '64, I discovered Pauline Kael, whom I fell in love with instantly!

Kael wasn't shy about her opinions.

R.S. GWYNN: She certainly wasn't, and I found her exhilarating. As you know, I do lots of book reviews and literary criticism, and I still think that Pauline Kael — along with Randall Jarrell — had the greatest influence on my overall style of criticism.

In 1965 you went to Davidson College, also in North Carolina, where you won the Vereen Bell Award for creative writing twice and started publishing in some very prestigious journals like The Sewanee Review. *Were you an English major?*

R.S. GWYNN: I was, and, I must admit, getting published in *The Sewanee Review* was a very lucky thing. I'd done some translations of François Villon, and Andrew Lytle took a few for *Sewanee*. I did manage to get a few poems in some other places, but my main literary stimulus at Davidson was a little magazine called *The Miscellany* that started in my freshman year and published a lot of good people. It was around that time, 1965, that I started to get really interested in poetry, and I discovered that some of my friends were also interested.

Who were your early models?

R.S. GWYNN: Browning was an especially important wake-up call for me. I first read him in a sophomore course in British Literature, and I soon wrote a number of dramatic monologues that were very Browning-esque. I was also greatly affected by Donne and Herbert, but I wasn't that big on the Romantics or any of the American poets, except for Frost and Robinson. As far as the contemporaries go, my most important influence was definitely Richard Wilbur. We studied his work in a modern poetry class, and I actually got to meet him — in the spring of '68 or '69 — when I went to Hollins College for a student literary festival.

While you were at Davidson, you were on the college's championship team in the

R.S. Gwynn

G.E. College Bowl. What was that like?

R.S. GWYNN: We were on television for five consecutive weeks, and we retired as champions! It was a wonderful experience, and now there's a new website about the G.E. College Bowl that lists all the old scores and other information.

Does any of the footage still exist?

R.S. GWYNN: Yes, I now have three of the tapes. The Davidson library still had those shows on an old large-tape format, and I was able to copy them to VHS. Then I started thinking, "I wonder where the other two tapes are?" On a whim, I searched the web for Robert Earle, who'd been the host of the program, and I found a phone number for Ithaca, New York. So I dialed the number, and his wife answered, and I said, "You don't know me, but I was on College Bowl many years ago, and I've found a few tapes, and I'm looking for more." Then there was a long pause. Finally, she said, "You have tapes? You have tapes! Bob! Bob!" So Mr. Earle got on the phone, and he was absolutely thrilled because he had nothing at all. So I ended up sending him copies of my tapes.

Where were the T.V. shows filmed?

R.S. GWYNN: In the NBC Building at Rockefeller Center. They put us up in the Warwick Hotel, we saw all the tourist attractions, and we had theater tickets every day! It was my first exposure to New York City, and it was a fantastic experience.

After graduating from Davidson, you got an M.A. and an M.F.A at the University of Arkansas. Why two Masters degrees?

R.S. GWYNN: That was the way the Arkansas program worked back then. Almost everyone who completed the M.F.A. program, which was a 60 hour degree, also picked up an M.A., which was a 30 hour degree, along the way. The masters was actually a literature degree. After I finished the M.F.A., I stayed on for another year in the Ph.D. program, but then I got my first job, and I decided to move on.

Who was more of a mentor for you at Arkansas, Jim Whitehead or Miller Williams?

R.S. GWYNN: It's hard to decide. I'd say it was about 50/50. Jim was quite a contentious guy, and he could be very difficult, but he was extremely generous with his time. He was also a great teacher. Then, during my second year at Arkansas, Miller came in, and he was extremely supportive of my work.

I always thought that Jim and Miller created the program together?

R.S. GWYNN: No, it was actually founded by Jim and Bill Harrison in either '65 or '66. Bill was the fiction writer.

Were you writing formal poetry at Arkansas?

R.S. GWYNN: When I arrived in Fayetteville, I was writing formalist poetry; and, fortunately, both Jim and Miller had no problem with that, even though, at the time, they were both writing in looser forms. Eventually, after I left, they both gravitated back toward form. As for me, for a number of years at Arkansas, I also experimented with a lot of free verse. Despite Jim and Miller's appreciation of formal poetry, I never really felt that there was "understanding" of it back then, so I tried other things. It was the early 70s, and everyone was writing deep-image surrealistic poetry, and I did some of that.

After you finished in Arkansas, you taught for three years at Southwest Texas State before going to Lamar University in Beaumont, Texas, where you still teach. Almost immediately, you published your first chapbook, Bearing and Distance, *which was followed in 1981 by another chapbook,* The Narcissiad, *which consisted of a long narrative poem in couplets about an inept but ambitious contemporary poet who, like Dryden's Shadwell, manages to outlast his poetic rivals. The poem was clever, funny, and well-written, but some people believe that it made you a number of enemies early in your career. Do you think that's true?*

R.S. Gwynn

R.S. GWYNN: It's hard to say. I'm certain that some people didn't like it, but I never received any negative feedback from the poets themselves. I guess they just ignored it.

Many poets were mentioned by name, and others were given rather transparent "new" names.

R.S. GWYNN: Yes, when you have two main characters named Merrilleus and Halpernus, it didn't take much imagination to get the references. When the book came out, I did mail a copy to James Merrill, and he sent back a wonderful card, which I still have framed at home. It's a funny little quatrain that I can't remember exactly, but it was very funny, and I was very grateful.

So he took it in stride. How about Daniel Halpern? Did he ever publish you in Antaeus?

R.S. GWYNN: No, I never submitted to *Antaeus*!

And how did The Narcissiad *come about?*

R.S. GWYNN: Back then, I was feeling kind of dead in the water creatively. My graduate thesis had provided most of the poems for *Bearing and Distance*, and I suddenly found myself overwhelmed with my first teaching job and my new life in San Marcos, so I wasn't producing much poetry. Then I read Christopher Lasch's *The Culture of Narcissism*, and it was a tremendous stimulus to write the poem, which kept me busy for six months or so. After a number of additions and revisions, I felt as though I'd gotten a lot off of my chest — venting my spleen! — and I found that I was able to return to writing more personal poems. The reason the book got published was because of David Yates, who'd started a tabloid poetry magazine at Texas State called *Cedar Rock*. Back in the mid-70s, the journal got around quite a bit, and I was one of its regular columnists. Anyway, one time I was stumped for a column, so I gave David about 150 lines of *The Narcissiad*, and I asked, "Could you run this instead of my column?" and he did. Then Judson Jerome, who was also a columnist for *Cedar*

R.S. GWYNN

Rock, did a piece about the poem in *Writer's Digest*, and the response was excellent. So David decided to bring it out as a chapbook.

A few years later, in 1986, the University of Missouri Press published your first full-length book, The Drive-In, *as part of its Breakthrough Series, and your next full-length collection,* No Word of Farewell: Selected Poems, 1970-2000, *came out in 2001 from Story Line Press. Both of those books, as well as several other chapbooks, contain poems which, despite their versatility, still have a distinctive identity or individuality. So I'd like to discuss a number of the characteristic aspects of your work, starting with your willingness to write hard-hitting poems, sometimes tempered with humor or irony, about a wide range of subjects, including violence itself. "Body Bags," for example, is a three-sonnet sequence about Vietnam, and "At Rose's Range" is a powerful sonnet about a woman preparing to shoot an ex-con who's coming back for her daughter.*

> *Earl's free next month. He says he wants some more*
> *Of what she's got, and she's my daughter so*
> *I reckon there's just one way this can end.*

Where did these poems come from?

R.S. GWYNN: Something definitely happened between *The Drive-In* and *No Word of Farewell*. My newer work gravitated more toward realism, and the language simplified. I realized that I'd written just about as many "literary" poems as I cared to, and there were quite a few of those in *The Drive-In*. So I felt that work like "At Rose's Range" or "Body Bags" was a way of combining the formalism that I'd locked into by the early 1980s with a subject matter that I felt comfortable with. I'm definitely attracted to writing poems that are on the edge, at least in terms of the situations they describe.

An occasional theme in your work is American consumerism run-amok. Yet poems like "Among Philistines" and "The Ballad of Burton and Bobby and Bill" do so with a certain good humor, even sympathy.

R.S. GWYNN: Yes, that's because I'm a consummate consumer. I'm an eBay maniac! When I wrote "Among Philistines," there seemed to be some kind of contemporary madness in the early '80s about "mall culture," so I tried to get that into the poem. As for "The Ballad of Burton and Bobby and Bill," it's an almost sentimental poem about a small-town clothing store, and it's one of my favorites. When I was a teenager, there was no Gap in the town, and other than television, the Town Squire, Ltd., was our only window into the world of savior faire and the Ivy League "look." So we spent a lot of time window shopping in those days.

You also like to poke fun at some of the quirks of modern academia, as in poems like "The Classroom at the Mall" or "The Professor's Lot."

R.S. GWYNN: I tend not to satirize the world of literary theory because it's been satirized so much. But I like to write poems about the academic process itself. A poem like "The Classroom at the Mall," for example, was based on my own experiences. We have a number of satellite classrooms around Beaumont, including one for a couple of years at Parkdale Mall, and the shoppers would often walk by and wonder what the heck was going on. I taught two different classes out there, and they were each three hours long. One of those classes was always quite terrible for the first hour and a half, but then, after the break, the students would return and everything would be great. This went on for about five weeks before I realized what was going on. During the break, my students were all going to the Mexican restaurant on the mall's food court and chugging margaritas!

Among my favorites of your poems are the creepy ones, like the sonnet "The Great Fear," about some kind of nursing home or terminal hospice which is, as the last line makes clear, "Ready for the next one, whose name is you." Another very effective and unsettling poem is the rather vague, interrogatory poem, "The Denouement," which ends your Selected Poems *with the creepy lines:*

> Who were my father and mother?
> Trust me to keep your secret.
>
> What is the mark on your forehead?
> What is the mark on your cheek?

R.S. GWYNN: Most of my poems are quite definite about the dramatic situation, but those poems — and another called "The Dark Place" — are much more evocative of various moods of paranoia or uncertainty. I suspect that these poems move a little closer to deep-image poetry, which was something I was affected by in the '70s, but they're also greatly influenced by Weldon Kees. I first discovered Kees in an anthology back in the '70s, and I thought, "Wow, who is this guy?" So Kees has always been a tremendous influence on some of my work, and eventually, through Kees, I discovered the poems of Don Justice, who also wrote some very moody and evocative pieces.

Your work is so full of humor, wit, satire, and parody, that it's impossible to discuss all your various modes and usages. So I'll just cite a personal favorite, "Horatio's Philosophy," about poor Horatio, under deadline, trying to satisfy Osric's demand to soup-up the Danish story line: "Keep the thing scandalous, and keep it brief. / Action and jokes." So Horatio writes the first draft quickly, in two days, then he hires a "ghost."

R.S. GWYNN: My old friend from Arkansas, Leon Stokesbury, wrote a wonderful poem about one of the most obscure of all of Shakespeare's characters, titled "Reynaldo in Paris." Reynaldo, you'll remember, was sent off to spy on Laertes, and then he vanishes from the play. So I was tempted to write a sort of sequel about how Horatio, who was not a very interesting or imaginative person, was going to fulfill Hamlet's last request that he set down the story. What would he come up with? So I turned him into a spin doctor of sorts. Or, at least, that's what his boss Osric is, and poor Horatio — like Shakespeare — has to find ways to improve on the original story. I very much enjoy working in parentheses around a known text, which is, I suppose, a form of parody.

In a number of your poems, you drop in a fair amount of pop culture, especially in the more satirical poems, and I wonder if you have any concerns about that? What if readers down the road don't know who Sting is, or Bill Blass, or Demi Moore?

R.S. GWYNN: I know what you mean. For the latest edition of my

R.S. Gwynn

poetry anthology, I decided to include B.H. Fairchild's wonderful poem about baseball, "Body and Soul," and it occurred to me that I should probably put in a footnote explaining who Mickey Mantle was since many younger readers simply won't know. There's always a risk in alluding to pop or sports culture, but I must admit I don't worry about it too much. Some of my poems aren't for the ages anyway, and if some do manage to survive, a helpful footnote could do the trick. A lot of 18th Century poetry is full of contemporary references and private jokes that need to be footnoted, yet we still read Pope and the others. But I certainly understand your point. Recently I had to footnote "Charlie Chaplin" when I reprinted Hart Crane's "Chaplinesque" since the vast majority of college students won't know who he was.

Maybe the most crucial aspect of your poetry's success is your ability, even within many of your hardest-hitting poems or humorous verse, to effectively drop into a lyric mode and give a sudden, often unexpected power to your work. A perfect example is the rather creepy poem "Untitled" about a man's "unlived life," which ends:

> . . . In which my days begin
> With scenes in which, across unblemished sands,
> Unborn, my children come to touch my hands.

Do you consciously remind yourself to occasionally invoke the lyric, or does it come naturally?

R.S. GWYNN: You're right. I like to use a kind of a "stealth" technology in some of my poems. "Untitled," for example, begins with numerous references to rather trivial missed opportunities — not making the big touchdown, not writing the great book, and so on — before it shifts. So I like to draw the reader in with a bit of a red herring before gently pulling out the carpet and moving the poem to a different emotional level.

And a different dictional level as well.

R. S. GWYNN: Yes, I've always thought that, whatever my strengths as a poet, my lyricism works best when it's counterpointed against something else, like irony, for example. A poem like "Among Philistines" begins as a purely satirical poem; but, by the end, it becomes a poem, admittedly rather obscurely, about faith. It's moved to a different level. But even though I do like to create contrasts for the lyric passages in my poems, when I'm actually writing the poems, I like to think this happens intuitively.

Dana Gioia has suggested that your more recent poems in No Word of Farewell *are darker in tone, and he suggests that your "painful bout with cancer casts its shadow across the new poems in the book." This is rather obvious in the poems that clearly relate to the illness, like "Bone Scan," "Before Prostate Surgery," and "At the Center," but do you sense this "darkening" in your overall work?*

R.S. GWYNN: Actually, I think the poems started getting darker even earlier. "The Great Fear," for example, was written before my diagnosis and surgery in 1996. But it's certainly true that having mortality thrust in the foreground — and that happened just a year after my father died — does a job on one's consciousness. It forces you to think about where you are in life and how you're seeing the world around you. It's a catalyst toward seeing things in a different, deeper, and more creative way.

Has Hardy become a more significant influence?

R.S. GWYNN: I do love Hardy. Back in high school, I didn't even realize he was a poet. We had to read *The Return of the Native*, which was on the standard reading list, and I hated the book. But I later discovered Hardy, the poet, around the same time that I discovered Robinson and Ransom — who are a bit like American Hardys. In truth, Hardy's ruralism and local color don't interest me that much, but he's certainly the great satirist of circumstance, the great ironist, and I revere him for that. I also think you can learn more about how to write in forms naturally by reading Hardy than by reading almost any other poet.

R.S. Gwynn

He seems to have written in more forms than any other writer.

R.S. GWYNN: I've heard it said that even in the huge *Collected Poems*, Hardy never repeats the same form more than three times. Some of the poems, of course, are peculiar and terrible, but others are truly amazing.

Returning to your own work, I feel that your more recent poems are a bit tighter than before — tighter in expression and sometimes shorter in length.

R.S. GWYNN: It's true that I've been writing many poems with shorter lines over the last few years. Previously, almost everything was pentameter, but recently, I've been writing some trimeter poems, and that certainly creates the imperative for succinctness. On the other hand, I'd like to do some longer pieces in the future. I've been toying with a long narrative poem, on and off, since about 1984. But I've never quite figured out how to do it, and I'm still hoping that it'll dawn on me.

What's it about?

R.S. GWYNN: It's a kind of Carveresque story about a man who becomes obsessed with listening to a garden show that comes on at 5:00 in the morning, and his compulsion is related to certain deficiencies in his life. The plot also includes the death of his daughter and his reaction to that loss. Years ago, when I was a young instructor, I took a job throwing daily newspapers to supplement my income. For about seven years, I got up at 5:00 every morning, and I'd listen to the farm report and the garden show, and when I'd drive around town, the idea for the poem slowly started to develop.

What was the show like?

R.S. GWYNN: Most of the people called in asking questions about their gardens and lawns, but occasionally some very strange people would call in. I remember one woman who wanted to know if she could grow cucumbers in her bedroom. I almost drove into a ditch when I heard that one!

A few years ago, X.J. Kennedy wrote that "Gwynn commands a wide range of forms, some of them daunting in their difficulty." You've written blank verse, couplets, sonnets, the French forms, and even Spenserian stanzas. What would you like to do more of?

R.S. GWYNN: If I could ever get this narrative poem going, I'd like to get back to blank verse. I've been working with rhyme so much over the years that I sometimes feel that I've tapped everything out. Richard Wilbur once said that a true poet should never repeat a rhyme, and I'm sure I've violated that principle numerous times.

Are there any forms that you haven't tried that you'd like to use in the future?

R.S. GWYNN: There aren't too many forms left for me to try! I must admit I never thought I'd write a Chant Royal, which is the most maddeningly difficult form I've ever seen. But then I was asked to write an introduction for Lew Turco's collected lyrics, and I'd written so much about Lew in the past that I realized that I didn't have anything new to say, so I thought, "The hell with it! I'll write a Chant Royal" — which is now the introduction to his collected poems. But I don't think I'll ever attempt a Rondeau Redoublé since Wendy Cope has driven the final nail into that coffin, and no one ever needs to write one again. I've also never written a terzanelle — although I've assigned them to my students — and just last year, for the first time, I finally wrote some limericks.

That's surprising. The limerick seems like a natural for you.

R.S. GWYNN: For some reason, it never occurred to me before. I guess the problem is that most of them are just bawdy, and it seemed ridiculous to try and come up with some new wrinkle on "Nantucket." But then I got this idea to write a sequence of limericks about religious denominations, so I started writing about the Methodists, the Baptists, the Episcopalians, and I just couldn't stop. I ended up with about forty, then I cut it down to twenty-six, and I told my wife that I'd written a twenty-six-part poem about "sects." When she got this very bemused look on her face — thinking that I'd said "sex" — I said, "No, Sects! S-e-c-t-s!"

Moving now to compositional questions, most contemporary formalist poets claim that their initial idea or impulse "finds" the form in the actual process of writing. Do you work that way as well, or are there times when you say, "I think I'll write a sonnet today"?

R.S. GWYNN: Well, it works both ways for me. "Among Philistines" ended up around sixty lines, but it had begun as a sonnet. Ideas just kept generating, and since I liked them, I thought, "Well, I won't throw this out," so I kept things going in quatrains. Other times, as with "Dogwatch," which you mentioned earlier, I've set out to specifically write a sonnet. That poem was composed on a tape recorder while I was driving from Pennsylvania to North Carolina in 2004. I'd thought of it as a sonnet right from the beginning, and it was one of the few poems I've written where I really had a definite sense, right from the beginning, of where the poem was going to end. Of course, the more you learn about forms, the more you understand how certain forms are adaptable to certain ideas. The first few villanelles I wrote were perfectly torturous, if not tortured, but eventually I've realized that there are certain specific things that you can do with this form that you can't do with any other structure. The same is true of the pantoum and other forms. So to answer you initial question, I would say that I probably write in intended forms about fifty percent of the time, and I "find" the others along the way. If a poem starts in blank verse, of course, it's probably going to remain in blank verse, and the same is true with heroic couplets.

Do you have any writing rituals?

R.S. GWYNN: Well, I don't write out many poems by hand. Occasionally, a line will pop into my head, and I'll jot it down and save it for later, but mostly I work at the computer. In recent years, my cross-country drives have been very beneficial because of the tape recorder. On a drive from Texas to North Carolina a few years back,

R.S. Gwynn

I worked out the whole poem of "Cléante to Elmire," and that's a poem of maybe 140 lines. While I was driving, I was composing into the recorder, then backing it up, listening, starting over, listening again, and so on. Eventually, I transcribed it onto the computer, and then I did lot of revision.

Do you write on a regular schedule?

R.S. GWYNN: I'm not a time-structured regular writer, except when I'm doing editorial or critical work. Sometimes months will pass before I write a line of poetry, and I've learned to accept that. When I was a young instructor — and feeling the pressure to publish — I'd put myself on a rigorous schedule, often staying up until two or three in the morning, churning out reams of stuff that never led anywhere. It was very frustrating, and I had to learn to wait and let the poem find me rather than trying to force it. The only exceptions have been a few occasional poems.

So how do the poems develop?

R.S. GWYNN: Most of my poems start with the ear, rather than the page. I'll be driving along or walking around, and a line will pop into my head, and I'll say it over and over, and maybe pick up another line or two that seems to match it in some way, and then I try to put the lines together. Then I'll get to the computer, and that's where the real work gets done.

Where do your initial ideas come from?

R.S. GWYNN: For me, pretty much everything's grist for the mill. Sometimes a poem comes out of a teaching experience, sometimes it comes out of a personal experience — like my marriage, or my relationships with my children, or my relationships with other people — and sometimes the poems begin with other poems, or television, or conversations.

Do you keep a list of ideas?

R.S. Gwynn

R.S. GWYNN: I don't keep notebooks or anything like that. But I do have a pretty good memory, and I store concepts in my head, sometimes for twenty years or more, before I know what to do with them. Then, someday, through some miraculous and mysterious process, a little voice in my head will insistently say, "*This* is what you can do with it." And I get excited, and I go to work. The poem I mentioned earlier, "Cléante to Elmire," was a story that was banging around in my head for eighteen years before I figured out what to do with it. Over the years, I'd had various false starts on the poem — usually six or seven lines — but I never got any further until a few years ago. But, in general, I never know exactly what's going to happen, or where, or when. It's a great mystery. Why, for example, when I'm driving through Pennsylvania, should the idea for "Dogwatch" just pop into my head? That image of my father standing on the deck of a Liberty Ship in WWII watching another ship get hit by a U-boat seemed as though it came from nowhere, and it insisted on being a poem.

You also do a fair amount of translating from a wide range of sources. I'm particularly impressed with your translation of Heine's longish and powerful poem "The Slave Ship."

R.S. GWYNN: When I first came across that poem, I was in Miller Williams' translation workshop in Arkansas. There was a German woman in the class who had never read the original before, and she was floored by the poem. She said, "I've been reading Heine all my life, but I've never heard that poem — or anything like it." She'd always associated Heine with his short lyrics, his lovely little songs, and she was amazed by this long narrative and its rather sardonic tone.

Did you have any difficulties with the ballad format?

R.S. GWYNN: Once I got into the poem, it went rather smoothly since the common measure gave me a lot of latitude, and the rhymes, for the most part, came easily. Some of the diction, however, created problems, and I certainly didn't know how to handle Heine's "neger." At first I thought the "n" word would be the more accurate translation, but later I came to believe that it was more of a distraction in the poem, so I changed it. I should admit that I am not much of a linguist. I've studied Spanish, French, and German, but all of that was a long time ago. I can still read some Spanish; French with a lot of help; but German not at all; and I've always worked closely with colleagues who speak the different languages.

You also spend a lot of time editing textbook anthologies. Do you enjoy it?

R.S. GWYNN: Well, it definitely keeps the boat in the driveway! But aside from that, there's, of course, a great deal of satisfaction in putting together books that'll be used by teachers and students. The hardest part is keeping track of everything — the galleys, the proofs, the manuscripts — especially since some of the books are now in their 4th or 5th editions. For those books, I have to do lots of minor revisions, updating the authors' biographies and changing certain selections. Fortunately, over the past few years, I've had student assistants who do a lot of the physical stuff — the copying, collating, and cutting-and-pasting — which is a great help.

In the "Introduction" to The Advocates of Poetry: A Reader of American Poet-Critics of the Modernist Era *(1996), you cite Robert Lowell's recollection that when he was a twenty year old in 1937, he and other young poets eagerly looked forward to the new essays being published by the New Critics, which "had the excitement of a new imaginative work." Then you point out that "This situation no longer exists" although there are "a good number of contemporary poets [who] write excellent criticism." In this age of pseudo-literary theory, which critics do you most enjoy reading?*

R.S. GWYNN: Aside from the excellent poet-critics like Wilbur, Hecht, and others, I don't read or even reread much pure criticism these days — not even the New Critics. When I look back, I'm most impressed with Randall Jarrell, whose great strength was not as a critic, but as a reviewer. The contemporary reviewers I most respect are people like Dave Mason, Bruce Bawer, Adam Kirsch, and William Logan, who's always fun to contend with. It's a shame

177

that serious criticism isn't being written these days, but maybe there's no audience for it anymore. I think Dana Gioia has addressed this situation well in his critical books.

Also in the "Introduction" to The Advocates of Poetry, *you mention your high regard for the poetry and prose of John Crowe Ransom, and you've been described as "A Southern Melancholic" by Lew Turco in* The Hollins Critic *(February, 2002). How strongly do you identify yourself and your work with the Southern literary tradition?*

R.S. GWYNN: That's always problematic for me. I realize that some Southern poets, like your own mentor, James Dickey, could work out of local conditions as well as expand to more cosmic levels — as Dickey does in *The Zodiac*. But I've written very few poems that I consider specifically "Southern." An exception might be something like "At Rose's Range" which was set in Ft. Worth, Texas, but I'm not much of a local colorist. I think what I've taken from the Southern tradition — and poets like Ransom — is more of an attitude rather than the "Southern" particulars. When you look at it closely, Ransom wasn't much on local color himself. A poem like "The Equilibrists" isn't necessarily a Southern poem, but it was clearly written by what we used to call a Southern gentleman. We can sense his manners, his high Southern culture, and his love of a more ornate manner of speaking — a different rhetoric — and I'm sure that all of those things have affected me over the years.

What about Southern themes?

R.S. GWYNN: For many years, I've wanted to write a poem about what it was like growing up in the segregationist South. My father was a segregationist — a "State's Rights" man — and he was the president of something called the "Patriots of North Carolina." In 1955 he ran for the school board on an anti-Brown vs. Board of Education platform, and I still have some of his campaign paraphernalia with the old slogan "separate but equal." When you grow up in the midst of all this, you eventually learn to grow past it. Then you live through the '60s, having nothing but for disdain for it, and then you eventually step into a new millennium with a longer perspective, and you realize that you've had a unique experience and that it's a lot more complex than it seemed at the time. I don't believe that people who grew up in the North or the West can fully understand the complexity of it — which is, of course, not excusing anything that happened back then. Faulkner understood the psyche of a typical small-town kid like myself growing up in the midst of that culture, but you never see the complexity dealt with anywhere else, and certainly not in the media. But I think what happened is important, and I'm still trying to puzzle out how to approach it. One idea is to write a verse epistle to a friend who lived in a different part of the country — maybe Dave Mason who grew up in Washington state, or Dana Gioia who grew up in California — and try to explain what that kind of childhood was really like. Neal Bowers wrote a fairly interesting book of poems about this subject called *Out of the South*.

Turning now to your teaching experiences, I wonder how you get young people interested in metrics?

R.S. GWYNN: In my beginning poetry class, the students do about ten assignments each semester, and about half of those have some kind of formal requirement. A lot of my kids seem to want to write rhymed, non-metrical ditties that are pretty terrible, so I try to open them up at the beginning of the semester by encouraging them to be outrageous. I often start with ballads, and I tell them to buy the sleaziest tabloid they can find — like the *Weekly World News* — and then find a ridiculous story and base their ballad on it. This produces some very lively stuff, and it's a great ice breaker. This year, for the first time, I also had them do some rap early on, which was also a lot of fun. Then I say, "Ok, we've had some fun with rhyming for a while, but now it's time to get to things like imagery, and metaphor, and meter." Near the end of the semester, we attempt the sonnet and some of the repeating forms.

I'm surprised that so many of your students expect to rhyme. Most college freshmen these days have written nothing but rather dreadful, free verse, "confessional"

R.S. Gwynn

lyrics, which have often been praised by their high school teachers.

R.S. GWYNN: Oh, yes, I get plenty of that too. I'd say I get about a 50/50 mix between those students and the ones who think poetry is rhymed, greeting card ditties. So I'm always trying to bring the one group in one direction — learning about form — and the others in the other direction — learning about language and originality. Whenever I teach the beginner's course, I always remind them, "This is a composition course, and you're going to have graded assignments. You may not be writing in the style that you think you've developed on your own, but this is a course in techniques to introduce you to other ways of doing things." Some students thrive, and some others resist and feel frustrated, but I remind the second group, "Look, this is an introductory class. We offer a second poetry course that's essentially a workshop class. So learn this stuff first." And most of the kids understand, and they do quite well.

At the beginning of The Narcissiad, *you cite Byron's famous remark that "there are more poets (soi-disant) than ever there were, and proportionately less poetry." You cited that quote nearly twenty-five years ago, and I wonder if you think things are better now.*

R.S. GWYNN: I do think things are better. That was before the boom in the creative writing programs, before the age of electronic information, and before the formalist revival — which *The Formalist* did so much to stimulate. After all, I'm a product of the M.F.A. system, and although I realize that creative writing programs have probably turned out way too many "degree-bearing" poets over the last thirty years, they've also turned out many good ones. It's been very exciting to see so many excellent books coming into print over the last ten years, especially by poets of the younger generation like Alicia Stallings, Catherine Tufariello, Joshua Mehigan, and others. For many years, I felt like I was one of the few formalist poets out there on the playground, but now there's plenty of competition! There are people in their 30s writing sonnets better than I can, and I'm asking myself, "How did this happen? Where did they come from?" I'm very pleased by what's happened over the past twenty-five years.

I'd like to finish up today by reading the ending of your poignant and rather complex poem, "1969," which begins No Word of Farewell. *In the poem, the narrator, addressing himself in the second person, remembers back to a birthday he spent in a bar in 1969.*

R.S. GWYNN: Yes, and the impetus for that poem came in 1999 when my son turned twenty-one. I wanted to write him a poem, but I didn't want it to have all the usual sentiments, so I tried to discuss the simple fact that the actual experiences of our various rites of passage will always be totally unique when they occur. No other glass of beer will ever taste like the first glass of beer — that fatal glass of beer! So the narrator in the poem tries to conjure up some of those things from his past, realizing that he can never truly capture the "newness" of things.

And here's how it ends:

> *Why bring it back? Because you want me to.*
> *Because you want to light your cigarette,*
> *Clutching a scene which you cannot forget*
> *Where everything you gaze upon is new.*

Thanks, Sam.

R.S. GWYNN: Thank you, Bill.

Frederick Turner

Frederick Turner is a distinguished poet and polymath, at home in the arts, the sciences, philosophy, and theology. As Michael Lind has described, Turner's poetry "unites wisdom and modern thought with the aid of timeless art."

Born in Northamptonshire, England, but raised in central Africa and Manchester, England, Frederick Turner received several degrees at Oxford University, including a B. Litt. in 1967. He subsequently taught at the University of California, Santa Barbara (1967-1972), and Kenyon College, Ohio (1972-1985), where he also served as the Co-editor of *The Kenyon Review* (1978-1982). He is currently the Founders Professor of Arts and Humanities at the University of Texas at Dallas.

He is the author of numerous books about the arts, literature, and culture, as well as various books of poetry. His works include *Shakespeare and the Nature of Time* (1971); *Natural Classicism: Essays on Literature and Science* (1985); *Beauty: The Value of Values* (1991); *Foamy Sky: The Major Poems of Miklós Radnóti* (1992, translated with Zsuzsanna Ozsváth); *The Culture of Hope: A New Birth of the Classical Spirit* (1995); and *Shakespeare's Twenty-First Century Economics: The Morality of Love and Money* (1999). His books of poetry include *The Garden* (1985); *The New World* (1985); *April Wind and Other Poems* (1992); *Hadean Eclogues* (1999); and *Paradise: Selected Poems 1990-2003* (2004), which received the David Robert Poetry Prize. Frederick Turner is also a past recipient of the Levinson Poetry Award, and he serves as a regular contributor to *American Arts Quarterly*.

This interview was conducted at the poet's home in Richardson, Texas.

You were born in Northamptonshire, England, but you spent much of your childhood in central Africa, where your parents were conducting anthropological research. Were you in Rhodesia most of the time?

FREDERICK TURNER: Yes, mostly in Northern Rhodesia,

which is now called Zambia. I also spent some time in present-day Zimbabwe, and about six months in Cape Town, which was the only way in or out back then.

Did you arrive from England by ship?

FREDERICK TURNER: Yes, it was a marvelous seven days on the ocean, sailing down the Atlantic Ocean and seeing Ascension Island and all the other sights along the way.

What were the living conditions like in Rhodesia?

FREDERICK TURNER: In Africa, we lived mostly in grass huts. They were quite wonderful, with a kind of smoky-hay smell.

How about things like food and supplies?

FREDERICK TURNER: We would truck in supplies occasionally, and there was also a small trading center called Mwinilunga, which had a few stores. We also bought a lot of bush meat, mostly goat and antelope, from the local people.

Your family didn't return to England until you were eleven years old. So how were you educated during those early years?

FREDERICK TURNER: My parents did it, and it was wonderful. My mother would teach me in the morning, and in the evenings, my father would read the great classics out loud.

Did you have textbooks?

FREDERICK TURNER: It was mostly the classics. My parents had the addresses of several secondhand bookstores — which had various catalogues — so we ordered from Africa. As a boy, I read all of the great politically-incorrect books! Lots of Kipling, and Rider Haggard, and all of Stevenson, like *Treasure Island* and *The Master of Ballantrae*.

Were these the books that your father read in the evenings?

FREDERICK TURNER: Yes, and then I would re-read them by myself: *The Swiss Family Robinson*, *Kim*, and *The Jungle Books*, of course. Later on, when it started coming out, he read us *The Lord of the Rings* series. I think he read it three times, and then I read it five or six more times on my own. Eventually we also read C.S. Lewis's *Narnia*, John Buchan, Arthur Conan Doyle, some Dickens, and lots of Shakespeare.

So despite their scientific interests, your parents clearly had literary interests?

FREDERICK TURNER: Very much so. In fact, my father was a poet, but he chose to be an anthropologist to put food on the family table. He used to say to me that I'd become a poet because he'd always wanted to be one.

Did he continue to write?

FREDERICK TURNER: He did, in bits and pieces, but he never publicized his poetry very much. It gave him pleasure, but he could never give it the full attention it needed. Yet he was quite good, and I now understand how he felt. I do a bit of painting myself, but I don't have the time to do it very well, but I still enjoy it a great deal.

Apparently, your own impulse to become a poet began at a very early age in present-day Zambia.

FREDERICK TURNER: Yes, I was with my father in his truck while we were driving about four hundred miles to the copper mining town of Chingola, which was also the headquarters of the Rhodes-Livingstone Institute, which funded my father's work. And during that long trip, two important things happened. The first was that I was overcome, in a way I'd never felt before, by the vastness and the beauty of the world around me — by the trees, the plains, the sky, and nature itself. At the same time, I had this peculiar awareness of my own consciousness. I was sitting right next to my father, and I could easily look over and see him, but I was fully aware of my own personal sense of innerness and interiority. Naturally, with all the arrogance of an eight year old, I thought that I had discovered something extraordinary, and I wanted to tell the whole world about it. It seemed miraculous to me, and I wanted to share it with everyone else. So that was the first time I first felt the impulse to write, to be a poet.

Three years later, when you were eleven, your father took a position at the University of Manchester, and the family returned from Africa. You've written that it was a difficult adjustment at first since you felt rather alienated and longed for Africa.

FREDERICK TURNER: I missed the whole fantastic landscape — that vast and exotic landscape that you could get lost in and be overwhelmed by. I greatly missed, for example, the Zambezi Rapids. On weekends in Africa, we would often drive out there in our truck, usually on Sundays, and we would go to the spot where the Zambezi River pours across a tremendous outcropping of granite. It was square mile after square mile of rapids and quiet pools, as the river divided into several streams and runnels, and then rumbled past with the thunder of a waterfall. In some places, the water would race over the vast sheets of granite at an incredible speed, yet the water was only an inch or so thick, so you could wade across it, which created these huge Mercury wings at your ankles as you moved through the coursing water. And I could see the thick forest, full of orchids and fruit trees, and it was like Kubla Khan's Xanadu. I also greatly missed the African people, especially my closest friends who were all Ndembu boys. There was one boy in particular named Sakeru — who is now, I understand, a Colonel in the Zambian Air Force — and he was the leader of our group. He ran around virtually naked, but he was a great hunter and a great trapper, and he was absolutely admirable. He seemed so perfectly good at everything he did, and I missed him and the others when we got to Manchester. I also missed the tribal rituals. The Ndembu were ritual people, and my friends and I always hung around for the rituals which were perfectly fascinating. My parents, of course, were studying the rituals, so I got to witness many of them, and sometimes even participate. Once I was actually initiated into some kind of cult, but the most fascinating of all were the women's puberty rituals. We boys were never allowed to attend, but we did our best to sneak around, although we were often driven away with terrible curses by the elderly women. What went on in those rituals was absolutely fascinating — and my mother has written about it rather extensively.

What was the objective of your parents' research?

FREDERICK TURNER: They went there as traditional, structuralist, functionalist anthropologists with a Marxist background. They were both atheists, and I was raised as a good atheist and a humanist — very idealistic, always believing in the brotherhood of man. Their primary interest was studying the structure of roles, statuses, and relationships — kinship — in the culture, and seeing them as a system for survival. They had expected to find that economic factors would be the primary forces in the culture, but they discovered, instead, that it was really ideology, ideas, religion, ritual, and ritual symbolism that were running the society — especially those occasions in the life of the society that had a powerful emotional impact. Even here in Texas, for example, our lives very much revolve around funerals, weddings, and births. So my parents were struck with the power of religion and ritual in the Ndembu culture, and they became world renowned experts on those subjects.

In England, you studied at the Manchester Grammar School, which you've always felt was an exceptional school.

FREDERICK TURNER: I think, back then, it was one of the two best schools in England.

What was the other?

FREDERICK TURNER: Eton.

Did any of your teachers have a particularly lasting influence?

FREDERICK TURNER: Yes, John Armstrong. He gave me private tutorials at his home, and he essentially got me into Oxford. He'd been a war hero, a commando in World War II, and he still had a limp from his experiences. He was a truly extraordinary person, and a highly literary man, and we studied a lot of Shakespeare, and Dickens, and Eliot.

At Oxford, you spent five years and earned three degrees, specializing in Shakespeare.

FREDERICK TURNER: Yes, the title of my thesis — we'd say "dissertation" over here — was *Shakespeare and the Nature of Time*, which was also the title of my book that was published later. I first got seriously interested in time while reading T.S. Eliot's "Four Quartets," and I've been interested ever since.

So you're one of the few people to publish his doctoral dissertation!

FREDERICK TURNER: Yes, Helen Gardner, who was my thesis supervisor at Oxford, made sure of that! My other examiners were David Cecil and John Bayley, who was the husband of Iris Murdoch. They were all wonderful, brilliant people, and very funny as well. Bayley stammered, and Cecil stuttered, and Cecil was under the impression that he knew exactly what Bayley was going to say, so he had a tendency to try and complete Bayley's sentences for him. They were delightful, marvelous people.

In those days, university courses in creative writing were almost non-existent in England. Did you get involved in any other kinds of literary workshops?

FREDERICK TURNER: Mostly, I was writing privately and just showing my work to a few friends and my family. My family was very encouraging, and in grammar school, I sent some pieces to the school's literary journal, and they must have liked them because they gave me a few prizes. There was, as you've said, no formal training in creative writing back them, but in my English courses, I learned about scansion, so I "reverse engineered" it, and figured out how

FREDERICK TURNER

to do it myself. At Oxford, we did have a little literary group called the Anonymous Society, and we would get together every once in a while and read each other's brilliant creations!

Who were your poetic influences at the time?

FREDERICK TURNER: I especially loved Gerard Manley Hopkins. I also loved Keats, and Yeats, and a bit later, Shakespeare, and a little bit later, Milton. I especially like Milton's conscientious program to make himself into a poet through self-education. It was Milton who eventually brought me to Virgil, and it was actually quite a bit later that I ran across the *Odyssey*. I was also greatly influenced by Kipling.

Who's shamelessly underrated today.

FREDERICK TURNER: Absolutely. His sound was remarkable, his political poems are brilliant, and his intellect was very subtle and provocative. He's certainly no Colonel Blimp, not by any means.

Even before matriculating at Oxford, you'd visited Palo Alto, California, where your father was teaching at the Stanford Center for Behavioral Studies. Right from the start, you were powerfully attracted to America.

FREDERICK TURNER: Yes, I was, and what first attracted me was the light, especially when the sky turns violet near the horizon, which was just like the sky in Zambia. After all those years in Manchester, which is sort of a dull, urban, industrial city — every house covered in soot — I was overwhelmed with the brilliant California sunshine and the brilliant Pacific Ocean. And there were other echoes of Africa as well, especially that sense of being free, the feeling that you could walk in any direction, and you might get lost in the wild. As a child in Africa, I'd once gotten lost in the wild, and it was terrifying. Sometimes children would get lost and not survive, eaten up by red ants. So you always knew that there was an "edge" beyond which you had no knowledge of, and it was both frightening and exhilarating, and I sensed that in California as well. These powerful feelings also led to my interest in science, which is also the "edge" beyond which we don't know much.

After graduating from Oxford, you returned to the States and began teaching at the University of California at Santa Barbara. At that point in your poetic development, you were apparently experimenting with open forms.

FREDERICK TURNER: Yes, I was quite excited about the Beatnik poets, and I got to know Ginsberg, Ferlinghetti, Duncan, and Creeley. I also knew Kenneth Rexroth quite well. We were colleagues for a while, and we did some readings together. At Santa Barbara, I directed the reading series, so I brought all the Beats down to read, and we had huge crowds, especially as they turned into war protests. I must admit that I enjoyed the whole scene enormously, although I was totally unable to smoke dope since inhaling made me sick. I also had no interest in the incredible sexual games they were playing at the time since I was rather straight-laced. But I did enjoy the exuberance of it all, but eventually I started writing in form and meter because I wanted to tell stories in poetry. I simply couldn't get the density I wanted in the sprawling lines of free-verse. I tried it endlessly, but it didn't work. I needed something that was more coherent, that would tie all of the parts of the poem together. So when I started composing in form and meter — for practical reasons, not ideological ones — a lot of my old friends and acquaintances on the west coast decided that I'd totally betrayed them. In fact, a few years later, when I came back to Santa Barbara to give a talk, Missy Maytag threw a party for me, and Kenneth Rexroth had a few drinks, and he announced to me, in front of everyone, that I had completely betrayed the whole of poetry. Insulted, I impulsively grabbed him by the lapels, stared in his face, and said, "Don't put your failures on me," or something like that. I still regret acting so rashly, but it shows how high the feelings ran. At that time, it became so hard to publish metrical poetry — as well as narrative poetry — that I simply gave up.

After leaving Santa Barbara, you took a position at Kenyon College.

FREDERICK TURNER: Yes, and my first year at Kenyon was

absolute bliss. I abandoned all my previous ambitions and set out to save my soul. I read immense amounts of philosophy, science, political philosophy, and theology from all over the world. And I also wrote poetry. That's when I wrote *The Garden*, which some people still think is my best book. It's always a bit annoying when people say an early book is your best work because that means you've been going downhill ever since!

So what got you publishing again?

FREDERICK TURNER: A man named Ed Watkins. Ed recently died, and I'm still in mourning for him right now. Back then, he more or less talked me into going "public" again. He started up a small press, primarily to publish *The Garden*, and he encouraged me to get out into the world again. Eventually, I helped revive *The Kenyon Review*.

Back in the Seventies, many other young poets, especially a number from the baby boom generation, began to question both the efficacy and the rigidity of the free verse poetic, and they began to experiment with traditional forms. From 1978 until 1982, you served as the co-editor of The Kenyon Review, *and you used this platform to encourage the young formalists by publishing their poems and essays. Did you get any resistance from the college?*

FREDERICK TURNER: In the beginning, Kenyon was very good to me, allowing a fair amount of latitude. But when I started proposing issues of *The Kenyon Review* which celebrated the beginnings of what is now called the New Formalism, I began to get a lot of opposition; and, eventually, the editorship was wrested away. Part of the problem was economic; we were in a bit of financial trouble. So the English Department offered to support the magazine out of its own budget, but that naturally meant that the department would set up an "editorial committee."

Whenever the "oversight" committee is formed, it's time to go.

FREDERICK TURNER: Exactly. And Ron Sharp, who was a

bit more far-sighted than I was, realized what was coming, and he retired.

Nevertheless, your editorship at Kenyon had quite an impact, and you were an important early figure in the formalist revival. Regarding your own work, when did you first start thinking seriously about form and meter, for either lyrics or narratives?

FREDERICK TURNER: I suppose it was around 1969 or 1970. I'd tried my hand at sonnets before that, but then I just started looking for other useful forms. I first turned to Latin and Greek verse, and then I started working with Anglo-Saxon poetry. I started writing a lot of poetry in the Anglo-Saxon alliterative metric, and I think that it greatly influenced my later narrative verse.

Because you now felt that contemporary narratives were viable? Or because the sound of the accentual meters still echoed in your later work?

FREDERICK TURNER: I believe those meters still linger in my later work. I'd always wanted to write narrative poetry — to tell stories — even when I was in grammar school, but I'd never found a way to do it effectively and gracefully. The inclusion of back-story and exposition always seemed very difficult and awkward, and I had to learn that it works best in the context of a dramatic situation, with irony, and with a strong metric to bind things together.

Before getting to some of your individual poems, I'd like to touch on one of your many intellectual passions: the interaction between the sciences and the arts, especially the biological foundations of aesthetics. One outcome of this interest was your seminal essay "The Neural Lyre: Poetic Meter, the Brain, and Time," written with the distinguished German neurophysiologist Ernst Pöppel, which revealed, among other things, that modern science has discovered that regular rhythm actually induces the brain to release pleasure-creating endorphins. How did that collaboration come about?

FREDERICK TURNER: My book *Shakespeare and the Nature of Time* came out soon after I'd arrived in California, and it attracted the interest of J.T. Fraser, the great philosopher and physicist. He was especially interested in physical patterns, and he had been the founder and secretary for the International Society for the Study of Time, which has tri-annual conferences all over the world. So I started attending those meetings — in Italy, France, Austria, and elsewhere — and I started meeting this extraordinary group of interdisciplinary scholars (scientists, artists, and writers), including a number of Nobel prize winners. At any rate, I eventually got involved with one of the subgroups at the Austrian conference which was interested in the neurobiological and evolutionary background of human aesthetics. Why do we find things beautiful? Why do we have the capacity to experience beauty? And why is this phenomenon so pan-cultural? Once we had the facts at our disposal, it was impossible to entertain any of these post-structuralist notions that such human forms and conventions are simply closed systems and culturally unique. In fact, it was clear that human aesthetic rose from human biology. Anyway, this subgroup got a grant from the Werner Reimers Stiftung, and we were able to involve even more interesting people from other disciplines ranging from physics to anthropology to music. So we began meeting over a nine year period, and that was where our ideas about the neural lyre initiated.

Where were the meetings?

FREDERICK TURNER: In a nice little town near Hamburg, Germany. Now Ernst had been a member of the time society, so we'd known each other for quite a while, and we used to hang out in the bar and talk about all sorts of things. At the same time, I'd already embarked on a serious study of world meter, and I'd noticed that all human societies had poetry, that it was always divided into lines, and that, even in pre-literate societies, all the lines were about three seconds long. Ernst had similarly concluded that humans have a three-second cycle in which we hear and understand language. At his lab at the Max Planck Institute of Neuroscience in Munich, for example, he'd noticed that when our words are played back to us over headphones as we continue to speak, if the playback is delayed and quite short, it sounds like an echo chamber, and we have no problem speaking. But if the delay is three seconds, we find it absolutely impossible to continue, and we mess up our words. On the other hand, if the delay is longer than three seconds, we're able to continue again — it sounds as though there's an ignorable cocktail conversation going on behind our backs. So there was clearly some kind of crucial three-second phenomenon going on. Then we hooked up with a group of bio-genetic structuralists who'd been studying, for instance, the neurophysiology of ritual chants, and we examined the effects of ritual chanting and learned that the chanting produces significant changes in the brain waves, so we started to put a lot of things together, and we wrote the essay.

Have there been any other developments regarding the physiological effects of regular rhythm?

FREDERICK TURNER: Well, the whole thing has cascaded into many other areas, like the prosody of whale song, or the prosody of mother/newborn interactions — which also takes place in three-second cycles — or the prosody of deaf and dumb poets who compose in sign language — also in three-second cycles.

Is the presumption that the completely deaf poet "hears" some version of the poem in his mind?

FREDERICK TURNER: I think the presumption is that there's something in the very nature of the brain itself that isn't limited to the hearing system. There's still a three-second lapse, and that's the limit, and if you drive the fundamental rhythm by an external rhythm, you get various changes in brain waves. That was a very interesting discovery, and people are still working with it. For example, it seems that children with Down's Syndrome have something closer to a four-second cycle, which might lead to further insights. In my own work, I became very interested in the nature of poetic variation, especially when the rhythm of a spoken line departs from the meter in ways that enhance emotional and psychological significance. Thus, when the line's recited, it's not spoken with an exaggerated iambic. For example, when we say, "Shall I compare thee to a summer's day?", we don't necessarily exaggerate all the beats, and those spoken differences are very meaningful. Thus the "meaning" of the poetry is being appreciated on the right side of the brain rather than on the linguistic left side of the brain, so I like to say that we're hearing the poetry in stereo.

You've written numerous love poems to your wife, and one of my favorites is "The Mei Lin Effect," which ends:

> *A soft gauss crackles even when she sits*
> *Reading where none can see her, deep within*
> *The dark event-horizon of her wits;*
> *The world-lines gather and turn outside in,*
> *And a new world begins to synthesize,*
> *Out of which looks a pair of clear brown eyes.*

Where did you meet?

FREDERICK TURNER: We first met at Oxford. Earlier, in Manchester, she was actually attending school right across the road from me, but we never met at the time, although some of her friends and some of my friends knew each other. Later, at Oxford, my fiancée introduced us, and that, of course, changed everything.

Is she also a writer?

FREDERICK TURNER: She writes beautiful prose, and she's an excellent copyeditor, which she does professionally. Occasionally, if I can talk her into it, she'll copyedit some of my own books!

As we've already discussed, you're a great proponent of narrative poetry, and you've written several contemporary epic poems including The New World *(1985) and* Genesis *(1988), which is about the settlement of Mars. While it's certainly true that epic poems have the ability to explore themes and develop narratives, do you think such poems can reach the general audience in our era of fast-everything and limited attention spans?*

Frederick Turner

FREDERICK TURNER: I think so. People are willing to read novels, and they're willing to read the classic epics. I suspect that Robert Fitzgerald's wonderful translation of the *Odyssey* has been read by as many people as most contemporary novels. So I don't think that there's anything inherently wrong with the form itself; it's rather a problem of fashioned "expectations," along with the general incompetence with which it's usually done in our times — when it's done at all. Also, the perceived "difficulty" of modern poetry is a problem. If readers struggle with a short modern poem, they'll often dread the idea of reading a 200-page poem, but if it's crafted correctly and really tells a story, then it isn't a problem. You can read Fitzgerald's *Odyssey* more easily than most novels. It's much more direct.

And people still read Shakespeare.

FREDERICK TURNER: They certainly do. I wish I was collecting his royalties!

How have sales been for The New World *and* Genesis*?*

FREDERICK TURNER: *The New World* had two printings, which is very rare for poetry, and its publisher, Princeton University Press, has declared it a poetry "bestseller"! *Genesis* has also done quite well, and it's even been adopted by NASA.

Several of your more recent lyrics express not only a humility in relationship to your friends and loved ones — like "To All My Friends" — but also the desire to be more submissive to God. Your short, deceptively-simple poem "Habits" is particularly telling:

> *First we make them,*
> *Then we break them,*
> *Then we make ourselves anew;*
>
> *We're completed,*
> *Self-conceited,*

Frederick Turner

> *Find there's one thing left to do:*
>
> *Break the habit*
> *Of the habit,*
> *Let ourselves be made by You.*

Derek Walcott once explained, "My calling as a poet is votive, sacred, outdated," and you've said that writing poetry is a kind of worship. Such "outdated" notions are actually much more common among contemporary poets than it might seem on the surface. Why do you think it's so seldom discussed?

FREDERICK TURNER: In the 20th century, it became more and more frowned on to advertise your religious views. Partly it was a reaction against the "tolerant hypocrisy" of the Victorians, but the primary reason, of course, was the intellectual fashion of the "death of God." You really couldn't be a respectable thinker unless you made an act of faith that there was nothing more than matter in the world. We now know, of course, from countless scientific discoveries, that matter itself has a relatively late appearance in the universe, and if the universe looks like anything, it looks like a gigantic "thought," which Eddington claimed a long time ago. The best metaphor for the universe is not a gigantic machine, but rather a "thought," which from a theological point of view is perfectly reasonable. But there's still a lot of pressure to conform in the arts and academia, and it also has professional ramifications. People could certainly lose their jobs for expressing themselves like Hopkins, or Dickinson, or Milton — or they wouldn't get those jobs in the first place.

In your sonnet "The Kite," the act of writing is compared to helping a young girl fly her birthday kite. The poem ends:

> *Such is the book that I would want to write,*
> *Whose power could haul a mile of line into*
> *The dark purple, and strangely out of sight.*

Is such an ambition more likely to be achieved in an epic poem than in a collection of lyrics?

Frederick Turner

FREDERICK TURNER: Yes, absolutely.

Over the years you've written in a wide range of poetic forms, from the epic to the epigram. What formats are you currently using?

FREDERICK TURNER: Recently, I've started writing more dramatic verse, especially in narrative voices that are not my own.

Interior monologues?

FREDERICK TURNER: Yes. *The Prayers of Dallas* is a series of about fifty interior monologues in the voices of fifty different people living in Dallas. Most of the characters are invented, but some of them are based on people I know. We've had a number of performances of the monologues here in Dallas, and audiences have enjoyed hearing what the different voices have to say — about themselves, and God, and basketball, and politics, and all kinds of things.

You've also told me about a series of sonnets.

FREDERICK TURNER: Yes, I'm beginning a narrative sequence of wayfarer sonnets about a man who has, in some way or another, died and then come back to life. It's unclear in the sequence whether he's been through some kind of major medical intervention, but he's definitely been declared legally dead. As a result, he's bequeathed a lot of money to other people, including his wife, and he seems to have lost much of his memory. So he wanders around the world, like a "snowbird" — like the undead — and many strange things happen. At one point, in a thunderstorm, he takes refuge in a deserted building in an old mining town, where he discovers some money and supplies, like food and whisky. Then he vaguely recalls that, in his former life, he'd left these things here for himself. At another time, he's off in the mountains, probably the Apennines, and as he watches the locals beating down the chestnuts, he sees a very interesting dark haired woman who seems familiar, but he can't quite place her. Later that night, he dreams about the woman, and the next day, he learns that she's an heiress and most probably his wife.

How long will the sequence be?

FREDERICK TURNER: About a hundred sonnets. I've finished twenty so far.

Your work covers a wide range of interesting ideas. Where do you think your poetic ideas come from?

FREDERICK TURNER: They come from a wide range of sources, but there are always a few central questions or "knots" which continually generate interest in my mind — especially the phenomenon of time. So I might be stimulated by an article in a scientific periodical, or a personal memory, or the death of a friend. I'm also fascinated by various other complexities that stimulate me creatively, like self-ordered systems including evolution and economics.

What about poetic form? Do these initial ideas "find" the form in the act of writing, or do you sense the appropriate form even before you start writing the poem?

FREDERICK TURNER: It can work both ways. Sometimes a poem will start almost wordlessly, or with a very short phrase, and then everything will generate around that beginning. But at other times, I'll run across some wonderful metrical form, say in Goethe, and I'll say to myself, "I've got to try that!" Then, amazingly, at the very moment that I start thinking about the form in my head, a wonderfully appropriate subject matter will begin to accumulate around the form. I must admit, I've never felt as though I don't have enough to write about. On the contrary, I always feel that I have far too many things to write about and never enough time. So I'm never out searching for "material" for my poetry; instead, I'm looking for more time to write. Fortunately, if I don't have the time for something I'd like to work on, I can usually set it aside in my head, and it'll go underground and marinate until I can get back to it. Occasionally,

I'll also write down some notes for the idea and then come back to it months later.

Do you have any writing rituals? Any favorite places or times?

FREDERICK TURNER: I actually like writing in airplanes because people can't "get at you" up there, and it's so terribly uncomfortable. So I need to do something to take my mind off the discomfort, and writing makes the time pass enjoyably. I also, of course, work a lot in my study, and when I'm working on a longer project, I'll set off certain bits of the day, usually the mid-morning.

Let's talk about translation. In 1992, with Zsuzsanna Ozsváth, you published Foamy Sky: The Major Poems of Miklós Radnóti. *Radnóti, a Hungarian Jew who perished in the Nazi slave camps, wrote his poems in elaborate formats. You once speculated that Radnóti's formality might have been a protest against the randomness of fascism. Is there anything in the poems or letters that supports that notion?*

FREDERICK TURNER: Yes, there is, especially in the poem "O Ancient Prisons":

> What is his fate who, while he breathes, will so
> speak of what is in measure and in form,
> and only thus he teaches how to know?
>
> He would teach more. But all things fall apart.
> He sits and gazes, helpless in his heart.

One day, one of Radnóti's friends saw him on the streets of Budapest, and the poet was mumbling something like, "du-duh-du-duh-du-duh," and his friend said, "Don't you understand! Hitler is invading Poland!", and Radnóti supposedly answered, "Yes, but this is the only thing I have to fight with." As his poetry makes clear, Radnóti believed that fascism was the destruction of order. It both destroyed and vulgarized civil society. It was as if you wanted to create an ideal cat, so you took your cat, killed it, removed its flesh, put it into some kind of mold, and then pressed it into the shape of a cat. That's what fascism does, and that's what communism does. They both destroy an intricate social order in order to set up a criminally simple-minded order. And that's the basic problem with socialist ideas, and I say that as one who was a socialist for many years. But I'm more of a Burkean now. I believe that many things can work themselves out in society. I believe that something like meter forms naturally — like the common law, or the great myths, or the rituals of religion, or the everyday working practices of scientists and engineers, or the marketplace.

Like Smith's "invisible hand"?

FREDERICK TURNER: Exactly.

Given Radnóti's belief in the power of forms and his complicated formats, how did you and Zsuzsanna Ozsváth approach his poems?

FREDERICK TURNER: Well, we made an agreement right from the start that we would maintain the Hungarian formats. We also wanted them to capture the sound of the Hungarian, which is often quite unusual. Fortunately, Hungarian poets use a lot of meters and forms that we also use. Iambs and sonnets, for example, but the language also has many more trochees and dactyls, and the Hungarians often combine the two falling rhythms in fascinating ways, and ways that work extremely well in English. As George Steiner once pointed out, Hungarian poems shouldn't sound like American poems. So we worked hard to create the Hungarian sounds.

How did you approach your translations from the Chinese, particularly the Tang poets?

FREDERICK TURNER: That was quite a bit more difficult, but eventually I realized that the Chinese syllable is roughly equivalent to two syllables in English, and that made things much easier. Chinese poetry needs to be recited much slower than English poetry, and when a line of Chinese poetry has five syllables, it will probably take ten syllables to render it into English. Whenever I translate, whether from the Hungarian or the Chinese, I always listen to the poems recited first. Then I write a "score" for the poem, marking stresses, and the rhyme scheme, and the cadence, and so forth.

So the sound precedes the content?

FREDERICK TURNER: Always. Only after I understand the poem's sound and have an emotional feel for it, will I begin to examine its meaning.

In our current age of pseudo-literary theory, which literary critics do you most enjoy reading?

FREDERICK TURNER: Well, I do like Stephen Greenblatt. In the past he's done some dancing around his subjects, but he's begun to commit himself more and more. His notion of Renaissance "self-fashioning" was truly an excellent insight.

Anyone else?

FREDERICK TURNER: To be quite frank, there aren't that many contemporary literary critics that I enjoy reading, and most of the ones I do read come from my own literary circle, like Frederick Feirstein, Dana Gioia, Kevin Walzer, and Sonny Williams. But, in general, I have to admit that I've given up on contemporary literary discourse, pretty much in disgust. But I'm always hopeful that something good and interesting will come along.

You're currently the Founders Professor of Arts and Humanities at the University of Texas in Dallas. What courses do you teach?

FREDERICK TURNER: I teach a course on time, and I also teach a class on literature and martial arts, which includes martial arts training, so the students can feel in their bodies what it's actually like to fight. I also do a Shakespeare course in which we perform scenes from the plays, and I act as the director, and I also teach a poetry course, which is like a boot camp in meters. I teach them as though they're apprentice shamans — so there's an "ordeal" involved as they prepare themselves spiritually for getting the meter right.

How do you get them excited about meter?

FREDERICK TURNER: Once I give them my little spiel about the biological and evolutionary roots of meter and its effects in the human brain, they're quite eager to learn how to do it. I make them realize that meter is not some kind of silly invention, like wigs, that belongs to a particular culture, but that it's universal, and human, and a part of them, and part of their inheritance.

When young poets ask you for advice, what do you tell them?

FREDERICK TURNER: The usual but necessary thing: learn the craft. It's crucial, and it needs to be said over and over again. Also, read, hugely, and not just poetry, and certainly not just contemporary poetry. Read the old poetry, and learn it, and enjoy it, and read out loud. Then read everything else. Serious poets should have a fairly decent grasp of what's going on in most of the sciences, as well as philosophy and theology, whatever their beliefs might be. They should definitely understand the different religious systems. That's not only fundamental knowledge, but it also heightens our sense of the moral relationship between the writer and the reader. Poets need to be responsible and communicate. Any fool can write "difficult" poetry, but the greatest literary achievement is to be both intelligent and intelligible at the same time. Poetry should run deep, but it shouldn't be so turgid that you can't see beneath the surface. It should be like a deep river where the water is so clear that you can see right to the bottom of things. Bai Juyi, the great Chinese poet, used to try out his poems on the cleaning women, and if there was anything they didn't understand, he'd go back and change the poem.

I'd like to finish up today by reading your lyric descriptions of the philosophers and artists in your poem "In the Villa Adriana." The sonnet ends:

Frederick Turner

> *The court philosophers murmur, under eaves*
> *Painted with porcelain, of qualia,*
> *Of atoms, phantasms and clinamens;*
> *Court-painters breathe the aromatic dust*
> *Of pigments powdered in a concave lens,*
> *And poets press a lyric from a lust,*
> *And all this summer-house of Hadrian*
> *Makes melody in its oblivion.*

Thanks, Fred.

FREDERICK TURNER: Thank you, Bill.

Mary Jo Salter

Mary Jo Salter is one of the most distinguished poetic voices of her generation. Her work, as described by Joseph Brodsky, "embodies the marriage of superb craftsmanship to the tragic sense of reality, which is the formula of true poetry."

Born in Grand Rapids, Michigan, she grew up in Detroit and then the Baltimore, Maryland, area. Completing her B.A. at Harvard University in English in 1976, she subsequently completed an M.A. in English at Cambridge University. She then worked as a staff editor at *The Atlantic Monthly* from 1978-1980 and married fellow writer Brad Leithauser in 1980. From 1984 to 2007, she taught at Mount Holyoke College, South Hadley, Massachusetts, where she and her husband shared an appointment as the Emily Dickinson Senior Lecturer in the Humanities.

She is the author of six books of poetry, all published by Knopf: *Henry Purcell in Japan* (1985), *Unfinished Painting* (1989), *Sunday Skaters* (1994), *A Kiss in Space* (1999), *Open Shutters* (2003), and *A Phone Call to the Future* (2008). She is also the co-editor of *The Norton Anthology of Poetry* (1996); the author of a children's book, *The Moon Comes Home* (Knopf, 1989); and the author of the play *Falling Bodies*. Her numerous recognitions include the Discovery Prize (1983), the Lamont Poetry Prize (1988), an Ingram-Merrill Fellowship (1989), and a Guggenheim (1993).

This interview was conducted at the Sewanee Writers' Conference at the University of the South, Sewanee, Tennessee. After this interview, Mary Jo Salter and her husband Brad Leithauser took tenured positions in The Writing Seminars at The Johns Hopkins University.

You were born in Grand Rapids, but your family eventually moved to Baltimore. Did you live in the city or the suburbs?

MARY JO SALTER: The first half of my childhood was spent in Michigan — first in Grand Rapids and then in Detroit. When I was

Mary Jo Salter

nine years old, we moved to the city of Baltimore for a year before moving out to Towson, which is a Baltimore suburb.

I've read that your father was an advertising executive. Did he write ad copy?

MARY JO SALTER: Absolutely. In his youth, he thought he might end up an English professor, so he went to Berkeley and got a Master's degree in English. But he eventually took a job as an ad man, and he wrote copy for about the first half of my childhood before he became an executive. My father's literary interests and his career in advertising definitely affected my own interest in poetry, and my mother was also quite literary as well. As you know, whenever you write ad copy, you have to get people's attention, usually very quickly, and you need to do it with a sense of both fun and creativity, and that approach to things was very much in the air when I was growing up.

Did your father write poems?

MARY JO SALTER: He did, and he also wrote a novel, although none of his writings have been published in book form. Later on, when he lived in West Virginia, he won many prizes for the column that he wrote for the local newspaper. So he's always been a writer in one way or another.

Your mother was an artist, and one of her unfinished paintings — a portrait of your brother — inspired the title poem of your collection Unfinished Painting, *and the picture was reproduced on the cover of the book. What was her background?*

MARY JO SALTER: She was the child of Italian parents. One of the most moving experiences of my life was when I returned with my mother to the town of Castellaneta, where her parents had been born in southern Italy. My mother grew up in a home in Lansing, Michigan, that was always full of people, and many of them had come to America from Castellaneta. They tended to emigrate to the same place, which was Seneca Falls, New York, and then many of them moved on to Lansing, where my mother was born. So the

Italian language was very much in her household growing up, but my mother was from the generation that felt it was embarrassing to have your friends hear a foreign language in your house, so she never became truly fluent in Italian, although she understood it. As for me, although I grew up listening to lots of Italian opera in the house, I really didn't study Italian until I was in college. A number of years ago, my husband Brad and I lived in Rome for a year, and I've been back to Italy many times. In fact, I've just returned. So one of my mother's many influences is that I grew up "feeling" Italian — far more than any other ethnicity.

And she was a painter as well.

MARY JO SALTER: Yes, she was excited about all of the arts, and that became important to me. When I look back at my youth, it was a time when young girls were generally not encouraged to think in terms of making a living, and this led many young women into various blind alleys without a sustaining career. But, on the other hand, if you grow up in a household in which the arts are highly valued and nobody is worrying about how you'll eventually make a living, you might end up being a poet. So I'm very grateful to my parents for that. They allowed me to believe that it was okay to become an artist of some kind.

Was poetry an integral part of your childhood?

MARY JO SALTER: It was. My father loved to listen to poetry records, especially Dylan Thomas. He was enchanted by the mellifluousness of Thomas's recitations. And my mother memorized lots of poetry, although she seldom recited whole poems. But she would naturally insert little excerpts into her conversation, maybe Lewis Carroll, or Shakespeare, or whoever was appropriate. In our home, there was also a rather laissez-faire attitude about reading, so if I wasn't supposed to be doing some specific chore, it was perfectly okay for me to disappear into my room and read books. It was a very good environment.

Mary Jo Salter

When did you start writing poetry?

MARY JO SALTER: I was seven. I wrote a little poem in school, and I still remember that I rhymed "flowers" with "towers." It seemed to me at the time that I'd actually invented that particular rhyme. That's one of the marvelous things about being young and innocent — you have no idea what's preceded you, so you tend to think that you're inventing things all the time. As I child I loved all the arts — especially playing the piano, drawing, and writing — but poetry was generally at the top of the list.

Through high school as well?

MARY JO SALTER: Absolutely. I even kept a notebook back then — which I wish I still had — in which I wrote down my favorite lines of poetry. I can still remember writing down Frost's little couplet that goes, "The old dog barks backwards without getting up. / I can remember when he was a pup." So even back then, I was very interested in the concept of the passage of time.

Who were your early models?

MARY JO SALTER: I remember very clearly the first time that I read Richard Wilbur, which was in high school, and how thrilling it was. Earlier, when I was eleven, I'd seen a production of *Tartuffe* — in Wilbur's translation — so I already knew who he was, but I'd never read his own poems until high school. Another favorite was Auden. For high school graduation, I was given his last collection, and I remember thinking that these poems seemed to be doing something far beyond what I'd thought poetry could do. It was truly amazing and inspiring. To this day, I still adore both Auden and Wilbur.

In 1972, you went to Harvard. What was your major?

MARY JO SALTER: English, but I was in one of the first classes to be allowed to emphasize creative writing. I was still an English major, but I was able to concentrate on creative writing, and my thesis advisor was Robert Fitzgerald.

Fitzgerald was an amazing translator, and some of his poems are wonderful as well. What do you think you learned from him?

MARY JO SALTER: A clear sense of the line. And the poetic foot. Fitzgerald was an extraordinary prosodist, and not just in the scholarly sense, but also within his own poetry. He was also a very witty poet, and I remember reading some of his poems back then and thinking, "Why don't people know about these poems?" But he didn't write that much poetry given all the time he spent on translation. I also think he taught me a lot about taste. He was a man of both restraint and taste without being prudish, and I wanted to please him. I suppose I wanted to emulate a little bit of his natural dignity — we all did. He was a very kind man, and we loved him.

When did you meet Elizabeth Bishop?

MARY JO SALTER: When I finally got to study with her in the fall of '74, she was approaching the end of her life, and she actually died soon after I graduated. I'd tried earlier to get into her class, and I remember going to her office door where she posted the class list, and when my name wasn't on the list, I was heartbroken.

Did you have to submit a manuscript?

MARY JO SALTER: Yes, and I was quite upset about it. Soon afterwards, I went to a party where I met this young man who I'd seen in the poetry library at Radcliffe. I didn't know his name; and, for some reason, I thought he was in one of the campus rock bands. So we started talking, and I found myself attracted to him, but I must have sounded quite negative, complaining, "I'm so bummed out that I didn't get into Elizabeth Bishop's class, and, to be honest, some of the people who did get in, I don't think are so hot." Then I thought that maybe I should say something more positive, so I added, "But there's this guy named Brad Leithauser who got in, and I recently read his poem in *The Harvard Advocate*, and I think he's terrific." Then the guy who was standing next to him said, "That's Brad you're talking to." So that's how we met. So something good came out of my rejection!

And you got into the class eventually.

MARY JO SALTER: Yes, the second time around, and Brad got permission from the University to take the course over again, so we took it together. I found Miss Bishop to be a quiet but rather daunting presence. I definitely wanted to please her as well, but there was more distance than with Fitzgerald. Back then, of course, there was much more of a separation between student and professor. Not only was she "Miss Bishop," but I was "Miss Salter," and that's the way she ran her class. It was clear that she felt that she didn't quite know what she was doing, and she definitely had difficulty coming up with ideas for assignments. In truth, she assigned very little in terms of either writing assignments or reading. She did assign the two-part memoirs of Mandelstam, *Hope Against Hope* and *Hope Abandoned*, and I remember her saying, "I want you to know about the people who've died for poetry." At the time, I was quite surprised that such a quiet and unassuming poet would have such strong views about what poetry could do politically. Another important thing that we learned in her class was patience. We learned that you needed to wait until you've got it right, and to assume that you don't have it right until you've worked on it long enough. She convinced us that there was no need to be rushing toward publication and that we needed to value poetry as something that was worth waiting for.

Did you also study with Richard Wilbur back then?

MARY JO SALTER: No, he wasn't teaching there at the time, but I did get to meet him in 1976 at Mount Holyoke College, where I now teach. For many years, Mount Holyoke has run a poetry competition called the Glascock Intercollegiate Poetry Contest, and during my senior year at Harvard, I was invited to represent Harvard at the contest. The judges that year were Stephen Spender, Marilyn Hacker, and Richard Wilbur, and Wilbur was extremely gracious to all of the young poets. He made us feel as if we were going somewhere, and I'll never forget his kindness — and the excitement of hearing him read his poems for the first time.

After graduation from Harvard in 1976, you went to Cambridge where you received a Master's degree in 1978. How did that come about, and what was your primary subject of interest?

MARY JO SALTER: A Harvard professor named Peter Dale, whom I'd never taken a course with, encouraged me to go to Cambridge. We both knew that I had no idea what I wanted to do with my life, except that I wanted to write. At the time, I was torn between pursuing a doctorate and going into publishing. But back in 1976, the job market was even worse than it is now, and I was uncertain if I wanted to invest seven or eight years in a Ph.D. that might not result in a job. Also, I wasn't really sure if I wanted to be a scholar, and I discovered at Cambridge that it wasn't my primary interest. Nevertheless, I loved my two years in England. I went to New Hall, which was, at the time, one of the university's three women's colleges — today, it's the only women's college at Cambridge. New Hall had been founded in the year of my birth — 1954 — and it was, back then, the newest college at Cambridge. Because it was so new and small, and because it was a poor college, I had the benefit of being farmed out to a variety of different tutors. I had, for example, a wonderful practical criticism tutor for two years named Arthur Sale at Magdalen. I also took two years of tragedy, and I remember not only reading George Steiner, but actually going to his lectures. I also went to a lot of lectures by Christopher Ricks about Shakespeare, and I spent two years studying Chaucer. Eventually, I did my master's thesis on George Herbert, who is still extremely important to me. So Cambridge was a wonderful experience that helped me to fill in many of the gaps in my undergraduate education.

When you returned to the States, you worked as a staff editor at The Atlantic *for two years. How do you think that experience affected your writing?*

MARY JO SALTER: Actually, I'd worked there a year earlier as a

Mary Jo Salter

summer job between my two years at Cambridge. Then, when I was about to graduate, the person who had the permanent job quit, so I never got to attend my graduation ceremony. I immediately got on a plane to Boston and took over the job. At the time, I was the first reader for the fiction editors — Mike Curtis, who's still there, and Dick Todd, who's since retired — and I was also the first reader for the poetry editor, Peter Davison, who died two years ago. Probably the most important things I learned at *The Atlantic* had to do with speed. First, I had to read very fast and make quick judgments, or I would never have been able to do my job. This experience has made me, for the rest of my life, very patient with editors. I fully understand the pressures they're under, and I realize that it's entirely possible for a good reader to make a poor decision. The other lesson relating to speed — and maybe this is also because I'm the daughter of an ad man — was that I wanted writers to get to the point. To this day, I have very little patience with unintentional slowness in writing. I realize that some very great writers have a style that depends upon the slow accumulation of detail — writers like Henry James or Anthony Hecht, for example — but, for the most part, I feel that such writers create a comfortable pace within the gradual buildup. Their readers know that they're getting somewhere, and they feel it's worthwhile. So, overall, I think that my years at *The Atlantic* heightened my respect and concern for the audience. We're not just writing for ourselves; we're writing for other people. Naturally, after reading those slush piles for two years, I was totally exhausted and ready to move on, yet I've always been very grateful for the experience. But when Brad decided that he didn't want to be a lawyer, and he was offered a job in Japan, I was ready to go.

In 1985, Knopf published your first collection, Henry Purcell in Japan, *and right from the beginning your work was praised for its effective use of formal elements. Your fifth collection,* Open Shutters, *begins with the poem "Trompe l'Oeil," which discusses the fact that in Genoa some of the houses have painted shutters on their exteriors. This poem, along with others in the collection, seems to appreciate both the limitations and the "focusing" effect of the shutters — as well as the artifice of the construction itself.*

MARY JO SALTER: That's true. In more than any other of my books, *Open Shutters* eventually started to coalesce around a theme, although it wasn't intentional. In "Trompe l'Oeil" that particular Genoese artifice is not only worthwhile, but it's delightful as well. It reminds us that there's fun in the arts and that we shouldn't forget it — whether we're painting or writing. Eventually, I realized that I'd written a number of poems with shutters in them, and I became fascinated with the idea that we frame events simply by looking at them — whether we're a photographer or a painter or an observer — and the notion of frames and shutters still intrigues me.

Relating to poetic themes, "Another Session," a very effective sonnet series in Open Shutters, *points out that:*

> *Therapists have themes, as writers do.*
> *(A few of mine, then: the repertoire includes*
> *clocks, hands, untimely death, snow-swollen clouds.)*

One of your most consistent themes, especially since Sunday Skaters *(1994), has been family relationships, and the poem "Marco Polo" reminds us that we have a natural interest in family "because family / is always interesting."*

MARY JO SALTER: There's a part of me that's aware that we really can't do that much on this earth, and that the people closest in our lives are really the most important thing. That's where the heart is. That's where we live. And when you listen to writers, whether they're talking about their work or reading from their work, over and over and over again, it's about love, and it's about *not* being loved, and it's about how much we can risk in our attachments to other people. Even people who've come from rather cold families can't renounce this impulse. It's fundamental, and it's necessary; but, I have to admit, there's a part of me that doesn't fully understand it. So when I wrote "Another Session," I was intrigued by the fact that the therapist — who's since died — knew everything about me, but I knew virtually nothing about him. I knew he had a family, and I saw them one time in a restaurant, but that was it. And it struck me that family, inevitably, is the doorway inside each of us and that

Mary Jo Salter

it always relates to the passage of time. We know members of our family for decades; and, as parents, we have the privilege of knowing our children from before they're even born. Then we watch them change and grow. So our attachment to our loved ones is a lot like our attachment to life itself. So family, for me, is a door into thinking about not only love but about time as well — both of which are endlessly mysterious.

A number of your poems discuss the necessity for endurance in love and marriage. "Argument," for example, ends with the flapping tails of the young man's coat seeming to say, "You must go back to her, go back." "A Benediction" is a longish meditation on marriage, which offers advice to the newlyweds. And "The Twelfth Year" ends:

> love made us green for no sure cause on earth
> and grew, like our children, from a miracle.

But we live in a world where poets are often hesitant to offer advice about such things, yet you don't seem to hesitate?

MARY JO SALTER: Yes, but it's a delicate business. I can think of two poets whom I greatly admire who'll write in this way — Richard Wilbur and Anthony Hecht. They're both willing to write about married love in a very affirmative way. Hecht, of course, does so within a universe which is somewhat darker than Wilbur's, although Wilbur certainly acknowledges the darkness. The danger of affirming long-term relationships in the face of all the difficulties is that it can appear simple-minded, or too self-satisfied, or even smug. So it's a difficult balance. On the one hand, I'm not really interested in exposing the specifics of my own private hurts and difficulties; but, on the other hand, it's important to acknowledge the dangers if one is going to affirm that it all can be worth it. So it's a difficult dance. Maybe my most daring attempt was in the relatively short poem "The Twelfth Year." Now that the "twelfth year" is sixteen years ago, I no longer feel as threatened by it, but no one really wants to look back at the worst years. So you hope that in writing about such things, you've been both specific and sweeping enough in a way that might affect the reader. In a way that might actually make a difference, however small, in some stranger's life. Again, it's the audience that truly matters, and I care very much about my audience.

I think it's important for writers to take that risk. Nowadays, so many poets pretend to be horrified by the old Horatian notion that poetry can "teach," even though they're full of proselytizing ideas about everything under the sun.

MARY JO SALTER: Well, I've certainly been criticized for that poem — and for some others. In fact, one of my very favorite poets, who's also a dear friend, advised me, "Don't publish that poem. Don't do it. It's all wrong." And it was very hard to reject her advice, but I stuck with it.

Many of your related poems express the wonder and difficulties of being a parent. "A Benediction" wonders:

> *But who could have foretold how deep*
> *a passion the newborn would arouse*
> *in her parents as they watch her sleep?*

It seems to me that the "baby boom" generation of poets, oddly enough, is particularly interested in this subject.

MARY JO SALTER: I suspect that, in many things, that generation isn't much different from any other generation. I think it's just the natural process of maturation. I had friends in college who were absolutely positive that they'd never have children, but eventually they not only became parents, but they became the kind who are incessantly preoccupied with their children — to the point that they can't talk about anything else!

You've written many effective humorous poems, and my favorite is the villanelle "Video Blues," in which the woman laments her husband's "crush on Myrna Loy" and several other female stars of the forties. Yet she only allows herself to reveal one of her own "dreamboats" — Cary Grant. Why just one!

Mary Jo Salter

MARY JO SALTER: Well, Bill, you're being very polite to call her "the woman" — but, of course, it's me! And I must admit to other crushes on Jimmy Stewart and Gary Cooper — all the elegant ones, who, except for Cary Grant, were also relatively naïve.

One of my favorite poems is "Advent," which portrays a mother and her daughter preparing for Christmas by making a gingerbread house on a windy December day. It's written in delicate trimeter tercets; and, at one poignant moment, the child looks inside the gingerbread house:

> *When she peers into the cold*
>
> *interior we've exposed,*
> *she half-expects to find*
> *three magi in the manger,*
>
> *a mother and her child.*

This kind of religious longing, what St. Paul called the "hungry heart," occurs in other poems as well. For example, in "The Age of Reason," the narrator explains that, at a certain point in her life, her family had become "Unitarian":

> *And marched off weekly, dutifully, to hear*
> *nothing in particular. . . .*

Henry Taylor has recognized "a strong and deep moral sense" in your work, and part of that sense seems to relate to the common need for some kind of religious substance.

MARY JO SALTER: I think that little girl is definitely looking for something, without fully knowing it. The gingerbread house, all frosted and looking like snow, is momentarily transformed into the stable which serves as a symbol that has all kinds of subtleties. In my own life, I've greatly vacillated over the depth of my belief in God. At one time, I seriously considered going to divinity school, and now I'm married to a man who's an absolute atheist. I do worry that my own yearnings for the divine are nothing more than personal complacency or a wish for a certainty that simply can't be had. But if there is a God, then the God that I find myself directed toward is a God of love. I do think there's something irreducible in the human soul, and I don't think that the mystery of why people love each other can adequately be explained by sociobiology. Of course, I have no idea if I'm right about any of this. But I do feel, on some level, that there's a force out there that teaches us how to love, or that, at least, makes it possible for us to love, and I'm certainly not the first poet to think that way. It seems to me that much of the very act of poetry — making likenesses, and metaphors, and similes — is consonant with human love. That's what Herbert thought poets were doing. Finding and acknowledging the likenesses in the universe. So even though I don't go to church or feel part of any organized religion, I can't, either as a person or a poet, completely discount the yearning for something divine.

It's clear in your work that you're not afraid to broach the subject seriously, which so many other writers seem to feel is a contemporary taboo.

MARY JO SALTER: Well, I appreciate that. Unfortunately, for some writers, the Bible and the Biblical stories are often used out of context, for an added sense of grandeur or erudition.

Or weight. There's no easier way to drop some heft into your poetry than a religious allusion. But if it doesn't come from the yearning you've discussed, it often feels contrived and inauthentic.

MARY JO SALTER: It's a real danger, and I don't pretend that I've overcome the difficulties, but I certainly take it seriously.

Over the years, you've written in numerous forms — sonnets, villanelles, tercets, even a ghazal — and recently, in "Night Thoughts" and "Tanker," the haiku and the tanka. Your first book, Henry Purcell in Japan, *had numerous poems relating to your experiences in Japan, but it's only now, many years later, that you've begun publishing the Japanese forms.*

MARY JO SALTER: It's true that I've come to the shorter forms

Mary Jo Salter

more recently, and I think it's partly the result of teaching — especially at conferences, or on visits to high schools — and needing to assign something practical as well as instructive. As we discussed earlier, I'm also a believer in getting to the heart of things, and I'm fully aware that in my own work — and in the work of many of my contemporaries — there can be a tendency to go on a bit and lose focus. So it's a very useful corrective to write in the shorter forms like haiku and tanka and force yourself to get to the point. It's excellent for crystallizing.

Part IV of Sunday Skaters *is titled "Two American Lives," and it consists of two longish meditations on historical figures, "The Hand of Thomas Jefferson" and "Frost at Midnight." These poems, which were heavily researched, are effectively written in the third person, but I wonder if you'd considered them as first-person dramatic monologues?*

MARY JO SALTER: I didn't back then, but nowadays I think that, especially in the case of the Jefferson poem, it might have worked better as a play.

Like Falling Bodies?

MARY JO SALTER: Exactly. For a long time I was working on a long poem about the meeting of Milton and Galileo. I was fascinated by the fact that Milton, as a young man, had traveled to Florence in 1638 to visit Galileo, who was nearing the end of his life. This is an historical fact, but nothing else is known about the actual meeting. So I tried to prepare myself by reading and rereading *Paradise Lost*. Then I read lots of Galileo, and more Milton, and I finally felt ready to start the poem. Since I'd written those earlier poems about Frost and Jefferson, I thought that I knew what I was doing, but when I started the Milton/Galileo poem, I realized that the subject matter really lent itself more to drama. So I wrote *Falling Bodies*, which was recently performed at Mount Holyoke, and it's opened up many more possibilities in my life as a writer. But it also taught me something about being a poet. I learned that even good ideas can't necessarily be forced into a poem. So when I look back at the Frost and Jefferson pieces, I still like them, but I do feel that the Jefferson poem is a bit too long and a bit too homeworky. If I were working with the same subject today, I'd probably write a play.

In a 2001 question-and-answer session at The Borzoi Reader Online, *you admitted that "I love very off-off-rhymes," and you sometimes use such rhymes in the more rigorous formats like the sonnet. But isn't there a danger that whatever sonic echoes they might create, they'll get lost in the poem and not create the traditional power at the end-of-line?*

MARY JO SALTER: That's a good question, but I feel that it's precisely because the sonnet is a form that we all know — and have in our bones — that we can effectively use off-rhymes at the end of the lines. The sonnet's iambic pentameter creates such a strong backbone that the end of the lines already have a powerful sense of closure — especially with well-chosen endings. I believe that it's the responsibility of the poet — whether rhyming or not — to always make sure that every line-break rounds out the line in some meaningful way. Even, for example, if the line ends with the word "of," there needs to be some telling reason why that's the last word before the break. And this, of course, is especially true in the sonnet, but the form itself is so powerful that I think it can not only accommodate off-rhymes, but that it actually benefits from them. Off-rhymes open up all kinds of possibilities and semantic associations. So if the form is strong enough, I'm very comfortable with off-rhyme. I think that Emily Dickinson set the standard back in the 1850s and '60s, and it's a very high standard.

The very first poem in your first book is entitled "For an Italian Cousin," and one critic has pointed out that the persona in the poem "makes rapid connections and associations, many of them metaphorical." In your first two collections, you had a number of poems written in that occasionally disjunctive format, whereas the poems in your more recent collections have taken up a style that's more flowing, more narrative, and more graceful. Carolyn Kizer, in discussing A Kiss in Space, *for example, has written that "These are poems of breathtaking elegance." I wonder if you've have any sense of a gradual smoothing-out of your poetic style?*

Mary Jo Salter

MARY JO SALTER: That's another interesting question, Bill, and I've never thought about it in that way before. But I do think you're right that there's been a shift of some kind. When I was a younger poet, like most young poets, I was in love with metaphor and simile — often for their own sake. So when I conjured up a likeness that pleased me, it was hard not to use it in the poem. Now "Italian Cousin" is a very old poem — I wrote it in 1977 when I was twenty-three — and I was flush with ideas that I wanted to get into the poem. "I'll put this in. And I'll put that in." But when you get older, if you do write something rather disjunctive like that, you do it for a more conscious reason. Maybe to create a certain kind of mood, or to recreate a certain kind of mindset for a character in the poem. So it feels more organic. Maybe the maturation of any poet relates to governing metaphor and moving in the direction of conceit. One of the poets who does this best is Derek Walcott, and I greatly admire his work.

Are there any particular poetic forms that you feel compelled to experiment with in the future?

MARY JO SALTER: Even though I've written many tercet poems, I've never used terza rima, and I'm sure I will whenever I get the right subject matter. I'd also love to write a canzone. People who aren't poets don't always understand this. They think that poets are exclusively moved by the subject — and very often they are — but there's also another part of the poet that's sometimes saying, "I'm just waiting for the moment when it's right to write a canzone!" As you know, I've come to the sonnet fairly late, and I've greatly enjoyed it, but as I've grown older, I've also become more and more interested in inventing my own stanza forms, although not particularly ornate ones. I'm certainly no Hardy, but I do like forms that have some elbow room built into them, yet which also have rhyme and an expected meter.

Over the years, you've had thirteen residencies at the MacDowell Colony, mostly in the month of January. Do most of your poems get written in these one-month periods?

MARY JO SALTER: A lot of them do, but certainly not all. I tend to be a binge poet, and I do very well in the summer. I also do well on airplanes and in hotel rooms. I guess I do well everywhere except during my daily routine as a teacher. Although I do manage to cram in some poems during the semester — I'd just die if I didn't! — I do, generally speaking, get much more done when I'm out of my normal routine.

When you go to MacDowell, do you bring a list of ideas that you plan to write about?

MARY JO SALTER: I do, and I often start with those ideas — some of which have been around for many years. But, quite often, thinking about those ideas leads to other ideas, and the process snowballs. It's like when you go on vacation, and you pack certain books in your suitcase, and you fully intend to read them, but then the first one you read inspires you in some other direction, and soon you're off to the library or the bookstore. Writing is often like that for me.

Do you have any rituals?

MARY JO SALTER: I often try to capitalize on the moments just before sleep and just after waking. Maybe this is related to my inability to remember my dreams. Sometimes when I wake up in the middle of the night, I won't know what I've been dreaming, but I'll get some other interesting and unanticipated idea, and I'll turn on the light and jot something down. The metaphor-making part of our brains is directly connected to our dreams, so it's not surprising that sleep and waking are closely related to my own poetry writing.

Do you write before you go to bed?

MARY JO SALTER: Sometimes, but waking up very early is even more common.

I know that you and your husband, the poet Brad Leithauser, will discuss each other's work after most of the initial draftings have been completed. I also know that you've had other helpful "consultants" who've given you feedback, like Alfred Corn, Amy Clampitt, and Anthony Hecht. But I wanted to ask you about your editor at Knopf, Ann Close, whom you've acknowledged in all your books. In what ways has she helped you over the years?

MARY JO SALTER: Ann almost never talks to me about particular lines. I understand that with her novelists, she's a very close line editor, but she doesn't tend to do that with poetry. One of Ann's natural talents as an editor is to say things like, "This poem doesn't belong here," or, "Maybe we should move these poems into this section?" Those kinds of suggestions are, of course, extremely valuable, but Ann's greatest gift is that she gives me confidence. She always wants to know what I'm working on, and she'll call me up and say: "What are you doing? What are you writing? Oh, that sounds good. Can I see that?"

Does she ever say, "Well, I'm not so sure about that one"?

MARY JO SALTER: Yes, she does. For example, you mentioned "Video Blues" earlier, and she convinced me to not publish it in *Sunday Skaters*, but I eventually stuck to my guns, and we published it in *A Kiss in Space*.

The book that you dedicated to her!

MARY JO SALTER: Yes!

And what was her thinking about "Video Blues"?

MARY JO SALTER: Well, Ann has an editor's reasonable distrust of how lighter poems will be received. Unfortunately, our culture doesn't properly respect light verse, and she was worried that the poem would be dismissed as frivolous. But I love humorous verse, and I have the highest regard for it.

In Open Shutters *you have a whole section for the lighter poems.*

Mary Jo Salter

MARY JO SALTER: Yes, I thought, "Why not be upfront about this? Here are my light poems, all in one place, and I hope you like them."

In 1989, you wrote the text for The Moon Comes Home, *a children's book with artwork by Stacey Schuett. It's a lovely story of a little girl who, after a visit to her grandparents, notices that the moon follows her all the way back to her own home. Have you decided against more children's books?*

MARY JO SALTER: No, I love children's books, and I've always wanted to write more. What's happened to me is the same thing that happened to my mother in the poem "Unfinished Painting" — becoming a mother just took over my life, and I gave up writing children's books. I'm aware that J.K. Rowling seems to have done well being both a mother and a writer, but I let it go for a while. But recently, I've written another children's book, *Are You Sleeping Yet?*, and I hope to send it out soon.

It's not uncommon for some poets to start writing children's books later in life, often after they're grandparents.

MARY JO SALTER: Yes, like Richard Wilbur, who's marvelous. About a year ago, I participated in a tribute to him at the 92nd Street Y, and each of us who were involved were asked to discuss a different aspect of his overall work, and I volunteered to do the children's books — like *Opposites*, and *More Opposites*, and *The Disappearing Alphabet*. In my opinion there's nobody better, and my own *Are You Sleeping Yet?* is certainly influenced by Wilbur's work.

Many of your well-known poems relate to your experiences in foreign cultures, but, unlike many of your contemporaries, you don't, as far as I know, do translations.

MARY JO SALTER: It's true, and I don't know why. Neither my Italian nor French are perfect, but they're good enough. Maybe, as with drama, I'll eventually move into a translating stage.

Along with Margaret Ferguson and Jon Stallworthy, you've edited two editions

Mary Jo Salter

of The Norton Anthology of Poetry. *How has screening all that poetry — the good and the bad — affected your own writing?*

MARY JO SALTER: It's affected my writing by broadening my taste, which I certainly didn't expect. As you know — whether it's a journal or an anthology — an editor generally ends up reading lots of bad stuff. Ideally, you want to be open-minded, but it's hard to overcome your prejudices. "Oh, I really don't want to read that person's work. I've never enjoyed it in the past, so why should I now?" But editing the anthology did give me some new appreciations. I've learned, for example, to like Whitman. I'd always subscribed to the notion that you're either a Dickinson person or a Whitman person, and I was always a Dickinson person. But preparing that anthology gave me a new appreciation for Whitman's work. Now, I'm not going to start writing like him, but I do enjoy his poems.

Let's talk more about Dickinson. In the past, you've written about her in poems like "The Upper Story," and you're now the Emily Dickinson Lecturer at the school that she once attended. Over the years, various critics have claimed that she's been a significant influence on your work, especially her propensity "for examination and introspection."

MARY JO SALTER: It's true that I feel very close to Emily Dickinson. I've written two essays about her, and one of them discusses the fact that she's served me as a model as a woman poet. Elizabeth Bishop used to say that she didn't want to be in any women's anthologies and that she didn't want to be thought of as a woman poet, and I agree with that, but I can't deny that, like everybody else, I've needed role models, and it's always greatly interested me that there's this great nineteenth century American poet who wrote from a woman's perspective. I'm also, as we discussed earlier, very interested in her use of rhyme and her ability to know when to cut things out — to stay focused. I'm also fascinated by her effective use of meditation and abstraction — both so potentially dangerous — and her profitable use of paradox, ambiguity, and syntactic ambiguity.

You once admitted in an interview with Meghan Cleary that you always wanted to be a composer. In recent years, you've been collaborating with musical composers, and I wonder how that's been progressing?

MARY JO SALTER: Well, I've just completed the first draft of a staged song cycle with the composer Fred Hersch, who's not only a distinguished jazz pianist but also a wonderful composer. It's called *Rooms of Light*, and all of the songs relate, in one way or another, to photographs. We're hoping to have some of the songs performed in January when Lincoln Center is doing a salute to Fred.

Are the pieces about particular photographs? Or about photographs by particular photographers?

MARY JO SALTER: All kinds. Everything from a post-Civil War family standing stiffly during a long exposure to a contemporary scene of kids called "School Picture Blues." It's really about how looking through a lens has changed our perceptions — how we see. Photography and film are the great artistic inventions of the last hundred years, and since we decided that it would be too difficult to deal with film, we've focused on photography.

You and Brad share a teaching position at Mount Holyoke College, the Emily Dickinson Senior Lecturer in the Humanities. When you teach your young students poetry writing, how do you get them interested in metrics?

MARY JO SALTER: I think my "rigid" reputation precedes me! Not that I'm really that rigid, but all the students know that when they sign up for my classes I'm a stickler for versification. They know that in both my Verse Writing One and Verse Writing Two there will be a different formal assignment every week, and, that at some point during the thirteen-week semester, they'll be allowed to invent some kind of formal structure, but they won't be writing any free verse. We always do sonnets, and villanelles, and syllabics, and so on, but I try to do things a little bit differently every year. They also have to memorize ten to fifteen lines of poetry every week, and the memorization has to connect to the current assignment. So I guess it's truth in advertising. The students know what they're going to get, and most of them do very well.

In your interview with Meghan Cleary, you said that "Writing a new poem always feels like falling in love." Could you talk about that? Is it still as exciting as it used to be?

MARY JO SALTER: It is. Definitely. Tom Stoppard once said that writing plays is the only respectable way of disagreeing with yourself, and I would say that writing poems is the only respectable way that I can keep falling in love. I do think it's a lot like that. The inarticulate stirrings, the yearnings, the tingliness, and the sense that something magical is coming — that some new and wonderful idea is on the way. And then there's that thing that we discussed earlier — the idea that making connections and metaphors is a lot like love. I truly believe it. Poetry *is* like love. And it's inspired by a heightened sense of the reality of the world around us — the tangible, tactile world that we can connect with.

I'd like to finish up today by reading the lovely ending of your short blank verse poem "June: The Gianicolo," in which two lovers have parked their car in a parking lot above the nightlights of Rome:

>   Below them at the base
> of an ancient hill, the million lamps of Rome
> light up in rosy approbation, each
> signalling to one chosen counterpart
> among the stars the nightly freshened wish
> to lie uniquely in its dazzled gaze.

Thanks, Mary Jo.

MARY JO SALTER: Thank you, Bill.

David Middleton

David Middleton is a renowned metrical poet from the American South. In his poems, as Catharine Savage Brosman writes, "His broad, sympathetic vision and the sense of order that it implies are supported throughout by his seasoned command of formal verse."

Born in Shreveport, Louisiana, he completed his B.A. at Louisiana Tech in 1971 and his Ph.D. in English at Louisiana State University in 1979. He then took a position at Nicholls State University in Thibodaux, Louisiana, where he has taught for the past thirty-two years. He now serves as an Alcee Fortier Distinguished Professor, Poet-in-Residence, and Head of the Department of Languages and Literature.

David Middleton is the author of three collections of poetry and six chapbooks. His three full-length collections, all published by the Louisiana State University Press, are *The Burning Fields* (1991); *Beyond the Chandeleurs* (1999); and *The Habitual Peacefulness of Gruchy: Poems After Pictures by Jean-François Millet* (2005). His chapbooks are *Reliquiae* (Robert L. Barth, 1983); *Under the Linden Tree* (Robert L. Barth, 1985); *As Far As Light Remains* (The Cummington Press, 1993); *Bonfires on the Levee* (Blue Heron Press, 1996); *The Undivided Realm* (Robert L. Barth, 2000); and *The Language of the Heart* (Louisiana Literature Press, 2003). Currently the poetry editor at *Modern Age* and *The Classical Outlook*, he has also served in that position at *The Louisiana English Journal* and *The Anglican Theological Review*.

This interview was conducted at the University of Evansville.

After you were born in Shreveport's North Louisiana Hospital, your parents brought you home to a crib that was uniquely prepared by your mother.

DAVID MIDDLETON: Yes, it was. It contained a semicircle of children's books which had one picture and one word on each page — like a picture of an apple and the word "apple." It was my parents' intention that, from the very beginning, I would think about words and language as a natural part of the world around me — as natural as the sun, the moon, and the stars. They also read to me every night until I was about ten years old, and we went through a children's Bible, the Greek and Roman myths, and the Arthurian legends. So language was an integral part of my life from the very beginning.

You once said that during your childhood and adolescence, your father, who was an artist and elementary school principal, read a chapter from the King James Bible every morning at breakfast.

DAVID MIDDLETON: That's true. It was a red-letter edition, and I loved the beautiful poetic prose rhythms of the King James Bible. I think it's interesting to note the prominence of poetry in the Bible — and not just in the Psalms. Even in the book of Matthew, for example, the last words that Jesus speaks are, "My God, my God, why hast thou forsaken me?" and that's poetry. It's the first line of the 22nd Psalm.

In your youth, you often left Shreveport in the summers for the small town of Saline, Louisiana (population 400), where your maternal grandparents lived. Saline was very special to you, and you've often called it your childhood "Eden."

DAVID MIDDLETON: It was my poetic home — my equivalent to Sligo for Yeats. Growing up in Shreveport, I was a city boy, so my trips to Saline were my only encounters with country life. My grandparents had a huge garden and a corn patch and a watermelon field, and an uncle would take me hunting and fishing. Southern writers are often deeply attached to agrarian life, and that was ingrained in me as a very young boy.

Do you ever get back to Saline?

DAVID MIDDLETON: Although I don't have any relatives living there now, I occasionally get back. When I was a boy, my grandfather was mayor of the town and president of the bank in Saline, and they recently turned that building into a small local library. Then, just last year, I had the thrill of a lifetime when I was able to bring copies of my books, which are full of poems set in the region, to the library in Saline. So now my poems are available in my grandfather's old bank building, and it felt as though a great family circle had closed. In fact, one of the poems is called "The Old Bank in Saline."

When in your youth did you first start writing poems?

DAVID MIDDLETON: I can recall my literary beginnings with more exactitude than may be the case for other poets. I was in the ninth grade, and our English teacher wanted us to write a short story. We'd recently read a short story version of Menotti's opera *Amahl and the Night Visitors*, and she said, "Write a story that tells what happened *after* Amahl and the Three Wise Men leave his home to make their way to Bethlehem." All I can remember of my own attempt is that I made some use of Superman to get them there quickly, but that experience made me want to write fiction. I soon discovered that I had very little talent in fiction, but my teacher had awakened in me the desire to be a writer, so I quickly turned to writing poetry.

I realize that Frost was an important early influence, but what other writers affected you before you went off to college?

DAVID MIDDLETON: Dylan Thomas was an important influence.

That seems a bit young for Dylan.

DAVID MIDDLETON: Well, I'd read a feature story about him in *The Atlantic Monthly*, and I immediately read all his work. Of course, at the age of fifteen or sixteen, you're naturally overwhelmed by his powerful use of language. I also became aware of T.S. Eliot around that time. When Eliot died in 1965, my high school English teacher talked about him in class, and that spurred my interest. I was also reading and enjoying E.E. Cummings to a lesser degree. But, as you mentioned, Robert Frost was the poet who meant the most to me in my earliest years. Later, I temporarily moved away from writing that kind of poetry, but eventually I returned to writing metrical verse set in a specific rural area in the way that Frost does so well. The impact

DAVID MIDDLETON

of Frost also fits in with the influence of the Bible because, in both cases, you find a poetic language that is simple, in the best sense of the word, yet deep. And that's always been my ideal: to write poems that are crystal clear on first reading, but in which there are other levels of meaning if the reader decides to go back for subsequent readings.

You've also spoken about your adolescent interest in the music of the times, particularly the lyrics of Bob Dylan, Donovan, Simon and Garfunkel, and others. Do you think those songwriters affected your development as a poet?

DAVID MIDDLETON: Absolutely. That was the one part of the '60s that I really enjoyed. I wasn't interested in the drugs and the promiscuity and the rest of it, but I did love the best of the music — and, of course, all of it was rhymed metrical verse! In fact, I remember the irony of those times when free verse poets would read at the colleges, and then, later, at the receptions and parties, they'd all listen to Joni Mitchell and Joan Baez and enjoy metrical verse — although they might not have realized it at the time.

When you went to Louisiana Tech as an undergraduate, you were writing free verse, which was perfectly reasonable for a young poet at the time. So what brought you back to formal poetry? Did it happen at L.S.U., or did it start at Louisiana Tech?

DAVID MIDDLETON: It really happened at L.S.U. During my senior year at Louisiana Tech, a good friend of mine had preceded me to L.S.U. His name is Lindon Stall, and he'd met another poet at L.S.U. named John Finlay. So I was hearing from Lindon that they were both changing the way they were writing verse, especially under the influence of Donald Stanford.

Let's talk about Professor Stanford, who'd been a student of Yvor Winters and was the co-editor of The Southern Review.

DAVID MIDDLETON: Donald Stanford was not only an influential teacher, but he was the driving force behind reviving *The Southern*

Review in 1965. Then he and Lewis P. Simpson co-edited the journal for the next twenty years.

When was the first series discontinued?

DAVID MIDDLETON: The first series ran from 1935 to 1942, and it was discontinued ostensibly because of World War II, although Mike the Tiger, the L.S.U. mascot, and his air-conditioned cage, managed to survive the same budget cut.

Did you study with Professor Stanford in your first year at L.S.U.?

DAVID MIDDLETON: I did, and I remember that when I took a number of my poems to him for criticism, he gave them the "Yvor Winters treatment," meaning that he told me that they were all terrible — except for one about a bird. He said, "This one isn't too bad," and I later learned that he had a special fondness for birds. He had hummingbird feeders in his backyard, and he'd written a number of beautiful poems about certain birds native to Western Massachusetts where he grew up. At any rate, he saw how disconsolate I was by his severe treatment, and he told me something that I've never forgotten. He said, "David, I'm comparing you to the great Southern poet Allen Tate. That's the mark I'm setting for you to reach." So he challenged me from the start to become a better poet. In time, I took his courses in modern poetry and in the poetry of New England, and I had many private conferences with him as well. I also attended the famous sherry parties that he and his wife Maryanna hosted for years, as well as his steak and beer cookouts for the group of poets who surrounded him. During those years, we talked about metrical verse, and I was introduced to Yvor Winters' poetry and the work of J.V. Cunningham, Edgar Bowers, and the other senior Wintersians. This was the '70s, and the New Formalist movement was just beginning, and Stanford was publishing young poets like Timothy Steele in *The Southern Review*, and I became aware that there were other poets out there, some not much older than me, who were writing metrical verse or returning to metrical verse. So this was the period of my own return to formal poetry, and the crucial turning point was meeting Donald Stanford. At the time, there were four of us who formed a little group of graduate student poets around Stanford. One was the well-known poet Wyatt Prunty, and the others were John Finlay from Alabama, and my old friend Lindon Stall. We were later dubbed "The L.S.U. Formalists," and that greatly pleased Don, who had once been part of a group of poets around Yvor Winters.

Did Stanford continue to write poetry himself?

DAVID MIDDLETON: Although he published two books of poetry in the '50s, he'd given up poetry for criticism and editing. But he was always proud of his poetry, and it certainly meant a lot to him that, late in his career, a number of poets had gathered around him for guidance. It was a wonderful experience for all of us.

Of that impressive group of young poets, it seems that John Finlay had the most influence on you.

DAVID MIDDLETON: At that time, very much so. John was about eight years older than I was, and he'd discovered Winters as a student at the University of Alabama, Tuscaloosa. So he enrolled at L.S.U. in 1970 with the intention of studying with Don Stanford. John had read an essay that Stanford had written for *The Southern Review* in 1969 entitled "Classicism and the Modern Poet," in which Don argued that Pound and Eliot, although they claimed to be classicists, were not, and that the real contemporary classicists were the metrical poets. So John arrived at L.S.U. a year before I did, and his primary influence on me was not so much *whether* I should return to metrical verse, but rather *what kind* of metrical verse I should write. At the time, I was writing in a very dense manner, reminiscent of Dylan Thomas. I'd also been influenced for a while by the poetry of Geoffrey Hill. But John took the opposite approach; he wanted to write in the "plain style," as it's called. And I eventually came to agree with him. Although I think my verse is a bit more highly colored than John's, I do, as an ideal, try to write in the plain style as Winters defined it, following Ben Jonson. So, aside from our friendship, that was John's most important influence on my own development.

Your doctoral dissertation at L.S.U. was about Dylan Thomas, and I wonder how you evaluate his overall achievement?

DAVID MIDDLETON: I think his best poems are truly excellent, most of them syllabic or rhyming; and, of course, he wrote the great villanelle, "Do Not Go Gentle into That Good Night." Fern Hill was to Dylan Thomas what Saline was to me, and, in the last few years of his life, he wrote a series of poems called "In Country Heaven," in which he went back to his agrarian roots in Wales. In retrospect, I think there were definitely points of contact between Thomas's life and work and my own interests. But, to be perfectly frank, the reason I did my dissertation on Dylan Thomas was because I'd done so much research on him during my first three years at L.S.U. I had an NDEA Fellowship, and I'd gone to the British Museum in the summer of 1973, and I'd read and taken notes from all the secondary criticism on Thomas that wasn't available in the United States. So when it came time to write my dissertation, although I was, at that point, clearly under the influence of Don Stanford, I didn't want to start over on some other project, so I pressed ahead with Thomas. It was a monster dissertation, and I hate to admit it, but it was 778 pages! I did a new critical analysis of every one of his poems, and there was a separate chapter on the history of the term "Romanticism" because I believed that Thomas was clearly a Romantic poet. In the end, I think he was a fine minor poet who wrote a handful of excellent poems, for which he'll be remembered.

While still working on your Ph.D. dissertation, you took a position in 1979 at Nicholls State University in Thibodaux, Louisiana, on the Bayou Lafourche. At the time, your wife, Francine, was a librarian there, and you originally took a temporary non-tenure-track position, but you've now been teaching there for over thirty years.

DAVID MIDDLETON: That's right. In those days, teaching jobs were hard to come by. In that sense, I suppose, the job market hasn't improved very much in all those years. As you mentioned, we originally moved to Thibodaux because Francine had a job in the library, and I was originally planning to have no association with Nicholls at all. I was determined to finish my dissertation, and then we would go on the job market nationally. But when a member of the English Department took a sabbatical to return to L.S.U. to finish her Ph.D., I was offered a one-year instructorship, which I gladly took to make some money. Back then, instructors taught a five-five load, four of which were comp classes. But that still left me enough time to read the books and articles I needed to research my dissertation. Then, the following year, they offered me another five-five load, but I turned it down to teach a two-two load so I could finish my dissertation. I was determined not to be ABD forever! Then, at the end of my second year, a senior faculty member took early retirement, and the department head came up to me in the hallway and said, "David, would you like a tenure-track assistant professorship?" and I said, "Yes!" And that was my whole experience of the academic job market. Eventually, Francine and I both got tenure, and we decided to stay where we were. I prefer working at a smaller college rather than an R-1 research institution because, even though the teaching load is heavy, I can publish whatever I want — at my own rate. I've never been pressured to crank out footnoted, peer-reviewed articles twice a year to maintain my status on the graduate faculty. If I want to take a year to research and write a long poem, I can do it at Nicholls State, and I'm very grateful for that. I'm also grateful for a class load reduction to three-three that I've had at Nicholls as poet-in-residence.

In your adolescence, as you've discussed quite candidly in a memoir, you turned away from your religious upbringing, formal poetry, and your Southern heritage, but I believe it was the Southern Literary Festival in 1985 that led you to reconsider your Southern roots.

DAVID MIDDLETON: That's correct. When I was a young boy growing up in Shreveport, it was still the era of formal segregation. I can clearly remember segregated buses, water fountains, bathrooms, and doctors' waiting offices. So, in my adolescence, like so many other young Southerners, I became very liberal in my political views. I was ashamed of many aspects of the history of the South, although, prior to that, like many white Southern boys at the time, I was totally fascinated by the Civil War, and I'd read numerous books about the conflict, and I could tell you about all the battles, and how many troops were on each side, where they were positioned, and all the rest of it.

Lee's Lieutenants.

DAVID MIDDLETON: Exactly. But during my undergraduate years, I definitely wanted to move away from all that. I also decided that north Louisiana offered me nothing to write about. It was just a rural part of a Southern state, with the exception of three or four medium-sized cities, and I was much more interested in writing about Greco-Roman myth or the Arthurian legends. I've always been an Anglophile. I have an aunt who's English, and I'd visited England several times in my early twenties, and I no longer thought the American South was worth writing about. But then, in 1985, when the Southern Literary Festival was held at Nicholls, my wife and I decided to do a book display in the library during the festival, and we were determined that this wouldn't simply be a matter of putting out a few books and standing some pretty vases around them. We carefully read the books — writers like Robert Penn Warren and Andrew Lytle — and took out interesting quotations and wrote them out on note cards with various props. For example, if one of the writers mentioned a particular kind of wine that one of the characters preferred, we'd find a bottle of the exact same wine and place it there next to the quotation. So it turned out to be a major undertaking, almost like a research project, and it gradually reawakened in me the idea of writing about what I knew best. I remembered the old story about Sherwood Anderson telling William Faulkner in some Parisian bar, "What are you doing here? Go back to northern Mississippi and write about what you know." Ironically, around the same time, a fine English poet named Clive Wilmer, whom we'd visited in Cambridge, England, had given me the same advice: "Why don't you go back to north Louisiana and write about what you know?" So that's what I decided to do. Even more influential was similar advice given to me years earlier by my lifelong friend, Dr. Susan Roach, our preeminent north Louisiana folklorist whom I first met in the 1960s at Louisiana Tech.

Then you met George Core.

DAVID MIDDLETON: Yes. At that same conference I was luckily chosen to drive to the New Orleans airport and pick up George Core, who then, as now, was editor of *The Sewanee Review*. On our ride back, I was able to talk with George in great detail about Southern literature — mainly because of the book display that Francine and I had put together. During my conversations with George, I never mentioned that I was a poet because he was a guest, and I didn't want him to think I was trying to work on him to get myself published in *The Sewanee Review*. But later, after a farewell cookout on the last day of the festival, my wife and I were leaving when we heard someone running down the driveway. It turned out to be George Core, and he tapped me on the shoulder and said, "Why didn't you tell me you write poetry? Send me something to consider for *The Sewanee Review*." So I did, and he eventually published my work. So I was very fortunate, at a relatively young age, to meet two of America's premier quarterly editors and receive their support. Don Stanford had published me earlier in *The Southern Review*, and George Core has been a great supporter from 1985 to the present time.

You once described yourself as an "inheritor of the Tate-Davidson school," and I wanted to ask you about the Fugitives. It seems to me that, with the exception of Robert Penn Warren, the Fugitives are, unfortunately, being forgotten — even John Crowe Ransom, whom I consider one of the best American poets of the Twentieth Century.

DAVID MIDDLETON: I think that's true, and I agree it's unfortunate. It's especially true in the case of Donald Davidson, whom I consider a fine metrical poet, but Davidson, unfortunately, never altered his views about segregation, and I think that's had an effect on his reputation because even in anthologies of Southern literature, you'll often get Ransom, Tate, and Warren, but not Davidson, even though his best poems are not about segregation. Also, interestingly enough, the Fugitives usually wrote formalist poetry, and they need to be included in the history of formal poetry in the Twentieth Century. It was Winters, and the Fugitives, and various others like Auden who kept the tradition alive during the '30s and '40s.

Let's turn to your own work. After two chapbooks with the distinguished publisher R.L. Barth, your first full-length collection, The Burning Fields, *was published by L.S.U. Press in 1991. Since that time, along with other chapbooks, you've published two more books with L.S.U.:* Beyond the Chandeleurs *(1999) and* The Habitual Peacefulness of Gruchy *(2005). In these books, certain subjects and themes predominate, and I'd like to start with your poems about family. Two of my favorites are "The Maker in Lent" and "Night Fears: A Lullaby," both related to your daughter Anna Marie, when she was very young. In the first poem, the poet is walking with his colicky infant after midnight, and he hums the child to sleep rather than trying to lull the child asleep by reciting poetry, and he reflects on the fact that someday the books that surround them will both comfort and instruct her.*

> *But now, how great the good*
> *We share in wordlessness,*
> *This Lenten fatherhood*
> *When love may quietly bless*
> *As much as those hard texts*
> *Where wifeless, childless, deep*
> *In their profound and sterile rest*
> *Cold Paul and Plato sleep.*

Thus faith, literature, and fatherhood all intermingle.

DAVID MIDDLETON: They do, and, for me, fatherhood was deeply involved with my return to faith. As you mentioned earlier, although I was raised a Southern Baptist, I eventually went through a long period of not attending church and not necessarily being a person of faith. The best part about my Southern Baptist upbringing was learning the King James Bible and my many years of close Bible study. This is, of course, crucial for anyone interested in literature, whether he or she's a person of faith or not, since, if you don't know the Bible thoroughly, you won't understand much of the great literature of the Western tradition. But, at that point, I no longer appreciated other aspects of the Southern Baptist denomination — such as the great emphasis on guilt — and, as a result, I lapsed from the church and my faith. But even before Anna was born, Francine and I felt that we had to raise her in a Christian church, whatever my doubts might have been. I didn't want her growing up in a community where everybody went to church and where she wouldn't even have the opportunity to decide for herself. Eventually, my wife and I decided to come back to the church as traditional, conservative, High-Church Anglicans. I did want to get all those adjectives in there because I feel less comfortable with many of the current teachings of the Episcopal Church than I do with Anglicanism as it was known and practiced by persons such as George Herbert, Samuel Johnson, C.S. Lewis, and T.S. Eliot, different as they are from one another in some ways (and not all of them Anglo-Catholics). So it was fatherhood that really brought me back to religion, and it also led me to shift from my previous liberal/moderate perspective on things to a more conservative one. It seems to me that there are certain givens in human nature and that there are certain innate God-given qualities in all of us, and this fits in with a belief in religious absolutes. As for the poem you mentioned earlier, it has to do with language and communication, which I think is one of the great mysteries of human life: that we're able to develop the ability to speak and to understand the world around us through words. As a father, like all parents, I was able to actually witness the process with my daughter. It was truly miraculous.

You've also written a lovely tribute to your wife, Francine, who's an accomplished needlewoman, once honored by the state of Louisiana for her craft. The poem is called "For a Needlewoman," and it reads in part:

> She soaks her strands in colors of the South
> And Old-World tinctures such as Pliny praised —

DAVID MIDDLETON

> *The saffron asphodel, bayberry gray,*
> *The yellow weld, blue woad and indigo…*

DAVID MIDDLETON: I'm very fortunate that Francine and I are fellow artists, and this has been an important part of our relationship throughout the years as we've encouraged each other to develop our separate crafts. A number of years ago, in fact, she needlepointed a couple of my poems which are now hanging in the house, and, in so doing, she brought our arts together. I tried to do the same thing in my poem about her and her artistry.

You've written about other relatives as well, including your mother.

DAVID MIDDLETON: My mother was a traditional housewife, a stay-at-home mom, and my poem "A Quiet Reply" was written in her honor. My mother was perfectly happy being a housewife. She didn't find it constricting, and she didn't harbor other ambitions, like being a lawyer, for example. She came from a generation where it was perfectly acceptable to be content caring for one's family and doing the cooking, and the cleaning, and, in her case, taking care of me, her only child. Those were wonderful things in her life, and I inherited that sensibility from her. So family life means a lot to me, and I try to observe it carefully and reflect it in some of my poems. I think that one of the most effective kinds of poetry is the kind that's rooted in the particulars of a locale that you're familiar with, but which can also have universal implications. Thomas Hardy is a perfect example. Or Robert Frost. They knew their landscapes, and even though they're so different, they knew the details of the life around them — like the specific dyes which I mentioned in my poem about Francine. So family and locale are crucial for me.

This brings us back to the South, and your acceptance and respect for your Southern heritage. This is discussed in many different ways in many of your poems — and very beautifully in the four quatrains of the poem "The South," where each stanza represents a season. For example, the second quatrain reads:

> *Then summer heat's oppressive strokes*

David Middleton

> *Made drunken sons of memory*
> *Raise Dixies under courthouse oaks*
> *To the sober bust of Lee.*

At the end of the poem, even in the chilling winter, the great oaks silently endure:

> *Now trembling ironweeds rust and fold*
> *At a touch of winter chill*
> *While round the courthouse, green and old,*
> *The pastoral oaks grow still.*

DAVID MIDDLETON: In the Middle Ages, there was what was known as the "Matter" of Greece and Rome. Later, there was the "Matter" of Britain that English poets wrote about. For my own purposes, as I wrote in the poem "Oak Alley," there's "the Matter of the South." The Matter, of course, is the inheritance of history, culture, and folktale. Some of it's myth, and some of its aspects are clearly over-idealized, and there's always a mixture of both good and evil. Obviously, slavery was a terrible blight on the South, and we're still dealing with its consequences today. On the other hand — and I'm certainly not the first writer to point this out — the South, although it's now becoming more and more industrialized and urbanized, still has its agrarian roots, and there's still the lingering suspicion that what we term "modernity" is not only the wrong way to live, but that it also might not be sustainable. Now I'm not suggesting that everyone in Manhattan should leave the city for forty acres and a mule. That's not going to happen. But maybe there is another way, and I'm a great admirer of the writings of the essayist Wendell Berry, who not only questions our urbanized society, but also works his own farm in Kentucky. In my opinion, he's a modern prophet, rightly pointing out that we can't go on forever using up our natural resources. All over America, we've lost the family farm, and we've lost the sense of living according to the slower rhythms of the agricultural year, which are so deeply intertwined, as you know, with the church calendar. So this is an important theme for me, and, of course, it comes straight from the Southern Agrarians and Robert Frost and from my own youthful experiences in Saline.

You're consciously concerned with what you call the "commonplace" aspects of life.

DAVID MIDDLETON: I am, and I find it to be one of the strangest things about life that we tend to overlook the "everyday" and the "commonplace." Personally, I've never understood people who say they're bored; I've never been bored a moment in my life because the world around me is fascinating. I can look out the window and watch the seasons change, and observe the trees and the other plants and the animals, and I can do it endlessly — with a true sense of wonder about life. I believe the universe was created by God; that it has intent and purpose; and I know that we're only here a short time. So things that others might not consider of much interest are truly fascinating to me. I don't want to waste my time playing video games. I want to enjoy the mystery and wonder of our lives. I believe it was Philip Larkin who said, "Everyday things are lovely to me." I feel the same way, and I like to write about them.

This is especially true in your most recent collection, The Habitual Peacefulness of Gruchy, *inspired by the pictures of the French artist Jean-François Millet. The poems in the collection deal with — as did Millet's pictures — the commonplace aspects of life, and even when the poems don't specifically dwell on the details, the insinuations are always there. For example, your wonderful poem about the Millet's picture "Farmyard in Winter," which ends with the quatrain:*

> *What farm folk do inside the distant house*
> *Is unexpressed, though through the chimney-keep*
> *Smoke slips from fires whose silent tongues caress*
> *Baked chicken, apple brandy, sex, and sleep.*

DAVID MIDDLETON: I definitely felt that I'd found a common spirit with Millet. My father was an artist, and even though he didn't do it for a living, I often watched him paint, and I watched him make wood sculptures. I also watched him build his own kiln in the backyard and take the pots out for the bisque fire and then back again for the glaze firing. I also accompanied him to art galleries and helped him to hang paintings, and so on. So I was very comfortable with art from a young age, and I found Millet's world to have many parallels with the American South since it was essentially an agrarian society. Millet clearly believed that his people, his subjects, were worthy of representation and study. Despite his realism, he wasn't afraid to elevate the dignity of these people in his pictures. I'm not enough of an expert on Millet to recognize all his classical models from Greco-Roman art, but many are obvious — like the Apollo Belvedere, which is clearly behind the central figure in "The Sower." So Millet was always saying that these hardworking agrarian people are worthy subjects, and Millet knew what he was talking about since he grew up on a farm.

It's a fascinating book, and the parallels with the American South are clear, but why did a Southern Anglophile decide to write a whole book set in Nineteenth Century France?

DAVID MIDDLETON: The truth is, after writing two books of poems set almost entirely in the South, I realized that I really didn't have anything else to say for a while about the rolling pinewood hills and cottonfields of north Louisiana, and the marshes and swamps and barrier islands of south Louisiana. I needed a new landscape — at least for the time being. But, originally, I'd only intended to do one Millet poem. I went to the library, and I found a catalogue from the Boston Museum of Fine Arts, which has the greatest Millet collection in America, and it was full of extraordinary color plates of different paintings. Now, I'd always admired the poem "Humility" by Fred Chappell. It's five quatrains of blank verse, and it's about life on a North Carolina farm. So I shortened Fred's form to four quatrains of blank verse, which created a four-by-four effect — like a picture frame — and I wrote the poem. Then I decided, "Well, that was fun; I'll do another one." Soon I was thinking, "Why not go for a chapbook? Maybe Bob Barth will publish it." But the white heat continued over a few years, and it expanded into a whole book. In truth, it seemed to come out of nowhere. I certainly didn't intend it. It was almost as if I was taken over by some inspirational force. Eventually, before I submitted the manuscript to L.S.U. Press, I sent it off to Fred Chappell, asking, "Would you mind critiquing this, Fred?" As always, he was completely generous with his time, and I mentioned in my cover letter that his poem "Humility" had been the model for the form for all the poems in the book. Then he wrote back and asked, "Did you know that 'Humility' was inspired by Millet's picture 'The Gleaners?'" I was truly amazed, and another circle had closed.

That's an amazing story, David, but I don't want to create the impression that all of your poems are of a single agrarian type. You also have a number of poems that move away from your more common subjects and themes. I'm particularly fond, for example, of "Blue Essences: The 1890s." And there are other poems like "From the Journal of Branwell Brontë," and your very affecting trimeter poem called "On the Suicide of the Chairman of the Math Department," which ends:

> *Until explosion triggered*
> *A final train of thought,*
> *Your brain reduced to naught.*
> *Factored out, beyond persuasion,*
> *You balanced the equation,*
> *Finding the terms you sought*
> *In the barrel's double-ought.*

DAVID MIDDLETON: I began each of those poems for a different reason. The one about Branwell Brontë was the result of a visit to Haworth Parsonage and reading about the brother of the Brontë sisters, who was supposedly the most artistically talented of them all. But he ended up an alcoholic and a drug addict, and he accomplished very little.

Wasn't he a pictorial artist of some kind?

DAVID MIDDLETON: Yes, he was, and the poem is about the relative value of different literary genres. "Blue Essences" is about a late 19th century aesthete who attempts to become a better writer by losing himself in absinthe and daydreaming. Maybe it's not unlike

"Miniver Cheevy," except without the humor. "On the Suicide of the Chairman of the Math Department," which is full of mathematical terms, is about a mathematician who's normally rational and logical, and yet he does something inexplicable and irrational.

In another vein, you've written some of the best Christian verse of recent times; and, as we know, religion is a subject that many contemporary poets shy away from. But you've written many poems that recognize our sinful failings while still maintaining optimism in the grace of Christ. I'll just cite one, "Azaleas in Epiphany," which ends:

> *Thus taken, in their stations,*
> *All things are angels sent*
> *Blazing into creation,*
> *The Word's embodiment.*

DAVID MIDDLETON: That comes out of the Aristotelian-Thomistic argument from design — that the world obviously has order. But the world also has evil, and suffering, and chaos, and that brings up something else that I often write about because I definitely believe that there was something that we refer to as "The Fall." It may be hard to reconcile that notion with modern theories of evolution, but it seems, nevertheless, that we're all haunted by this sense that there was once another way in which we lived: something we call Eden, something which we've lost. From a completely rationalist point of view, many of the things that Christians believe may be hard to comprehend, but I prefer the vision of someone like William Blake who saw beyond simple Deism. So I'm comfortable with the mysteries of life and the mysteries of Christianity, and I believe in a universe that's providentially ordered. In my case, I believe that the radical specificity of the Incarnation and the Passion are the key to everything.

I'm particularly fond of your translation, "Final Prayer," from the Latin of Samuel Johnson. Have you done many other translations?

DAVID MIDDLETON: Just a few. I'd studied Latin in graduate

DAVID MIDDLETON

school at L.S.U., and when R.L. Barth decided to do a small anthology of Johnson's Latin poetry in English translations, I was glad to translate a few of the poems. It's clear that Johnson put many of his deepest personal feelings in his Latin verses, and in one of those poems, "On Recovering the Use of His Eyes," he relates his profound gratitude to God for curing him of an eye ailment, which was quite terrible, and which the poet believed might lead to blindness. It's also about using one's personal "gifts," and I often close my poetry readings with that poem. Johnson is clearly saying to God, "You've given me a gift to be a writer, and I want to be able to realize that gift, and I thank you for giving me my eyesight back." It's like a happier version of Milton's famous sonnet on his blindness. He's saying that all such gifts come from heaven, and I end my poetry readings by reminding the audience, especially the young students, that they all have special gifts that they should pursue, whether they're religious or not.

Over the years, you've written in a variety of poetic forms, but much of your work is either blank verse or quatrains. I wonder if there are any forms you'd like to try?

DAVID MIDDLETON: I'd like to try writing longer narrative poems. I've done a few in the past, but the problem is that they're so hard to publish, and when you put them in a collection, they take up so much room that they can often make the whole book seem lopsided. But there are a number of poems that I'd like to write about north Louisiana and various people I knew there, and those poems would require an extended narrative. But I'll probably have to wait until I'm retired, because, like a novelist, I'd really have to have the time to re-immerse myself in that world, and time for that is hard to find now that I'm department head.

I know that you're a firm believer in what you call the "habitude of craft," and I wonder if you could describe your own writing practice? Do you have favorite places to write? Favorite times of day? Or any rituals?

DAVID MIDDLETON: These days, now that I'm the department head, I work from 7:30 to 4:00, five days a week. So I can't come home in the early afternoon as I'd done for so many years in the past. So I get off at 4:00, I come home, I check the mail, look at the paper, take the dogs out, and by 4:30, I'm sitting in my big rocking chair in my study. Usually I'll have some Medieval or Renaissance music playing — maybe Tallis or Byrd — and I immediately start writing, and, except for a supper break, I work until bedtime, and I do that every night, even on the weekends. So it's a discipline that I'm comfortable with; but, I must admit, poetry isn't first on my list. First are family, church, and my job, but after that, it's almost exclusively poetry — or reading and meditating in preparation to write poetry. I don't socialize very much, or attend many readings or conferences, simply because there's not time enough for everything. When I'm actually writing, I use a ball point pen on either long legal sheets or in little notebooks that I've used for many years. They have a dark blue cover, with even darker blue tape on the spine, and when you open them up, it's light green inside and the pages are numbered from one to one hundred twenty. I do all my rough drafts by hand, but once I'm into the second or third draft, I'll type it up on the computer screen and edit from there. Fortunately, I'm able to work in unfavorable conditions. I'm not someone who has to have some sort of clinically pure and silent environment. For example, when my daughter was home, and the T.V. was tuned to MTV, I still found that I was able to work.

You've done a lot of editing over the years, serving as the poetry editor at The Classical Outlook, The Louisiana English Journal, The Anglican Theological Review, *and, currently, at* Modern Age.

DAVID MIDDLETON: I've always had the desire to serve the world of poetry in some way, and I seem to do that best by editing. After all, I expect other people to edit the journals that print my poetry, so why shouldn't I help out as well? Anytime that I can have the opportunity to publish good poets, I'm delighted. It also allows me to promote the kind of poetry I prefer: metrical verse.

Like me, you're a great proponent of Timothy Steele's brilliant and brilliantly original book, Missing Measures: Modern Poetry and the Revolt

DAVID MIDDLETON

Against Meter *(1990)*. *What do you feel are some of Tim's main points that we need to constantly reconsider?*

DAVID MIDDLETON: The most important point is that we shouldn't confuse revolutions in poetic diction with a revolt against metrical verse. This was the great mistake that the Modernists made when Ezra Pound decided to get rid of the pentameter line. Every other poetic revolution, as Tim clearly illustrates, from the Greco-Roman period through the Romantics, was a renewal of poetic diction by bringing it closer to the speech of the time but never by revolting against meter. This was the tragic mistake that Pound and others made, and I feel Tim's arguments are irrefutable. He writes in such a reasonable, cool, restrained, and inviting manner that unless you're irredeemably prejudiced, his book will convince you — whether you write free verse or not — that metrical verse has a continuous 3,000-year tradition that goes back to Homer, a tradition poets should know and try to master. Why should anyone think that meter is a "straitjacket" when it accommodated the poetry of Dante, Shakespeare, and Milton, and all the rest? It defies common sense to ignore the power of the tradition.

All forms have constraints, and constraints create opportunities.

DAVID MIDDLETON: Exactly. I like to think of the game of chess. If the players could move any piece to any square on any move, there'd be no game. It's only because there are a limited number of squares and because individual pieces can only move in set ways that one can experience the joy and beauty and innovation of the game. I always found it interesting that in John Frederick Nims's book *Western Wind*, he and David Mason take a number of lines from Whitman, and they illustrate that they're all metrical. Maybe not perfectly metrical, but it's clearly not "free." So I always tell my students in my writing classes, "Even if you write free verse, you still have to know what a trochee is, and what an anapest is, or else you'll end up writing chopped-up prose." If we want our verse to be effective, we have to master the same techniques as the great metrical poets.

DAVID MIDDLETON

Do you have any new projects under way?

DAVID MIDDLETON: I have a new collection that's about 95% finished. It's called *The Fiddler of Driskill Hill: Poems of Louisiana North and South*. Driskill Hill is the highest point of elevation in north Louisiana, although it's only 535 feet. It's located near Saline, my poetic home, and the fiddler represents the artist, perhaps myself, and the collection contains a ballad called "The Fiddler of Driskill Hill." So, in this newest collection, I've returned to and extended the interests of my first two books for L.S.U. Press, having renewed myself by working with Millet.

I'd like to ask the inevitable but still important question: What advice do you have for aspiring poets?

DAVID MIDDLETON: I believe that we need to master our craft before we seek publication. I know this is hard for young poets, but they need to be patient. After the death of my good friend John Finlay, I became his literary executor, and when I opened up his very first notebook, I saw that he had written the words "BE PATIENT!" in capital letters with an exclamation point on the very first page. I would also suggest that young aspiring poets read widely, and, by that, I mean not only literature, but history, philosophy, and theology. In addition, serious writers need to read more than contemporary poetry; they need to read the classics. You can learn a lot more from Shakespeare and Dante and Homer than you can from the comments of your classmates in your creative writing class. Poetry takes a lifetime of commitment. It's something you have to devote yourself to, and it has to be very high on your list of priorities.

I'd like to end today with the final lines of your tribute to your friend and fellow poet, John Finlay. The poem is called "For John Finlay (1941-1991)," and it closes with a remembrance of two young poets trying to establish their priorities in graduate school:

> Both natives of the South trying to reclaim
> Something of Greece and Christendom, we'd walk

David Middleton

To the Union from our desks in Allen Hall
Talking of Homer, Dante, Winters, Tate,
A "Stanford" or a "Simpson" Southern Review,
Finding ourselves as poets and as friends
There, at LSU, in those sweet-olive days,
Summer seeming endless in sunlit colonnades.

Thank you, David.

DAVID MIDDLETON: Thank you, Bill.

Dick Davis

Dick Davis is both a distinguished poet and a world-renowned translator from the Persian. Regarding Davis's own poems, X.J. Kennedy has written: "To read Dick Davis is to be reminded of what poetry used to be, and can still become."

Born in Portsmouth, England, he was educated at Cambridge University and received his Ph.D. in Persian studies at the University of Manchester in 1988. He has taught in Greece, Italy, Iran, England, and at the University of California, Santa Barbara. He is currently the Chair of the Department of Near Eastern Languages and Cultures and Professor of Persian at The Ohio State University.

He is the author of nine collections of poetry, including *In the Distance* (1975); *Seeing the World* (1980); *A Kind of Love: New and Selected Poems* (1991); *Touchwood: Poems 1991-1995* (1996); *Belonging* (2002); and *A Trick of Sunlight* (2006). His many translations from the Persian include *The Conference of Birds* (with Afkham Darbandi, 1984); *Borrowed Ware: Medieval Persian Epigrams* (1997); *The Shahnameh: The Persian Book of Kings* (2006); and *Vis and Ramin* (2009). He is also the author of *Wisdom and Wilderness: The Achievement of Yvor Winters* (1983), and the editor of *Selected Writings of Thomas Traherne* (1980) and the Penguin edition of *The Rubaiyat of Omar Khayyam* (1989).

This interview was conducted at the Exploring Form and Narrative Poetry Conference at West Chester University.

You were born in Portsmouth on the southern coast of England. Were you raised there as well?

DICK DAVIS: We lived in Portsmouth when I was very small, and we went back there occasionally throughout my childhood because my mother's mother lived there. But mostly I grew up in Yorkshire in the north of England. Portsmouth is a big naval town with a large sailor population. It's a noisy, busy, and dirty place. Our Yorkshire home was in a small village by the sea. In the past, it had been primarily a fishing village, but that was winding down when I was a child, although the boats still went out in the morning to fish in the North Sea. But mainly the village was dependent on summer tourism. Yet I can still remember that whenever there were bad storms at sea, there was a particular hymn that we always sang in school because the fathers of some of the boys still went out in their fishing boats. The hymn was "O, Hear Us When We Cry to Thee, For Those in Peril on the Sea," and, to this day, I still can't hear that hymn without a lump in my throat.

So if the weather got ominous, the teacher would stop class and you'd all sing the hymn?

DICK DAVIS: Actually, it would always happen at the assembly at the beginning of the school day. If the weather was bad, we would sing the hymn.

What was the name of the village?

The village is called Withernsea, and it's located in a fairly isolated part of England — about twenty miles from the nearest big town, which is Hull. I was very lucky because they decided to set up an experimental school, what they called a "comprehensive" school, which was quite similar to public schools in the U.S. Previously in England, when you went to a state school, you were divided into two groups at the age of eleven: those who went to grammar school and those who didn't. But, back then, they were considering allowing everyone to go to the same school, and our little rural community was chosen as a pilot area. Since this was unique and experimental at the time, it attracted some very dedicated and excellent teachers who moved to Withernsea. So even though I lived in a very small and isolated village, I had some extremely good teachers, and because of them I was later able to go to Cambridge. I came from a family where nobody had ever been to University, let alone Cambridge, and I believe that if I'd gone to a regular state school and didn't have all those dedicated teachers, I probably wouldn't have made it.

Were your parents interested in the arts?

Dick Davis

DICK DAVIS: My mother always read a lot, and she's now in her eighties, and she's still a voracious reader. One of my earliest memories is of my mother reading poetry to me. During the Second World War, she'd left school at sixteen, so she wasn't an educated woman, but she always loved verse, and she always loved novels. In truth, she reads anything. One minute, she'll be reading some trashy romance novel, and the next minute she'll be reading *Madame Bovary*, and she'll love the both of them. I never knew my biological father, who left when I was two years old, but my stepfather, although not very well-educated, has always been a very thoughtful and studious man, with a life-long and passionate obsession with history, especially classical history, European history, and British history. So even though my family wasn't very well educated, they were very bookish, and there were many books around the house, and I was expected to read them like everyone else.

Do you remember when you first became attracted to poetry?

DICK DAVIS: It was very early. *Very* early. I honestly can't remember a time in my life that I didn't want to write poetry. I was certainly writing poems before I was ten, and I've never really stopped. It was always right there from the beginning. Probably the first poem that I wrote that I wouldn't be totally ashamed of was when I was nineteen. But it was still a nineteen year old's poem, and I certainly wasn't an exceptional teenage poet. I don't think I really found my voice — if I have — until I was about thirty, but I'd been writing steadily since I was a child.

Which poets influenced you the most before you went to Cambridge?

DICK DAVIS: I read the people you were supposed to read, and by the time I went to Cambridge, I'd pretty well read the entire canon of English poetry. I was very fortunate to have an extremely good English master at school, John Gibson, who's still a dear friend. I still remember, for example, John telling me to read Milton's *Paradise Lost* over the summer, and saying, "Then come back and tell me about it in the fall." Another summer he had me read *The Prelude*.

He was always pushing me, but he never made it onerous — he made it fun. Looking back, one of the poets I especially loved in my youth was Blake — whom I can't stand now. Later, when I was about sixteen, I won a prize at school for something or other, and I was allowed to choose a book, so I chose D.H. Lawrence's *Collected Poems*, and I enjoyed his work very much back then, even though I can't stand Lawrence now either. Much more important to my own development was my interest in Wyatt and Emily Dickinson. Somehow I discovered Dickinson, which was strange back then because American poetry was never taught in English schools. But somehow I got hold of a copy of her poems, and I loved them and imitated them. I loved the epigrammatic aspect of her work — poems that were short, sharp, and to the point, and I thought to myself: "That's the kind of poetry I want to write."

Who were your primary influences at Cambridge?

DICK DAVIS: Once again, I was very lucky. When I went to King's College, Cambridge, the director of studies in English was Tony Tanner, a young man about ten years older than I was. Tony was a very good friend of Thom Gunn, although his main interest was fiction. He wrote primarily about American fiction, including *The Reign of Wonder* about 19th century American fiction, and he also wrote those wonderful introductions for the Everyman series of Shakespeare's plays. He was a great guide to literature for me, and he was very kind as well. He introduced me to Thom Gunn, and it was through Gunn that I learned about Yvor Winters, J.V. Cunningham, and that interesting school of American poets.

Was Gunn in San Francisco at that point?

DICK DAVIS: Gunn was living in San Francisco, but he still visited Cambridge occasionally. When he did, Tony would give a party and invite all the undergraduates, and Gunn was young, approachable, and very charming. He also gave me reading suggestions, saying, "You should read this person, or you should read that person."

Dick Davis

Did you know any of the other Movement poets? Like Conquest, or Davie, or Larkin?

DICK DAVIS: I got to know Davie later when we both became involved in a British literary magazine called *PN Review*. Davie was an editor for a while, and I was an associate editor for three or four years. But I never really got to know Davie that well, and we didn't, to be honest, hit it off that well, but I did think he was a wonderful poet. Like many poets, I think he wrote too much, but some of his work was excellent, as were many of his translations from the Polish. I never got to meet Conquest, but I did meet Larkin once, and it was a bit frosty on both sides. Unless you were one of his buddies, Larkin wasn't very pleasant; but, of course, I admired his poetry very much, and I still do.

Did you ever write free verse?

DICK DAVIS: I tried it for a very short time, less than a year, when I was about eighteen. Back then, it seemed to be what people were doing, and what you were *supposed* to do. But I very quickly realized that I wasn't interested in writing free verse. I think it was Raymond Chandler who once said that you should write the kind of novels that you'd like to read, and I'd never particularly enjoyed reading free verse. I read it dutifully, of course. I read Gunn's free verse because I admired Gunn so much, and I read a lot of the American free verse poets, but I never wanted to do it myself.

After your B.A. and M.A. in English literature at Cambridge, you taught abroad for nearly a decade.

DICK DAVIS: I left Cambridge in my early twenties, and I taught first in Greece and then in Italy, but I was feeling the urge to go somewhere outside of Europe, and a friend of mine who'd been working as an archaeologist in Iran said that it was a wonderful country and that he was planning to teach there for a while. So he said, "Why don't you come, too? We can share an apartment." So that's what I did. I got a job teaching English at Tehran University on a two-year contract. During that time, I fell in love with the woman I'd eventually marry, so when the two-year contract ended, I looked for another job so I could stay in Iran and be near her and get married. There were, of course, problems because her parents were very against it. It was the usual concerns: marrying a foreigner, we don't know who he is, and all of that. So I stayed in Iran for two more years, and we were married in 1974. At the end of '78, it was obvious that the country was falling apart politically, and at the beginning of the next year, the Islamic Revolution happened. All the universities had been closed at the end of 1978, so I no longer had a job, and it became clear to both of us that it was going to be difficult to stay in Iran. So we left and went to England.

Did you ever feel that you were in physical danger in Tehran?

DICK DAVIS: No, on the contrary. There was certainly danger out there, of course, but I never felt specifically in danger because I was a Westerner. In fact, my students would often try to protect me, saying, "There's going to be a big demonstration downtown, and it's going to be at such-and-such a time and such-and-such a place, so don't go down there." Or, if I wanted to go out of curiosity, they'd say, "If you really need to go, then we'll go along and make sure you're okay." The people who experienced the real hostility in Tehran were the people who were officially associated with Western governments. As for the rest of us, the Iranians would often say things like, "Tell people in your country what's happening here. The world should know." So I personally never experienced any problems, but my wife and I did have an apartment on a main road where there were many demonstrations, and sometimes there was some shooting going on. We lived on the third floor, with large plate-glass windows, and we could look out and see the tanks outside, and that didn't feel too good. At the time, we had a couple of friends who were Indians who lived on a back street, and they said, "Why don't you come and stay with us until all this quiets down?" So we moved in with them for about three weeks, but it soon became clear that it wasn't going to quiet down in the foreseeable future, so we made arrangements to leave the country.

DICK DAVIS

Were you interested in Persian culture before you went to Tehran, or did it start while you were living there?

DICK DAVIS: It's a bit complicated. As an adolescent, one of my favorite books was Fitzgerald's *Rubaiyat*, which, as you know, is a very romanticized version of Iran. Fitzgerald himself had never visited Iran, and, as a matter of fact, he never got further east than Paris. So his translation presents a kind of imaginative vision of Iran, one which I found very attractive. Later, when I was at Cambridge, I got to know E.M. Forster a little bit, and he had a great love of both Indian and Persian culture. So when I ended up in Iran in 1970, I really did feel a kinship with the culture, but I didn't go there thinking that it would be a spiritual home for me, although I felt very drawn to it.

So when you finally left Tehran, did you go directly to Manchester?

DICK DAVIS: Not immediately. The first thing my wife and I did when we got back to England was translate *The Conference of the Birds*. The other thing that happened that year, in 1984, was that our second daughter was born, and I realized that I had to start thinking seriously about my future. Since we'd found a publisher for *The Conference of the Birds*, and since I'd enjoyed doing it, I thought that I'd like to study Persian more seriously. So I first went back to Cambridge, and Peter Avery, who taught Persian at the university, said, "Yes, we'd love to have you, but, unfortunately, we can't offer you any money." But I needed money to support the family since we were living off the proceeds of my literary reviews. I was writing hundreds of reviews for all sorts of publications, but it wasn't enough, and then Manchester offered me a bursary for two years.

Was there any particular professor there who helped you?

DICK DAVIS: Norman Calder, whom I'd first met in Iran, arranged for me to get the bursary. He was a very nice man, a bit younger than I was, and a very good scholar. But he was really an Arabist, and the Persianist at Manchester was Edmund Bosworth, an historian of medieval Iran and another very good scholar. So I officially studied under Bosworth, but I didn't do very much under his direction. Mostly, I wandered around and found people — most of them not in Manchester — who could help me.

So you were essentially finding your own way?

DICK DAVIS: Exactly. A Ph.D. in England is a much more informal affair than it is in America. Basically they say, "Oh, you're interested in this? Then go away and write a book about it." And that's pretty much what you do. So I went out and found all kinds of people whom I thought could help me, provide bibliographies to read, and look over and make suggestions about what I was writing.

Was it after your Ph.D. that you went to Santa Barbara?

DICK DAVIS: I was in the process of finishing things up when we moved to Santa Barbara.

Did you know Edgar Bowers before you went there?

DICK DAVIS: Yes, I first met Edgar in the late '70s. When I'd published my first book of poems in the mid-'70s, I'd sent him a copy with a fan letter telling him how much I admired his poems. Eventually, he sent me back a very guarded letter, thanking me for what I'd said about his poems. He said almost nothing about my own poems, although he did mention two that he seemed to think were okay. So I realized that he was very serious and that he wasn't going to praise my work just to be nice, and I appreciated that. Then he also said, "I'm going to England this summer. Will you be there?" So that's how I met him. And that's how I first met Tim Steele, too, since he came along with Edgar. So Edgar and I stayed in touch; and, after my wife and I moved back to England from Tehran in late 1978, Edgar would come and visit us every summer. Eventually, he said, "So why don't you come to Santa Barbara as a guest teacher?" And that's how it happened.

How long were you there?

DICK DAVIS: I was there for a year and a half — as a visiting professor.

In 1979, you received an award from The Arts Council of Great Britain to write a book about Yvor Winters, and the book, Wisdom and Wilderness: The Achievement of Yvor Winters, *was published in the U.S. in 1983. Did you ever meet Winters?*

DICK DAVIS: I never met Winters, and I do wonder if we would have got on very well. I really don't know. But I did meet his widow, Janet Lewis, when I was in Santa Barbara, and she was just wonderful. She was a very good friend of Edgar Bowers, and it was Edgar who introduced us, and I saw her quite often.

Like Bowers, another disciple of Winters was Donald Stanford, who later taught a new generation of poets at L.S.U. that included Wyatt Prunty, David Middleton, and Jon Finlay. So the Winters tradition continued in various parts of the country.

DICK DAVIS: Yes, and even though I was British, I felt very at home in that tradition. Some people found Edgar very difficult to deal with, but I found him an angel, and I loved being with him. Tim Steele is one of the nicest people I know, and Don Stanford was charming as well. Like Janet Lewis, they were great people to be around, and I could really talk to them about poetry and enjoy it.

The first of your nine books of poetry, In the Distance, *was published by Anvil Press in London in 1975. I'd like to discuss a number of subjects and themes that recur in your subsequent books, beginning with the poems that refer to your brother's death. The first poem in* In the Distance *is entitled "To the Memory of My Brother," and in a later poem, "Out of Time," the narrator wakes up one day "with sorrow in my mind," but he only realizes later in the day why he feels that way:*

> *Then in the dusk I recognized*

Dick Davis

> *The day I fear and know:*
> *Grief had not lied, my brother died*
> *On this date, years ago.*

DICK DAVIS: My brother committed suicide when he was nineteen and I was twenty-one. We had the kind of relationship that brothers often have: we were very close, but we also had a strong rivalry. He was a very unhappy child, and he was diagnosed as being mentally unstable — as a schizophrenic — and he spent a lot of his adolescence in and out of institutions. It was clear from about the age of fifteen — when I was seventeen — that life was going to be difficult for him, and my years at Cambridge were shadowed by my brother since he was often ill. He also had very bad relations with my parents, and they'd effectively turned over his care to me. So I spent quite a lot of time seeing him into institutions, although he would often run away. It was a very strange existence for both of us, and I took his death very hard. For a long time, I couldn't deal with it; and, to be honest, it's the reason that I left England. He died shortly before I graduated from Cambridge, and as soon as I graduated, I said, "I have to get away from here." Just being in England reminded me all the time, and I felt very guilty about his death. I was the last person to see him alive before he killed himself, and I felt that I'd failed him in some way. I couldn't even write about his death for a very long time, and then I wrote that tiny poem at the beginning of *In the Distance*, which was an acknowledgement of my feelings about him, but it wasn't exactly *about* him. Finally, about twenty years after his death, I wrote a number of poems about him that are included in my book *Touchwood*. That was the first time that I was able to approach the subject and actually write about it. If I had to isolate the one major event in my life, it would be my brother's death. It changed everything for me; and, in a strange way, I owe a great deal to it. I left England because of it; and, in the end, I think that was a very positive thing for me to do. I discovered that I could be happy living in other cultures and living with people from other cultures, and I discovered a whole new part of myself.

In your powerful poem "Secrets," the narrator admits that he sought refuge from family problems:

> *I ran away to books, fantastic lands,*
> *To verse, where things add up: . . .*

DICK DAVIS: That's true. I did run away to books, and that was going on even before my brother's death, because my family was very dysfunctional when I was young, and I believe that it's one of the reasons that my brother went to pieces. He simply couldn't deal with it. I learned to deal with it by losing myself in literature, which I believe many young people do when things are difficult. Later, as I mentioned, after my brother's death, I tried to deal with it by leaving England. But you can't run away from your own past. You discover that it goes with you everywhere, and eventually when I realized that, I was able to write about it.

Related to these family concerns, your poetry also indicates a natural attraction to other worlds. In "West South West," the narrator discusses fantasizing in his youth about Nelson's adventurous life, which, of course, ends with both victory and death at Trafalgar. The poem ends:

> *My west south west was more a stealthy game*
> *To be elsewhere, escape, rewrite my fate*
> *As one who got away. But all the same*
> *I find I walk the shattered deck and wait*
> *For when the marksmen see me, and take aim.*

DICK DAVIS: Yes, there was that natural attraction, and it was certainly influenced by my stepfather's interest in history. My stepfather, in many way, is a very noble man, and he always was. He served in the Second World War, and he was highly decorated for bravery. He never talked about it, but I'm certain that he killed people in combat and felt quite terrible about it. When I was a very young boy, I remember him bringing a German guest into the house. In those days, that was a terrible thing to do in a little village. Naturally, the Germans had an awful reputation in England in the 1950s. But he didn't care. He wanted to show his hospitality. A few years later, when I was about eight or nine, we had a West Indian staying at our house, and he was the first black person to ever appear in the village. My stepfather had befriended the young man in London, and he'd always had this belief that nations shouldn't be isolated from each other. That people should get to know each other. He believed that the world could improve itself if we interacted more. So he had a very internationalist heart, and I always saw him as a good man who was very kind to me, and I admired the things he believed in.

In an early poem, "Touring a Past," the narrator seems to identify with a figure from the Middle-Eastern past when reflecting on the ruins:

> *I read that now there is*
> *Almost no evidence —*
> *No walls or pottery —*
> *Of what I know were once*
> *The walks and palaces*
> *Love lent to you and me.*

DICK DAVIS: I can't remember the exact circumstances in which I wrote that poem, and perhaps it's a bit obscure. At the time, I'd just ended a long relationship of several years. This was before I met my wife, and it was a very sweet and poignant relationship — the first serious love affair of my life. Then I ended up in Iran, and I read in a guidebook the quote about the ruin that I used as the epigraph for the poem which said that you can't get to the ruins but that it's not worth the bother anyway, and it seemed a useful metaphor for the end of my relationship.

In a more recent single-quatrain poem, "A World Dies . . . ," the concept of one's individual perspective is even more startling, especially in the opening line:

> *A world dies when a person dies; who sees*
> *And savors life as he did who is dead?*
> *No one now lives the myriad privacies*
> *That made the life that ends, now, on this bed.*

DICK DAVIS: That poem was about Edgar Bowers, and it was written shortly after Edgar died. I was very aware that Edgar and I had shared a great deal — in terms of the things we loved, the things that moved us, and the things that we admired. Yet Edgar's life had been so utterly different from mine, and the privacies in his head were also so different from mine. So even though we shared so much together, we were still strangers to each other in so many other and important ways. There's a remarkable line from Wittgenstein in which he says, "The limits of my language are the limits of my world." The truth is, everybody lives in that private place. *Everybody*. And it's so strange. We all interact, and we live publicly, and we share all kinds of things, but when an individual person dies, a world goes out. It's gone. That person's particular take on the world is gone forever.

Another theme that reoccurs in your work is the plight of the exile. Your poem "Exiles," wonderfully crafted in couplets, portrays two exiles playing chess who are distracted by — and interested in — their wives' gossip. Much more poignant is "In the Gallery," where the narrator observes a woman mesmerized by a painting with an Eastern scene that clearly revives untold memories. Equally powerful is the poem entitled "Political Asylum" which begins:

> *My closest friends were killed. I have a life*
> *That's comfortable in almost every way.*

DICK DAVIS: I'm fascinated by exiles. I'm fascinated by people who can make a new life in a new place. I've done it myself, but I had a choice. I've been privileged because I could choose, of my own free will, to go to a country, and I could choose to return, or to go to another country. But some people don't have those choices, and their plight greatly affects me, and I know many people in this situation. They've been forced from their native countries and forced to live between two cultures. They have to live in the culture they moved to, but ineluctably they still live in the old culture. They feel split between them, as if living in some kind of limbo. I'm very drawn to people like that. I find their stories powerfully moving, and I've written a lot of poems about people in that situation.

Dick Davis

The U.S., of course, is full of exiles, both forced and unforced.

DICK DAVIS: I realized that when we lived in Santa Barbara, and I found it fascinating. I was always coming across people who, with very little prompting, would tell me about their journeys from China or Iraq or Vietnam. They were extraordinary stories of loss and adaptation, which is really one of the great historical sagas of the last hundred years or so. It might sound strange, but it's one of the reasons I love America. It's so accommodating to people like that, and so welcoming. Many people claim that America is very hard on foreigners; but, in fact, it's much more welcoming than almost anywhere else, and I find it a very noble aspect of American history.

Another persistent theme in your work is a kind of reluctant pessimism — one that's often tempered by longing. In "Guides for the Soul," the poem ends with a dead person encountering a crowd of accusatory ghosts in the afterlife:

> *They are the pleas you had no patience for,*
> *The pathos you brushed off: the waiting shore*
>
> *Is filled with those you failed. You recognize*
> *The sum of what you are in their blank eyes.*

Yet in "Aubade," which reflects "the dawn thoughts of an atheist," the narrator, although admitting that "colors don't objectively exist," concludes:

> *Still, still we long for Light's communion*
> *To pierce and flood our solitary gloom:*
> *Still I am grateful as the rising sun*
> *Picks out the solid colors of my room.*

So even within your pessimism, there always seems to be a kind of hopefulness.

DICK DAVIS: It's true. I feel both. Obviously, there's the potential for enormous joy and pleasure in life, and I'm very grateful for that. On the other hand, I think I have a very realistic view of life. "Guides for the Soul" is about those things that we do that we regret, and often in life, when the pleasure has passed, the regret remains. I'd like to believe that that's more realistic than pessimistic.

It's true that many of your poems, like "Growing Up," for example, are full of words with powerful spiritual resonance: "grace," "soul," "salvation," "heaven," "communion," and "sacrament," to cite a few. You've also written a number of poems about specifically religious subjects, such as "Maximilian Kolbe," "Rembrandt's Return of the Prodigal Son," "A Christmas Poem," and others. Some of the poems, like the quatrain poem "There," even admit to unexpected things like prayer:

> *Absence becomes unbearable: old men*
> *Spell out the scriptures from a distant childhood.*
> *I shall be one of them I know, despite*
> *The incredulity of some I pray for.*

Do you feel that there's some accommodation to spiritual possibilities within your realistic outlook?

DICK DAVIS: Spirituality has always been very difficult for me, and I think that I'm an atheist. On the other hand, I'm very sympathetic to religious emotion. If I'd lived in the Middle Ages, I probably would have been a monk. I would have been a very bad monk because I would have been tormented by lots of non-monkish desires. But I'm very drawn to spirituality, and I'm very drawn to those people who can live a truly spiritual life. Having said that, I'm often revolted by the way in which most religions are actually practiced in the world. I lived in the Middle East, and I've seen the damage that religious sectarianism can do. I'm not picking out any particular religion, but I feel that, overall, they often do more harm than good. So I feel very conflicted about organized religion, but I must admit that there's some religious art, both visual and musical, but especially musical, that takes away my will to resist it. There are particular pieces of Christian music that are so moving that I find myself assenting to their spirituality while I'm listening to the music. I suppose I tend to think of my religious feelings as kind of an "evening" thing. At the end of the day, you often allow it. But when you wake up in the morning and the sunlight comes in, you think, "Oh, that can't be true." But later, when the evening comes again, you're ready for it once again. I also have the feeling that the same thing might happen in the "evening" of life.

Another important group of poems deals with domestic life — both as a husband and a father. In the humorous poem, "Farewell to the Mentors," the narrator now finds the bachelor poets (like Edward Fitzgerald, Edgar Bowers, Auden, and Housman) not very helpful regarding the practical matters of fatherhood, like dealing with such problems as "teenage rage" and "sibling rivalry." Another more serious poem, "A Bit of Paternity," deals with the difficulty of comforting a weeping child, and the poem "Shadows" catches a magical moment when:

> *Delighted my daughter runs*
> *Twisting from my embrace*
> *To touch the fragile snow*
> *Before it leaves no trace.*

DICK DAVIS: It's often occurred to me that there are so few poems that celebrate love within a marriage. It's been suggested that Petrarch would have never written all those sonnets about Laura if he'd slept with her. But marriage is something that exists all over the world, and it's very real for many people. It's not some fantasy or illusion, and it's something that I've wanted to write about. As for my children, they're immensely important to me. You certainly don't want to burden them with your emotions; but, on the other hand, the emotions are still there, and I've tried to write about it. I must admit that I find those poems very hard to write, much more difficult than writing poems about my wife.

You have a number of lovely poems that refer to your wife, from the humorous "Monorhyme for the Shower" to the very touching quatrain poem that's simply entitled "Afkham":

> *I wanted otherness*
> *And met your gaze, in which the world shone unreproved;*
> *You were the world itself,*

The uninterpretable strangeness to be loved.

Then there's "Memories of Cochin" in which the narrator remembers his marriage in the coastal melting-pot city in India where so "many faiths and peoples mingle" and where the lovers, "though strangers," didn't "fear / To invoke, in honor of our sacrament":

> *The sensual wise genius of the place.*
> *Approach, kind god: bestow your gifts on two,*
>   *Your votaries, of different race*
> *Made one, by love, by marriage, and by you.*

Were you and your wife Afkham married in India?

DICK DAVIS: No, we were married in Tehran, but we had our honeymoon in India. Cochin is a truly magical place, and that poem was written about ten years after our honeymoon.

A number of your poems deal with poetry itself. I particularly like your translation, rendered as a couplet epigram, from the Persian of Amarah-ye Marvazi:

> *I'll hide within my poems as I write them*
> *Hoping to kiss your lips as you recite them.*

"Déjà Lu" is a wonderful self-evaluation of the narrator's earlier work, and the poem "Preferences" begins, a bit like Marianne Moore, admitting:

>   *To my surprise*
> *I've come to realize*
> *I don't like poetry*

Then the narrator explains what he really likes, after rejecting "poetry" as a poor drunken "floozy":

>   *By her pert, terse,*
> *Accomplished sibling: verse.*
> *She's the right gal for me.*

Dick Davis

DICK DAVIS: I do love those kinds of poems — light verse as it's called. I love the technical joy and pleasure that takes place in the writing of such poems, and the hope that those reading them will sense the pleasure that the poet experienced while writing them.

What kind of distinction are you making between verse and poetry?

DICK DAVIS: In that poem, I was trying to say that what many people think of as poetry doesn't really interest me. Whereas, I'm much more interested in the kind of poetry that many people relegate to the category of "verse." Like light verse, for example.

Aside from your own poetry, you're also a world renowned translator of Persian poetry and prose, including Attar's The Conference of Birds *(translated with your wife Afkham Darbandi);* Borrowed Ware: Medieval Persian Epigrams; *and Abolqasem Ferdowsi's monumental* Shahnameh: The Persian Book of Kings, *the national epic of Persia. What motivated you to undertake such a huge project as the Shahnameh?*

DICK DAVIS: Originally, I didn't plan to do the whole epic. My publisher, who's also become a very good friend of mine, said, "Why don't we do a little book of the best stories from the *Shahnameh*? You'll enjoy it." So I said okay, and I started to translate them, and I liked them so much I said, "You know, we should do more of this." So I kept moving along until I finally said, "Why don't we do the whole lot?" So we did. Since some parts near the end of the poem are quite repetitious, I actually translated about nine-tenths of the entire epic.

How long did it take?

DICK DAVIS: Seven years

In 1989, you wrote the introduction for Penguin's new edition of Edward Fitzgerald's 1859 translation of Omar Khayyam's Rubaiyat. *In your introduction, you praised Fitzgerald's decision to render the quatrains with an AABA rhyme scheme, now famously referred to as the Rubaiyat stanza. I wonder if you've ever considered translating Khayyam's poem?*

DICK DAVIS: Fitzgerald definitely made the right choice since the *AABA* rhyme scheme is the actual rhyme scheme used in the original quatrains. They use a different meter, of course, but they have the same rhyme scheme. In the originals, however, each stanza is a separate poem, but Fitzgerald combined them as he wished into one long poem, thus radically altering the structural flow of the original poems. In one of his letters, Fitzgerald says, "I see how a very pretty eclogue might be tesselated out of Khayyam's quatrains," and that's exactly what he did. So the narrative is entirely his own invention, meaning that Fitzgerald essentially translated a poem that doesn't exist. Nevertheless, Fitzgerald really does "get" the feel of the Persian much better than any other translator. People always talk about Fitzgerald's translating mistakes, but I don't think he made any mistakes. When he was doing his translation, he was in contact with the person who'd taught him Persian, and their letters make it perfectly clear that Fitzgerald knew exactly what he was doing. He was a pretty good Persianist, and although he does change things, that's not the same as making mistakes since he knows what he's doing. Many Persianists are rather snooty about Fitzgerald until they take a closer look, and then they say, "Hey, he's pretty good." As far as I'm concerned, nobody captures the feeling of Persian medieval poetry as well as Edward Fitzgerald does.

Would you consider translating the original quatrains?

DICK DAVIS: I don't think that any version I could do would ever replace Fitzgerald's *Rubaiyat*. After all, it's a major English poem. Many other translators have attempted the individual quatrains, but they're not very good. Although I've done one or two of Khayyam's quatrains, I feel that there's so much excellent Persian verse from the Middle Ages that's still untranslated that there's no reason to go back and do something that someone has already done so well. Besides, there are many Persian poets who are better than Khayyam.

You have a wonderful epigram in A Trick of Sunlight *about translating called "Author, Translator . . .":*

Dick Davis

> *Author, translator; now their voices switch.*
> *Ventriloquist and doll; but which is which?*

What advice do you have for translators, especially for translators of poetry?

DICK DAVIS: There's a great 17th century poem by Wentworth Dillon about translation that has the line: "Choose an author as you choose a friend," and that would be my best advice. Unless you feel a real sympathy for the poet, there's no point in trying to translate his work. You need a certain zeal and eagerness to proselytize — to bring the original work out into the open for other people to appreciate. The translator also, obviously, needs to be a very good reader and truly understand the original. It's undeniable that the translator's voice will always be present in the translation, but you have to keep it as muted as possible. You also need to resist the temptation to "improve" the original. You need to be faithful to the original and not incorporate what you "wish" was included in the original. These skills can only come with practice. The act of translation is a much more self-consciously cerebral moment-to-moment activity than writing one's own poems. When you're writing your own poems, you have to be alert and intelligent, but you also have to be open to the subconscious and to moments of inspiration — those moments when the right word comes out of nowhere. When you're writing your own poems, you have to successfully navigate between those two hyper-alert states of mind. Now when you're translating, the same two things are going on, but the balance is different. The consciously alert state of mind needs to predominate, but you can't totally suppress the subconscious either. You still have to be ready for those moments when it says, "This is how it needs to be done." So finding the balance is quite difficult, and it takes lots of practice. In the end, you need to allow the original text to "speak" through you, and you need to keep yourself out of it as much as possible — and put yourself in service to the poet and the original poem.

Your carefully-crafted verse has been composed in a wide range of forms — sonnets, couplets, quatrains, terza rima, and many other formats. Are there any forms you haven't tried that you'd like to? Or ones that you'd like to do more of?

DICK DAVIS: I've never written a good sestina. Most sestinas, if you leave out Dante's and Rossetti's versions of Dante, tend to break down in the middle and don't seem to know what to do with themselves. So it would be nice to do a good sestina. Auden once said, "I go around with subjects in my head, and I go around with forms in my head, and when they come together, I have a poem." I feel that way too. When the idea of a poem and an appropriate form come together, it's very pleasing. Unfortunately, there's one form I have to stop myself from writing, and that's couplets. I can write in couplets until the cows come home, and they've become, unfortunately, my "lazy" form. My most recent translation, *Vis and Ramin*, is an 11th century Persian romance, and I feel it's my very best translation. When I was working on the poem, I would often feel, "This is the work I was born to do." But it's *all* couplets — 400 pages of couplets!

I wonder if you could describe your own writing habits? Do you have a favorite place to write? Or a favorite time of day? Or any personal rituals?

DICK DAVIS: I always write my own poems in long hand in pencil before I transfer them to the computer, usually pretty far along in the editing process. The translations, however, I generally do straight onto the computer. Although the ideas for my poems can come anytime, I always write early in the morning. I usually get up before dawn, at five or six, and write before the rest of the family gets up. I'm one of those people who wakes up alert, and then my brain tends to get duller and duller as the day goes on. I have no actual rituals, but I do need total silence. That's why I love the dawn. Fortunately, I don't mind the distant chirping of the birds.

As you look back over your work, and as you look ahead to writing more poems, which poets do you feel have had the greatest influence on your writing?

DICK DAVIS: A few years ago I was reading an article about Auden in the *Times*, and the author claimed that Auden was the greatest poet in English since Milton. Well, that's quite a claim. And I remember thinking about it and saying to myself, "Well, who's better?" I have the greatest admiration for Auden, so I'm very comfortable going along with that claim. But my favorite poet in English, bar none, is Chaucer. I'm absolutely besotted with Chaucer. I'm crazy about his work, and I love his versatility. If you look at *Troilus and Criseyde*, and then look at the fabliaux in *The Canterbury Tales*, there's such a different sensibility going on, but they're both done with such grace, such deftness, and such beautiful craftsmanship. Also, there's no pretension in Chaucer — no showing off. Obviously he wants to show you that he can write an excellent poem, but there's none of that "Watch me" attitude. He's just a marvelous poet. So I guess I'd say that Chaucer and Auden are my two favorite poets overall. But there are many poets that I like for particular things. For example, I love Herbert both for his tone and for the quietness of his technical dexterity. He doesn't make a fuss about it, and I love that. In general, I don't like poets who show off. I don't really care much for Donne because he shows off so much, and I don't find his sensibility very attractive. I also don't like poets who fight with the language, and push it around and try to bully it. So I find Hopkins, for example, very difficult to deal with.

Aside from Auden, how about the 20th century?

DICK DAVIS: I love J.V. Cunningham and Edgar Bowers, and I think they're both very underrated. There are also a few younger poets whose work I greatly admire. Poets like Joshua Mehigan and Catherine Tufariello. One of the reasons I'm so grateful to this annual poetry conference at West Chester is that it's introduced me to a whole generation of younger poets who are keeping the tradition alive and thriving, and that's very exciting.

You're currently the Chair of the Department of Near Eastern Languages and Cultures and Professor of Persian at The Ohio State University. Do you ever teach creative writing classes?

DICK DAVIS: I haven't for a very long time, not since I was teaching in Santa Barbara. If people bring me their poems, which occasionally happens, I'll always read them and comment on them and try to be honest within the limits of what I think the person can deal with. But that's about it. One problem with teaching poetry writing classes is that you always have people who sign up for the course who have no real interest in learning and no real interest in working at the craft. I always found that very discouraging, so I don't miss teaching those kinds of classes.

Metrical poetry has certainly made a comeback since the days when formal verse was seldom published in the literary journals. I wonder if you're pleased with the effects of the formalist revival that's taken place over the past few decades?

DICK DAVIS: It's certainly increased the level of metrical competence, which was so sadly lacking before. Of course, metrical competence doesn't guarantee great poems, and some clunky poems are certainly being written, but when you have a milieu in which metrical competence is expected and accepted and admired, then you have the potential to produce some great poetry within that tradition. For a long time, the soil wasn't there, but now I believe that we have an environment in which great poems can appear, and I do think they're appearing. There are some excellent young poets out there, and sometimes when I read their work, I feel that I could never write a poem that good, and I'm very impressed. So, overall, I think that the formal revival has been terrific.

Do you have any new projects under way?

DICK DAVIS: I'm working on a new translation project. In the 14th century, there were three poets who lived in the same town in the south of Iran, and they all knew each other, and they even referenced each other in their poems. But they were all completely different. Hafez, who's, without question, the most famous lyric poet in Iranian history, wrote with a strange personal sort of mysticism. Jahan Khatun is the only medieval woman poet whose complete works have come down to us — well over a thousand poems. She was a princess, and her family lost power halfway through her life, and she was nearly killed in a *coup d'état*. The poems that she wrote when she was young are very conventional, but elegant and

Dick Davis

beautiful. The poems that she wrote after her family's loss of power are often sad and sometimes angry, bitter, and satirical. The third poet is Obeid Zakani, the most famous obscene poet from medieval Iran. So they're all very different, and I'm planning to do about forty to fifty poems from each one. Then I'll write a commentary that will discuss their friendship and give the background for their poems.

My last question is a difficult one, but an important one: What advice do you have for aspiring poets?

DICK DAVIS: Read. Read a lot! Read much more than you write. A lot of young poets write more than they read, and they end up reinventing the wheel. They're trying to do things that other people have already done so much better. Also, I think it's important that young poets don't obsess too much about finding their voice. Instead, they should obsess about learning their craft. If they've read widely and worked at the craft, their own unique voice will eventually come. But if you try to force it, you'll just end up sounding bombastic, pretentious, and pushy. I would also suggest that young people should imitate what they like, and not be ashamed of imitating. You nurture your talent by practicing it. You have to play a lot of scales before you can play at Carnegie Hall. So do the equivalent. Write sonnets, write blank verse, write couplets, even write free verse if that's what you want to do, but always be conscious of *what* you are doing — ask yourself why you're ending your lines where you are, etc. You have to work at it. There's a line from Dryden that I can't remember exactly, but he says that the wheel captures fire by turning. Nothing will happen unless you're continually turning the wheel. Stravinsky, in his lectures *On Music*, says that the inspiration comes when you're practicing, when you're trying things out — when you're trying to figure out what will work. That's when the inspiration comes. You can't sit around and wait for inspiration before you start to write. If you do that, you'll never produce anything that's any good. You have to work at it, constantly.

I'd like to end today with the final lines of one of your poems that happens to be one of my particular favorites: "6 A.M. Thoughts." It's a poem about pressing on with things, and it begins with the narrator waking up to a flood of thoughts that "come blundering in / Like puppies or importunate children" and which immediately make a mess of the new day:

> And the mess they trail with them! Embarrassments,
>   Anger, lust, fear — in fact the whole pig-pen;
> And who'll clean it up? No hope for sleep now —
>   Just heave yourself out, make the tea, and give in.

Thanks, Dick.

DICK DAVIS: Thank you, Bill.

Rhina P. Espaillat

Rhina P. Espaillat is a distinguished bilingual poet and translator. Samuel Maio has called her "a poet of truth and experience," and Robert Mezey has written, quite to the point, "She is one of our finest poets."

Born in the Dominican Republic, she came to New York City when she was seven years old after her parents were exiled during the dictatorship of Rafael Trujillo. A graduate of Hunter College, she married the teacher and sculptor, Alfred Moskowitz; raised a family; and taught for many years in the New York City Public School System. Her first collection, *Lapsing to Grace*, appeared in 1992 and was followed by *Where Horizons Go* (1998), winner of the T.S. Eliot Poetry Prize, and *Rehearsing Absence* (2001), recipient of the Richard Wilbur Poetry Award. Her subsequent books include *The Shadow I Dress In* (2004); *Playing at Stillness* (2005); *Agua de do rios/Water from Two Rivers* (2006); *El olor de la memoria: cuentos/The Scent of Memory: Short Stories* (2007); and *Her Place in These Designs* (2008).

A two-time winner of the Howard Nemerov Sonnet Award, she was also a founding member and former director of the Powow River Poets. Her poems and translations have appeared in numerous literary journals including *Poetry*, *The Hudson Review*, *The American Scholar*, *Measure*, and *First Things*.

This interview was conducted at the Exploring Form and Narrative Poetry Conference at West Chester University.

Your parents, along with many other relatives, were political exiles from the Dominican Republic during the dictatorship of General Rafael Trujillo — specifically in the aftermath of the infamous El Corte Massacre of 1937. Could you explain how your family ended up in New York City?

RHINA ESPAILLAT: In 1937, my father and his uncle, Rafael Brache, were working in Washington, D.C., representing the Dominican Republic. My great uncle was a *ministro*, which is a kind of ambassador, and he was there representing the country's financial concerns. After the massacre, in which about 17,000 Haitians were murdered on the border, my great uncle Rafael courageously wrote a letter to President Trujillo saying that he could no longer be associated with a government that had committed such a terrible criminal act. Before the letter was actually mailed, my father read it and said to my great uncle, "Do you realize what this will bring about?" And Rafael said, "Yes, I know, but I have to do it." As a result, the *ministro*'s whole group was exiled, my father included. At the time, my mother and I were also in Washington, D.C., and since she was concerned that she'd never see her family again, we went back to the Dominican Republic. I was five years old at the time, and after my mother's short visit, she left me with my paternal grandmother before she went to New York to meet with my father who was trying to find work and a place to live. It was a very difficult time to settle in New York City, at the end of the Depression, so I stayed with my grandmother until 1939 before my parents felt settled enough to bring me to New York. And my mother was right. She never did see her family again, and my father never saw his mother again.

Does anyone in the family have a copy of that letter?

RHINA ESPAILLAT: No, unfortunately, but we did learn that the dictator was absolutely furious when he received it.

Apparently, your father had always hoped that the family could return to the Dominican Republic. Wasn't that a possibility after the assassination of Trujillo in 1961?

RHINA ESPAILLAT: It was, and my great uncle and his wife and some of their sons moved back to the Dominican Republic. But, by that time, I was married with children, and my parents didn't want to leave us. They'd also made many close friends in the United States; and, of course, many of the people back home had already died, including both of my grandmothers. I believe that it's very common in immigrant communities to have powerful longings for home, but by 1961, my parents' lives were centered in the U.S.

Rhina P. Espaillat

Is it true that when you were a child in the Dominican Republic, your poet grandmother encouraged you to compose poems in Spanish?

RHINA ESPAILLAT: Yes, but I can't remember a single one! But I do remember that she was very proud of me whenever I spouted something out, and she would always write them down for me — since I couldn't write yet — and she'd save them. But I have no idea what happened to them.

Do you think they were poems that you composed spontaneously? Or do you think that you practiced them and then recited them for your grandmother?

RHINA ESPAILLAT: I really can't remember. But I grew up hearing the adults reciting and singing, and it sounded like so much fun, so I wanted to do it as well. I'm sure that my childhood poems were dreadful, but you know how grandmothers are. She told me that they were all wonderful and that I was a "poet," and it made me very happy.

At the age of seven, you joined your parents in New York in a mostly immigrant section of the city on the West Side. What were your first impressions of New York City as a little girl?

RHINA ESPAILLAT: It was both amazing and bewildering. I'd never seen so many people in one place at the same time before — or so many cars. In my town back home, whenever a single car drove through town, it was a big deal. Even when a stranger visited town, it was a big deal. And now I was surrounded by strangers and this new and very exciting environment. I remember that I loved to run down the subway stairs and then run up the other side. It was such an adventure. It seemed amazing to me that there was actually a train running beneath the street, and I found the city terribly exciting and all the people fascinating. Naturally, I was dying to communicate with the other children and hoping to make new friends, but I also missed my hometown, and my friends back home, and, especially, my two grandmothers. I missed them desperately. So, despite all the excitement, I definitely experienced that deep sense of loss that every immigrant experiences, even if the final result is something terrific and wonderful.

As you mention in your poem "Bilingual/Bilingüe," your father had a family rule about language: "English outside this door; Spanish inside." I realize that this caused you some frustrations as a child, but, looking back, how do you feel about it now?

RHINA ESPAILLAT: I'm infinitely grateful because he made me truly bilingual. It was also part of his rule that I had to speak both languages grammatically correctly and that I was forbidden to mix the two — putting English words into Spanish conversation and vice-versa. He made it clear that these were both "world" languages and that they both deserved respect. At first, of course, it was quite difficult since I wanted to use all the words together, and sometimes I would get frustrated and even end up crying. For example, I might want to repeat something funny that I'd heard in class, but my father would say, *"No, habla en castellano. Si se puede decir, se puede decir en castellano."* If it can be said at all, it can be said in Spanish.

How good was your parents' English?

RHINA ESPAILLAT: They both spoke English, but my father had a very strong accent. My mother was much more comfortable with English, and her accent lightened over the years, and she spoke it very well — and she could also write in English very well. Eventually, my father became a businessman, ending up an exporter, and he dealt with customers who spoke both languages. He also read the newspapers every day and various magazines; but, for him, literature, especially poetry, was always Spanish. He loved poetry, and he always clung to the poetry he'd learned in his youth.

At the age of seven, did learning a new language come easily?

RHINA ESPAILLAT: Yes, I didn't have any difficulty learning English, and it took me less than a year. By the time I'd been living in Manhattan eight or nine months, I was speaking the language, and by the end of the year I was writing as well. But the first few months were pretty rough because I've always been very talkative. I'm a real chatterbox, as you know, and the fact that I couldn't sit down with my new school friends and yack, yack, yack, the way I used to do with my million cousins back home was very frustrating. But being naturally gregarious, I learned very quickly, and the school system helped a lot.

I believe you attended public schools in Manhattan. Which ones?

RHINA ESPAILLAT: I started out at a Catholic school for about five months, but when we moved to another apartment, I transferred to a public school — PS 94. In the public school, there was a tremendous variety of students — kids from Asia and all over Europe, and lots of Polish kids and Jewish kids. And this made me feel less "different" and less solitary because all the kids were in the same boat. Most of us, for example, had parents at home who didn't speak English very well.

In high school, under the guidance of one of your teachers, Catherine Haydon Jacobs, you began — amazingly — to publish in national magazines like The Ladies' Home Journal. *Could you discuss that a bit?*

RHINA ESPAILLAT: Well, it came about because my teacher was a poet herself. She used to write under her real name, Catherine Haydon Jacobs, but in class we all knew her as Miss Jones, which was her "teaching" name. She published her poetry in various magazines, although she never published a book. Then one day, when I was fifteen, she read some of my poems, and she got a bit suspicious, and she asked me, "What have you been reading?" and I said, "Edna St. Vincent Millay and Sara Teasdale." But she was still suspicious that I'd been "borrowing too much," so she sat me down in a classroom and said, "Now, Rhina, dear, I'm going to give you a subject and I want you to write a sonnet." So I did, and then she believed me, and she took a real interest. In time, I showed her other poems that I'd written, and then, without telling me, she sent them off to *The Ladies' Home Journal.* When the letter arrived that my poems had been accepted — three poems — I couldn't believe it. I remember thinking, "This can't be happening! This only happens to poets!" At that point, I was a junior in high school, age 16, and it was a turning point in my life. I realized that writing poetry is not simply something that you do for fun and then share with your family, it's also something that can be published and reach many other readers. Needless to say, it was *very* exciting. Then Miss Jones sent some of my work to the Poetry Society of America, and they accepted me as the youngest member they'd ever had, and I couldn't believe it. Suddenly, grown-ups were listening to me read my work!

Who were your favorite poets back then?

RHINA ESPAILLAT: I liked Thomas Hardy very much, and I also liked A.E. Housman. Around that time, I'd discovered T.S. Eliot, and even though I couldn't fully understand his poems, I loved them anyway. I was a voracious reader, and then, one Christmas, my great uncle gave me that big fat Untermeyer anthology, and that was another turning point in my life. I ate it up! It's such a marvelous book, and it became my poetic Bible. Over the years, I was very fortunate because I had many great teachers — in both elementary school and high school — who loved poetry and would read it to us, very beautifully, in class. I was, and still am, extremely grateful to all those teachers, and it made me want to become a teacher just like them.

Eventually, you went to Hunter College in Manhattan. What was your major?

RHINA ESPAILLAT: I majored in English, and I minored in Latin and Humanities, and I was already determined to become a teacher.

How did you meet your husband, the teacher and sculptor, Alfred Moskowitz?

RHINA ESPAILLAT: I met him at the wedding of my best friend, Mimi, and his best friend, Harry. I was still at Hunter College, in my junior year, and we ended up sitting at the same table at the wedding on Thanksgiving Day in 1951. And we started talking, then dancing, and — I know this sounds like madness — he proposed five weeks later on New Year's Eve, and we were married in June of 1952.

A real whirlwind!

RHINA ESPAILLAT: Yes, it was!

After graduate study at Queens College, you started teaching in the New York school system. What subjects did you teach?

RHINA ESPAILLAT: My very first year, I taught eighth grade in a public school in Queens, and I taught back-to-back English and Social Studies classes, and I had a tremendous amount of fun. Very quickly, I learned the first rule: get their attention immediately. Don't say a word until you have their attention. That was very useful, and I enjoyed it very much. But, eventually, when our own children came along, I stopped teaching for ten years since I was so busy childrearing. Then I got my Master's degree and returned to teaching.

In Queens?

RHINA ESPAILLAT: Yes, at Jamaica High School. In those days, it was a very good school, well-known for its Westinghouse winners. The math and science departments were very strong, but so was the English department. Nowadays, the public school system in New York gets a terrible rap, but I think it was magnificent back then, and whatever might be wrong with it now is from a lack of serious attention — from an unfortunate lack of desire to keep those schools alive and vibrant. I believe that the public school system in this country is an extremely important institution because it opens all kinds of doors for young children. Kids like me, who arrive in New York speaking another language, would never find their way without the public school system. So we need to get back to the idea that the culture belongs to everyone and that the school system is the place that can open the door to that culture. It's absolutely necessary for children to learn how to live together and how work together to form a society. I really believe that. It's one of my strongest personal convictions.

Years later, you were one of the founding members of the Fresh Meadows Poetry Workshop in Queens. How did that come about?

RHINA ESPAILLAT: That was a wonderful group, and I fell into it by accident. When I was still teaching at Jamaica High School, I had a colleague named Rose Kirchman who was both a poet and an actress, and she was also the head of the drama department. Eventually, after I left my teaching position, I ran into Rose in a store one day in 1980, and she invited me to a poetry workshop. When I asked her about it, she said, "Oh, it's no big deal. We just meet at the library on Saturdays." So I started going, and it was a small group and quite uneven in the quality of the work. Eventually those of us who were further advanced and more interested in publication — like Rose Kirchman and Yala Korwin — created another group, which we called the Fresh Meadows Poets.

How many years did you participate in that group?

RHINA ESPAILLAT: Until we moved to Massachusetts in 1990. Four years earlier, in 1986, we'd started doing public readings in New York, and that was very exciting — actually taking our work out to the community. We read everywhere: in libraries, in schools, in old age homes, in residences, and in all sorts of other places. I must admit that when we moved to Massachusetts, I was heartbroken about leaving the group. We'd become very close, like an extended family, and they're still going strong today.

After both you and your husband Alfred had retired from teaching, you eventually moved to Newburyport, an historic seaport on the northeastern coast of Massachusetts. Why Newburyport?

RHINA ESPAILLAT: When Alfred retired from teaching after thirty years, I took early retirement. As much as we both loved teaching, we felt that it didn't leave us time to do anything else — like focus on our own work, visit the kids, travel, and many other things. At the time, my mother had Alzheimer's, and she was doing very badly and needed twenty-four-hour-a-day services. We tried to find help in New York, but there was nothing available, so our sons suggested Massachusetts. They're both physicists, who'd done their doctorates at MIT, so we went up for a visit, and in one weekend we found a wonderful residence for my mother and a house for ourselves that were only eight blocks apart. So we moved to Newburyport, and my mother spent the last four and a half years of her life very well cared for and very well treated in a wonderful place. She was very happy there, and I was able to visit her every day. At the same time, both Alfred and I, although true New Yorkers, also fell in love with Newburyport, which is a lovely town with a lot going on.

So once you were settled, you could finally focus on your poetry?

RHINA ESPAILLAT: Absolutely! For almost three decades, over twenty-five years, I'd done very little writing, maybe producing about a half-dozen poems a year. I simply didn't have the time. I wasn't overly frustrated about it because I was happily busy. I enjoyed making lesson plans, teaching, and even marking student papers, but there was still something always nagging at me — something I missed. I was, of course, very grateful when I had the opportunity to be in the workshops, and it made me feel revitalized — as if I'd grown younger. I felt as though I'd suddenly regained something that I'd feared I'd lost. When Alfred said, "Why don't you retire early and give more time to what you really love?" I was very excited by the idea, and I started writing immediately. It was a matter of weeks.

In Newburyport, you became the founding director of the Powow River Poets Workshop, which has produced some of the finest poets in America. Aside from the natural talents of those involved, why do you think the Powow group has had such great success?

RHINA ESPAILLAT: I certainly agree that they're a tremendously talented group, but even in talented groups, there can be ego problems that can ruin everything. But we've never had that problem. There's always been a marvelous civility in the group. It's true that they care greatly about the craft of writing, but they also care about each other. Everyone roots for everyone else, and if someone gets something published in a really good journal, everybody breaks into applause. We also realize that writing poetry isn't just a hobby, it's a craft — an art — and everyone is there to learn how to do it better. The comments at our monthly meetings are very specific and craft-oriented, and never personal. As a result, the sessions are very stimulating, and the discussions continue long after the meetings end. For the rest of the month, the emails are flying back and forth, and the dialogue continues. As a result, it touches our whole lives, and we feel like a family.

Your first collection of poems, Lapsing to Grace, *was published in 1992, and your second collection,* Rehearsing Absence, *was published in 2001. These books established many of the themes that would remain important in your subsequent work. X.J. Kennedy once praised your collection* Where Horizons Go *by saying, "I'm won over by the way the poet writes of the most commonplace experience — she's a warm affirmer of life," and it's certainly true than many of your best poems deal with domestic concerns. In your poem, "Workshop," the narrator explains to a poet friend:*

> *Well, I've been coring apples, layering them*
> *in raisins and brown sugar; I've been finding*
> *what's always lost, mending and brushing,*
> *pruning houseplants, remembering birthdays.*

The list continues, and the poem ends:

> *I've been putting a life together, like*
> *supper, like a poem, with what I have.*

There's both a sense of humility and a sense of practicality in the narrator's explanation.

RHINA ESPAILLAT: I do believe that all we have to work with is what life has given us. I don't feel that I could invent battlefield experiences or write about heated love affairs. If I did, I would have to hold my fingers crossed behind my back because I've actually lived a very simple life, and I don't think that's necessarily a loss for a poet. *All* human life, no matter how simple it might seem, has the potential for drama and meaning. I learned that early from Thomas Hardy. It's not just his outrageous characters who matter, but all of his common country people as well. *All* lives are worth recording because they all have value.

That idea is reinforced in another poem with the same title, "Workshop," in which an older poet gives advice to another writer by comparing the writer's poem to a messy room and suggesting:

> *. . . Then, after you clean it,*
> *make the room say your life, as if it wanted*
> *to keep your life a secret, but must tell*
> *despite itself; . . .*

RHINA ESPAILLAT: Yes, you have to tell the truth, but you also have to tell the truth through the craft. It's not a diary, and it's not just a recording of everyday life. Even if you manage to tell the truth, that's not good enough, it has to be filtered through the craft and through the art. I really have no use for a certain school of poetry that consists of listing what someone ate, what she said, and what she did next, and so on. That's not the "ordinary" that I'm after. I'm after the *meaningful* ordinary. I'm after the ordinary that everyone else can understand and that can serve as a bridge between my life and everybody else's. But in order to express that, you need discipline, and that's what "Workshop" is all about: get disciplined. Make the bed. Wash the dishes. Get the meter right. For heaven's sake, get the meter right!

You have many excellent poems about family in which you explore a situation that's both poignant and telling. One of my favorites is "Evan, Breathing," where the two grandparents are listening on the phone and trying to hear their son's reluctant baby say something. The poem ends:

> *Evan, your breath is all we sense,*

Rhina P. Espaillat

> *minutely bridging, puff by puff,*
> *the miles, the days, from there to here.*
> *It isn't much. But it's enough.*

Was this poem based on a true story?

RHINA ESPAILLAT: Yes, it was. It was about my son Philip's first son, our first grandson, who's now studying musicology in New York City. He's now twenty-four and grown up, but back when he was little, we used to thrive on those little sounds of his breathing over the phone. At the time, we were still living in New York City, but the rest of the family — the boys and their families — lived in Newburyport, and we missed them very much. Then, when the first grandchild came, it made us even more willing to give up New York City — which we both adored — and move to Massachusetts.

As with the "Workshop" poems, you've written a number of poems about poetry and the "poet's life," both humorous poems like "For the Lady in the Black Raincoat Who Slept through an Entire Poetry Reading" and more serious poems like "Prosody," which expresses the necessary power of music in poetry. It concludes:

> *The words are a name*
> *for the shadow I dress in.*
> *The radiance that wears me*
> *answers only to the music.*

Could you discuss this a bit?

RHINA ESPAILLAT: I was hoping that the word "music" would grow with the repetitions of the word in the poem since it's used in every stanza. On one level, it means the music of prosody, the overall music of poetry, and all of the ear-pleasing devices that poets use. But, in addition to that, it's also about a music that's fundamentally human, something that transcends the individual, something that's capable of reaching out to other human beings. I think, by the end of the poem, that I'm talking about the music of human lives. Poetry is a music that will outlive all of us, and we're the individual notes in that music. I also believe that it's a music of the love of those that we love, the love of our family and of friends, which transcends the individual.

I know how much you love music, and I read somewhere that you're very fond of Rodrigo's guitar compositions. Do you think that Rodrigo and the other Spanish guitarists have affected your poetry?

RHINA ESPAILLAT: Oh, yes! The sound of Spanish music, especially the guitar, has had a great influence on me personally and has affected the way I approach poetry. When I was very young, my grandmother used to play classical Spanish guitar, and she played it wonderfully. I think those experiences made me much more of an "ear" poet than an "eye" poet. I tend to hear the poetry much more than I imagine it — much more than I see it — which is why I write more formal verse than free verse. I *hear* the meter just as I hear the rhythms of the Spanish guitar. I've also been very influenced by Spanish poetry. Sor Juana has been a major influence in my life from the very beginning, and, of course, St. John of the Cross, who was my father's favorite poet. Also, Lorca and all those 19th Century Spanish and Latin American poets whom my father used to love and frequently recite.

Despite your love of poetry and its possibilities, you're also very aware of its limitations. Your poem, "Warning:," begins:

> *Don't ask my poem*
> *too feed you:*
> *it lives on hunger.*

Then, after two more "warnings," the last stanza begins:

> *Don't ask my poem*
> *to think straight:*

Similarly, in your poem entitled "Poetry Reading," the narrator, although welcoming a potential listener, does point out:

> *Well, you've been warned: whatever world you came*
> *to find or curse or grieve may not be listed*
> *in our small menu . . .*

So poetry can only do so much.

RHINA ESPAILLAT: I think it's unfair to ask too much of poetry. For example, I don't think poetry should be asked to change political systems or rectify the economy, even though poets can certainly express how they feel about such things. Poets can, of course, write about their fears and hopes and wishes, but I don't think that poetry should be used for political sloganeering. I personally don't care for that kind of poetry, regardless of which side of the political spectrum it comes from.

Another important theme in your work is a sense of the randomness of life — the awareness that things might have turned out differently. This is very clear in your clever yet serious sonnet, "If There Had Been," which begins:

> *If there had been more time; if you had stayed;*
> *if you had spoken sooner or said less;*

This idea is reinforced in your excellent sonnet "Contingencies," in which a number of seemingly random occurrences end up being life-altering, such as the one cited in the final couplet:

> *or in some public room, the stranger's name*
> *half-heard, and nothing afterward the same.*

This theme occurs most powerfully in one of my favorites — another sonnet — entitled "Almost," in which a mother sees her son's car in a parking lot and suddenly reflects on the fact that her child's conception might never have occurred. The poem ends:

> *And think how easily — by blindest chance —*

Rhina P. Espaillat

> *this cell or that could have flicked elsewhere, failed*
> *to clasp in that first moment of the dance*
> *that life begins with, how you could have sailed*
> *out of all possibility, downstream,*
> *lost to my flesh forever, like a dream.*

RHINA ESPAILLAT: Yes, "randomness" is exactly the right word, and that last poem came out of an actual incident. One day, I walked into a parking lot, and I saw a car, and it looked very familiar. Sure enough, my grandchildren's toys were in the backseat, and I said, "Oh, I'll just wait around a bit and see if Philip comes out," but after I'd waited a bit, I needed to get going, so I got in my own car and drove away. And I actually started laughing on the way home because it struck me that it was just like conception. You don't know whether or not you're going to make that connection; and, whatever happens, it could change your life dramatically. So the idea stuck in my mind, and the poem was written very quickly — being one of those poems that practically "wrote itself." I also think that the idea of the poem reflected many conversations that I've had with Alfred over the years. Conversations when we'd consider how we'd come from such different backgrounds, different cultures, even different boroughs, and yet, ultimately, we came together so quickly. And sometimes we'd talk about how various small turns in our earlier lives would have altered everything, and that we would have ended up living completely different lives, with different spouses, different children, and so on — which is quite a frightening thought for two people who are happy together. There were so many earlier "ifs" that could have changed things. If I'd gone back to Oswego instead of going to school in New York City, if I'd taken that scholarship to Ohio instead of staying at Hunter College, and so on. In life, we never know when the important things are going to happen. When Alfred and I first met at that wedding, neither one of us was expecting anything major to happen. But it did.

I feel that a number of your more recent poems, especially some of those collected in Her Place in These Designs *(2008), are more hard-hitting than your previous work. Poems, for example, like "Triptych" and "January '41," about a*

Rhina P. Espaillat

young child's frightening encounter with a predator in Central Park, which ends:

> Those six blocks flew past me, numb and cold
> as in a dream through which my body went
> unmoving. It was years before I told,
> before I knew what harm it was he meant.

I suspect that it took you a long time to write a poem about that.

RHINA ESPAILLAT: Oh, it certainly did. At the time it happened, I didn't know anything about sex, but I still knew that something was happening that shouldn't be happening. I was nine years old, and I'd stayed too late at the playground, and the man called out to me, "Little girl, little girl, look what I have!" So I turned around to face him because I'd been taught to be respectful of adults, and to answer them whenever they talk to you. But then I saw his face, and I also saw that he was holding up something in his hand. It was a condom, and I didn't know what it was, but something about the look on his face told me that I needed to get out of there. It was 1941, and I still remember that he was wearing one of those pea collars that sailors used to wear back then, and I reacted on pure instinct, turned around, and ran all the way home. It took me a long time to tell anyone about what had happened because I think the first impulse that children have is to feel guilty about things like that, even if they've done nothing wrong. It also took me a long time to write about it.

Do you feel that you're now more willing to deal with harsher subjects?

RHINA ESPAILLAT: I think that I am. I see all kinds of things happening in the world that are quite outside of my own cheerful and quiet sphere — things that other people have had to suffer through that I haven't had to deal with — minority issues, women's issues, and so on. I don't see these things as merely political issues, but I do see them as demanding an enlargement of one's empathy. As I've gotten older, I've heard all kinds of stories about women who have been physically abused, and emotionally abused, and professionally abused, and these were things that I never had to deal with. In my own professional life, for example, I always felt that I was getting a fair deal as a teacher in New York City, but I've come to understand that that certainly isn't universal. There were a great many things that I took for granted when I was younger that I now need to reconsider, and that's naturally being reflected in my poems, and I certainly agree that *Her Place in These Designs* is my most socially engaged book.

I'd like to take a few moments to discuss your writing process. I understand that you always do the first draft in your head. Is that correct?

RHINA ESPAILLAT: That's right. Almost always, a poem starts for me as a kind of restlessness, something that's nagging at me, and it comes with an accompanying beat so that I immediately have some sense of what it wants to sound like. Then the words and phrases begin to slip into my consciousness, and I start to have an inkling of what I want to write about, but it's always the sound that comes first. It's as if the sound wants to say something, which is why I refer to myself as an "ear" poet. So I continue to work on the poem in my mind, and I don't put anything down on the page until the initial version of the poem is pretty clear. Then, once I've written it down, I begin to make a million alterations since so much of the *real* writing process is rewriting.

Do you recite the poem out loud or do you just hear the sound in your head?

RHINA ESPAILLAT: I hear it in my head, but I always need some peace and quiet and isolation to do so.

Have there been times when you've written it down and there wasn't that much revision to be done?

RHINA ESPAILLAT: Some of them need very little revision, but they all need some. Of course, sometimes some of them turn into something else entirely. It happens with fiction as well. Not long ago, I had an idea that seemed to be a short story, but every time I started to write it down, I hated it. Then, eventually, I dreamed about it one night, and I realized that it really wanted to be a poem, and it eventually became "The Ballad of San Isidro." I think that when I approach things too intellectually, it causes problems, but when I let the poem tell me what it wants, things go much smoother.

Do you have any writing rituals? Any special time of the day? Or any special place?

RHINA ESPAILLAT: Not really, because I never know when it's going to come. A lot of them seem to arrive when I'm busy doing housework, looking out of the window, or cooking. Often when I'm multi-tasking. Alfred says that he can always tell when I'm writing in my head because he sees the "look." I never know when the poems are coming, and sometimes they formulate very quickly in my mind, and sometimes they can kick around for weeks or months before they come out right. And even when I do get to the point that I write them down, many of them end up thrown away. I tear up lots of paper! And that's something I always tell my students, "Don't be afraid to write, because if you hate it when it's finished, you can always throw it away." There's nothing sacred about it once it's written down, so keep a wastebasket handy at all times!

Aside from your own poems, you've been doing a lot of translations from the work of St. John of the Cross, Sor Juana Ines de la Cruz, Miguel Hernandez, and others. In you poem, "Translation," you begin with an apt analogy that "This is an art difficult as marriage," but if the "compromise" is done correctly, it can be "miraculous." Even your poem, "On the Impossibility of Translation," which begins by saying, "Of course impossible," then goes on to point out:

> *. . . Yet lovers, each*
> *mute in one skin, can learn to speak in tongues,*

and the poem ends by reminding its readers that we've all

> *. . . seen, in shallow pools in every town*
> *how rain translates the sky and writes it down.*

Rhina P. Espaillat

RHINA ESPAILLAT: I can't imagine a world without translation because we'd have no Bible, no Homer, and no Virgil. All of our libraries would shrink down to a single room. So we desperately need translation, but it's crucial for the translator to face the fact that he's not going to get it all. There are going to be losses, which he should try to keep to a minimum, but he can never flatter himself that's he's really bringing that other poem into another language because it simply can't be done. I think the translator needs to begin with humility. As far as the actual process goes, I think a translator first needs to understand the poem as well as he can, try to get under the author's skin, and see if he can reconstruct the thought processes of the original author. The primary job of the translator is to carry the poem from one language to the other with as little damage as possible. Personally, I enjoy the challenge very much, even though I'm never fully satisfied.

What advice do you give to your Spanish-speaking poetry students?

RHINA ESPAILLAT: Whenever I speak to Hispanic groups, I tell the young people to make sure they hold onto their Spanish, and keep it clean, and constantly increase their vocabulary, just as they're doing with English. Then I encourage them and say, "Now, since you know two languages, for heaven's sake, translate! We need you. Both languages need you to bridge the gap."

You've also, on occasion, translated your own poems. What was that like?

RHINA ESPAILLAT: It's a lot of fun because you're already inside your own head. Sometimes things get so intertwined in my mind that I can't remember which version was written first, so I actually have to look back to my records to see if the Spanish version or the English version came first. And that's a good sign because it indicates that both versions are feeling perfectly natural.

Do you tend to go more from English to Spanish, or more from Spanish to English?

RHINA ESPAILLAT: Since I write more in English, they tend to

Rhina P. Espaillat

start that way. But sometimes a poem comes to me in Spanish, and I'm always happy about that. As for essays and short stories, they seem to arrive with greater frequency in Spanish.

Recently, you've begun translating Frost into Spanish.

RHINA ESPAILLAT: Yes, and I'm enjoying it very much. I've finished over forty poems, and I think that may be the entire manuscript. But I haven't had much success with the long narratives.

How about "The Death of the Hired Man?"

RHINA ESPAILLAT: I did that one, and it's the longest one I've done. But something like "The Witch of Coos" seems to be written in a kind of New Hampshirese that's very hard to translate into Spanish. It's too idiosyncratic. But I've been pleased with the shorter lyrics I've done. In the past, I've only seen a few translations of Frost into Spanish, and I didn't care for any of them. One of them actually translated Frost into free verse, which I don't think is appropriate at all, and I'm sure that Frost was turning in his grave.

I understand that you're also translating Richard Wilbur?

RHINA ESPAILLAT: I am, and I'm having such a wonderful time!

Have you discussed it with Mr. Wilbur?

RHINA ESPAILLAT: Yes. I've been working on one or two or three poems at a time, and then I send them to him and ask, "Please, please, please, complain about whatever doesn't strike you right" — because his Spanish is good enough to know the difference. But he's very modest about it.

Has he made any suggestions?

RHINA ESPAILLAT: Not yet. So far he's been very pleased with everything, but I keep on insisting, "Please, tell me whatever's not quite right." I love these poems, and I'm trying not to do them any injury.

Looking back, which poets do you feel have influenced you the most?

RHINA ESPAILLAT: Emily Dickinson has been a crucial influence. Even though my work doesn't resemble hers very much, I feel I've learned from her unique ways of looking at the world — and her need to "surprise" in her poetry. I think she's one of the world's best poets, and I adore her work. Of course, other influences are Richard Wilbur, and Robert Frost, and Thomas Hardy, who's still one of my favorites. Like Frost, Hardy is so deceptively simple that you find yourself learning new things after countless re-readings. I also love the poetry of Stanley Kunitz, who eventually moved from formal to free verse. I love what he does with vocabulary — how he mixes the simplest words with the six-syllable ones. He also writes incredible lines and creates incredible similes. He's one of my favorites.

You've been teaching for many years, both in the classroom and in various workshops. What advice do you have for new aspiring poets?

RHINA ESPAILLAT: I would say to read lots and lots from every age, not simply what's being written today, although that's important, but also the writings of the past, which is still speaking to us as powerfully as ever. I would also say, learn the rules of prosody, even if you change your mind after you learn all the rules, all the tricks, what I call the "tricks of the trade." It's like saying to a young carpenter, "Learn to use the hammer, learn the plane, learn the ruler, learn the screwdriver, learn the use of the different screws and the different nails." It seems so obvious, but it needs to be said over and over nowadays. Master the craft, and then decide how much of it you want to use.

I'd like to finish up today by reading one of my favorites, the short quatrain poem, "Nativity":

> *How shall I fashion for my boy*

Rhina P. Espaillat

the marvel of that winter night?
His reason shall deny its joy,
my very breath blow out the light;

and still that haloed head, absurd
as winged children treading sky,
is truer than the seen and heard
within whose nets we daily die.

Thank you, Rhina.

RHINA ESPAILLAT: Thank you, Bill.

A.E. Stallings

A.E. Stallings is a distinguished poet and translator, generally considered one of the foremost poets of her generation. As *The Yale Review* has written: "A.E. Stallings is not a perfect poet but a poet of perfection, with the patience and courage to bring to her poems what American poetry so rarely knows how to give, and American readers hardly dare to receive: lapidary finish of both form and reading."

Raised in Decatur, Georgia, she was educated at the University of Georgia and received her master's degree in Classics at Oxford University. She is an editor of the *Atlanta Review* and the poetry program director at the Athens Centre. She lives in Athens, Greece, with her husband, John Psaropoulos, a freelance journalist, and their two children, Jason and Atalanta.

She is the author of three collections of poetry: *Archaic Smile* (1999), recipient of the Richard Wilbur Award; *Hapax* (2006), recipient of the Poets Prize; and *Olives* (2012), a finalist for the National Book Critics Circle Award. She also published a verse translation of Lucretius' *De Rerum Natura* (*The Nature of Things*) for Penguin Classics in 2007.

In 2011, she received a MacArthur Foundation Fellowship and a Guggenheim Fellowship. Her other recognitions include a Pushcart Prize, the Howard Nemerov Sonnet Award, the Eunice Tietjens Prize, an NEA grant in translation, and the Willis Barnstone Translation Prize.

This interview was conducted at the Exploring Form and Narrative Poetry Conference at West Chester University.

James Dickey once said that John Crowe Ransom spoke Greek with a Southern accent, and your own life has deep connections to both Greece and the South. Let's start in Georgia: did you grow up in Atlanta or in the city's suburbs?

A.E. STALLINGS: It was the suburbs then, but now it's considered part of the city. Back then, it was quite wooded, and our first house in Atlanta — which was actually unincorporated Decatur — was right next to a forest. As very little kids, we weren't allowed to play in the backyard without supervision because it led right into the forest. These days, I think it's all been built up, but back then it was very woodsy and green and wild.

What subject did your dad teach at Georgia State University?

A.E. STALLINGS: He was in the department of education (Educational Psychology), although he taught statistics. He was kind of a polymath who read everything and who ended up on all kinds of diverse committees, including some with the English department.

Your mom was a librarian. What kind of libraries did she work at?

A.E. STALLINGS: She worked at various things. Mostly, she was an elementary school librarian, although the official title was "media specialist." Eventually, she ended up teaching English as a second language. As young kids, we spent a lot of time in libraries; and, at least once a week, we would go to the Avis G. Williams Library with a big laundry basket to carry home the books we wanted. I don't know if kids still do that anymore, but it was very special back then.

As a child, you were deeply affected by fairy tales, and your poetry still reflects that interest. Could you discuss your life-long attraction?

A.E. STALLINGS: I think it began with my grandfather on my mother's side, who was an Episcopal priest. His parents were from Germany and Norway, and there wasn't much "child-appropriate" reading material in his library, except for the Grimm stories and Hans Christian Anderson. A lot of those stories, especially the Grimm tales, are very scary, and some of them are strange and long and mysterious. I don't know if they'd be considered child-appropriate these days. I can still remember stories where people would get their thumbs cut off — and other creepy stuff like that.

Did you read them with your grandfather, or just go off by yourself?

A.E. STALLINGS: I think I mostly went off by myself; I don't have many memories of Hop-Pop reading to us.

What was his name?

A.E. STALLINGS: Hop-Pop. I think I was the one who gave him that name. I was reading *Hop on Pop*, and the adults were trying to get me to say Pop-Pop, but I kept saying Hop-Pop instead, and the name stuck.

Did your parents read to you as a child?

A.E. STALLINGS: Yes, up to the point where I began reading on my own. On the other side of the family, my father's father was a terrific storyteller, and we would often listen for hours to his stories, mostly about his childhood in Kentucky, but he also knew all the old Uncle Remus stories. So my mother's side was more literary, but my father's side was more in the oral tradition. We'd sit there mesmerized, in a trance, and listen for hours. Sometimes they'd be stories we'd already heard before, because we'd say, "Granddaddy, tell us about the time you did this or you did that."

You once said that even as a child you always wanted to write books. Was that before or after you first heard "Tyger! Tyger!"?

A.E. STALLINGS: I think it was even earlier, and I still have a few of the little "books" I made back then. I was about four or so, and I would dictate the books, which were stapled with my name on the front. Often my name would include various initials, which I didn't fully understand, like "Alicia E. S." Maybe it was because my mother was a librarian that I had the sense that some people wrote books and that this was something you could actually do if you wanted.

Apparently, Blake's "The Tyger" made quite an impression.

A.E. STALLINGS: Yes, my father would recite a lot of poetry, and I was really into tigers at the time. I was in a "tiger phase," and I thought it was really cool that there was a poem about tigers.

What kinds of poems did your dad recite?

A.E. STALLINGS: A lot of the old classics, like *Hiawatha* or "The Rime of the Ancient Mariner." Things from his own education, but he'd also recite advertising jingles and song lyrics from his youth.

So you were already writing poetry in grammar school?

A.E. STALLINGS: Yes. I was writing poems and stories in my journals, which also included drawings.

When you were at Briarcliff High School, you actually published some poems in Seventeen Magazine, *which seems rather remarkable.*

A.E. STALLINGS: Early on, I was very focused on being a published writer. I'm not sure why. I wanted to send things out and be "professional," and I managed to get published in a number of little literary magazines, and I would also write for some of the glossy magazines, like *Horse Illustrated* or *Cat Magazine*. I never mentioned my age or gender or anything else, and eventually the little checks would come in the mail, and I would pretend I was a grown-up person.

Were you aware, say with a magazine like Seventeen, *that your poem was in a journal that was on newsstands all over the country? That you could go anywhere in America and go to a newsstand and find your work?*

A.E. STALLINGS: I guess so, but, for whatever reason, I seemed more focused on "selling" the poems. I really liked getting those checks in the mail!

You were quite the entrepreneur!

A.E. STALLINGS: I guess I was.

A.E. Stallings

Tell me a little bit about Mary Mecom, one of your high school English teachers.

A.E. STALLINGS: She was actually kind of a prickly teacher, and she scared a lot of us early on, which I think was part of her shtick. In the first few weeks of the class, she'd give you a D for something like a comma splice, when you were used to getting A's all the time, and it was a scare tactic that definitely worked — you'd never have a comma splice again! But she was very bright, and very interested in literature, as well as very demanding and uncompromising, and I liked all of those things.

Did she read your poems?

A.E. STALLINGS: I think she did read some of my poems, but not that many. In general, she wasn't very effusive, so any praise you could get would mean quite a lot. I remember one time she nominated me for a National Council of Teachers of English award, and I would sit during recess and write the appropriate essays, and when I won the award, she seemed very pleased.

Do you remember what poets you were reading at the time?

A.E. STALLINGS: In earlyish high school, I discovered Tennyson and Poe — probably in those *Harvard Classic* volumes — and their overall gloominess appealed to me, and I would carry their books around with me. Then, maybe in junior year, I became obsessed with T.S. Eliot. I wanted to *be* T.S. Eliot!

Is that where the "A.E." comes from?

A.E. STALLINGS: I think I believed that that's what professional writers did. You know, C.S. Lewis, J.R.R. Tolkien, W.H. Auden — and T.S. Eliot.

I thought you were also reading a lot of Hardy and Housman?

A.E. STALLINGS: That actually came a bit later. In high school, I struggled with my affection for Housman because it seemed like we were "supposed" to be heading in the direction of T.S. Eliot, but, later, I gave into it.

After you received a scholarship to the University of Georgia, you eventually switched your major from English and Music to Latin. How did that come about?

A.E. STALLINGS: The University of Georgia is a huge school, and it was a little hard to find your niche, and I wasn't terribly happy in the English department. And I had this idea, probably from T.S. Eliot, that there are important Latin and Greek tags that every writer needed to know. But I'd never had any Latin before, so I took a basic Latin course, and I loved it. I also loved how the department focused on the appreciation of literature — and how literature actually works — as opposed to the theoretical.

Were there any particular professors who influenced you at Georgia?

A.E. STALLINGS: There were a few, beginning with Robert Harris, who taught Latin 101, a course that made a tremendous difference in my life. He was a very eccentric teacher, but very appealing as well, and as soon as I'd expressed a flicker of interest in changing majors, Rick LaFleur, the department head, swooped me up, showed me the department, and made me feel very welcome. It really did feel like a little home within that big university. I never had the feeling that the English department really cared whether I was a major or not, but the Classics department certainly did, and I also liked my fellow students very much. We had a lot in common, and I'm still friends with almost half of them.

After graduation, you went to London to work, as you've described it, as a canteen manager at the Institute of Classical Studies.

A.E. STALLINGS: "Tea girl!" On my resume, I would put down "canteen manager," but I was really known as the tea girl.

So what was that all about? And what where you plans or motives?

A.E. Stallings

A.E. STALLINGS: To be honest, I didn't know what I was going to do. Back then, there was a program called BUNAC, which allowed graduates from British and North American universities to get a visa and work in Britain for six months to a year. You could travel or work to earn some money, and you were covered by National Health, which was a great deal. So my roommate at Georgia and I went over, and she ended up working in a pub, but I saw a notice on the BUNAC bulletin board about an opening for the "tea girl at the Institute of Classical Studies," and I said, "Of course, that sounds perfect, I'll apply for that," even though I never expected to get the job. But I did, and I was there for six months, and I got to know the director quite well — a very sweet man named Professor John Baron — who allowed me to audit some classes and get my Greek up to speed. So I was able to work within an academic milieu, but I also had time to write a lot of poems, and it was a very productive period. I guess washing teacups and gazing out the window was very conducive!

So how did Oxford come about?

A.E. STALLINGS: It was actually John Baron who suggested it, so I applied.

Had you applied to graduate school after you finished up at Georgia?

A.E. STALLINGS: Yes, and I was accepted in the Ph.D. program at Texas at Austin, but I deferred going so I could spend the six months in England, and then ended up at Oxford, although I eventually decided that I really didn't really want to do the Ph.D.

Wasn't one of your goals at Oxford to work with Richard Jenkyns?

A.E. STALLINGS: Yes, I'd read some of his books, and I felt that he really understood how poets wrote. About how, for example, someone like Virgil would have actually written, and how he would have made the choices he made. He was also especially interested in the classics and the English tradition, which is really my own primary interest — how the classics affect the English tradition and how the English tradition reflects back on the classics.

So how did things go at Oxford?

A.E. STALLINGS: Well, the Oxford tutorial system was quite a shock, especially after being in the American system, where you're constantly getting little pats on the back that you're doing okay, and taking this exam and then that exam. But at Oxford my whole degree was entirely dependent on a single exam. There were no grades leading up to that exam, or any other tests, and you had no idea if you were going to pass or not, and I found it very stressful. Also, the workload was so much heavier than I was used to. It felt like I was doing in one week what I might have done in a semester at Georgia in terms of sheer reading. You might get an assignment like, "Read Book Two of the *Aeneid*, bring in an essay, and here's the reading list." So I'd plow through the reading list, skipping the articles in German, and then start on my essay. And when I asked, "How long should my essay be?" Professor Jenkyns looked totally puzzled and said something like, "However long it needs to be." So I'd turn up at my tutorial, totally exhausted and stressed out and feeling a lot of insecurity because I was coming from the University of Georgia and not from Harvard — especially since all the other Americans seemed to be from Harvard — and I wasn't sure if my credentials would stand up. So I'd come in clutching my essay, handwritten in black felt-tipped pen the previous night in the college library — which is a very spooky place at night — and hand it in. And he'd say, "No, no, no, you must read it aloud." So it was a completely different experience from what I was used to in the U.S. Now I was expected to read aloud my own arguments and my own poorly-constructed sentences and my own little jokes in front of Richard Jenkins. And one time when I cut a corner in my paper by quoting only half of a line, he actually quoted the other half of the line because he knew it all from memory! So it was quite an experience; but, in time, I started to get the hang of it.

What about the time you couldn't do the assignment at all?

A.E. STALLINGS: Oh, yes! I was given an essay assignment about the Fall of Troy, Book Two of the *Aeneid*, and I did all the reading, and I read all the Latin, and I couldn't write a single word. I had a case of complete writer's block, and I stayed up all night, and since I couldn't write the essay, I wrote a poem, which is "Crazy to Hear the Tale Again," which ended up in *Archaic Smile*. So I walked into the tutorial, and he said, "Where's your essay?" and I said, "Well, I didn't write an essay. I wrote a poem." And he looked at me in a rather bemused fashion, and he said, "Well, then, read the poem." So I read the poem, and he said, "Well, all right, but you still need to write the essay." But before I left the room, he insisted on keeping the fair copy of the poem. So, in a way, it was sort of a compliment, although he didn't let me off on the essay.

Did he look at you as some kind of eccentric?

A.E. STALLINGS: Well, I think I was a bit atypical to begin with. Most of the American students were very, very diligent, and they would have *never* brought in a poem.

Earlier, at the Institute, you met John Psaropoulos, a Greek national, and after you finished at Oxford, you both came back to Atlanta. Were you married at that point?

A.E. STALLINGS: No, not yet — for many years we were "living in sin," but eventually we got married.

So what were you and John planning to do when you went to Atlanta?

A.E. STALLINGS: John had a job at CNN, which is where he got his start in journalism and producing for television, and I was just trying to write. I had this optimistic idea that I was going to support myself by writing novels, so I could have time to write my poems — just for pleasure. So I got a part-time job in my father's department at Georgia State with Professor Asa Hilliard, who was very prominent in African American studies, and it was a terrific job. It was a half-time job, with full benefits, and I had an office with a window, and he was a joy to work for. He gave me a free hand, and when my work was done, I'd just stay there in my office and work on my novel and my poems.

So how did you end up in Athens permanently?

A.E. STALLINGS: Well, we'd visited Greece quite a bit, so I had a reasonable idea what it would be like to live there; but, at the time in Atlanta, we were just cruising along and not very sure what was going to happen. But whenever the idea would come up, I'd say, "Well, I'm not going there as anyone's girlfriend." I'd seen that happen before, and it never worked out, and I felt that if you're going to make that kind of leap and commitment, then you should be doing it as a married couple, so we did.

Wasn't it around that time that you published what you've called your first "grown-up poem" in the Beloit Poetry Journal*?*

A.E. STALLINGS: That was around 1994.

So what became of the novel?

A.E. STALLINGS: When I was younger, I *always* wrote both poems and short stories, and I wrote a fantasy novel in high school. Then, at Oxford, I published a short story that actually got a favorable mention in the *London Times* by Margaret Drabble. So after graduate school, I decided to write a novel set at the University of Georgia in the classics department. I still don't think it's a bad novel, but back in '93, '94, and '95, I couldn't get anyone to look at it. I tried to get it to agents, but I made no progress at all, and that was around the same time that *Beloit* published my poem, which then got taken by *Best American Poetry*. So I realized that I probably wasn't going to make a living writing novels, and I also felt more comfortable dealing with things from my own life in poetry — in a more oblique way — rather than writing about such things in fiction, which felt more exposed.

Have you ever returned to writing fiction?

A.E. STALLINGS

A.E. STALLINGS: No, and I don't know whether I ever will again. But if I do get the overwhelming urge to start a story, I probably will. But these days, most of my prose energy goes into critical writing,

Returning to the poetry, I believe that you were not only reading Richard Wilbur and Seamus Heaney at the time, but also the English Georgians, who certainly weren't being given their due in those days.

A.E. STALLINGS: I really didn't know any better. I was very much autodidactic, and I would go into the London bookstores, and I'd find books and anthologies with poems by the old Georgians. I was especially into Robert Graves back then, and I read everything that I could lay my hands on *about* Robert Graves and *by* Robert Graves. And he and the other poets of that period were very important influences on my own writings.

Shifting back to the States, you once said that you admired the early work of your fellow Georgian, James Dickey, who was my mentor at South Carolina.

A.E. STALLINGS: Yes, I particularly love poems like "The Lifeguard" and "The Heaven of Animals." Even though he was no longer living in Georgia, he was considered one of the few "real" Atlanta writers back then, along with Turner Cassity and David Bottoms. They were poets who'd come from a place that, in many ways, doesn't seem very poetic. Atlanta had become a kind of carpetbagger town, but we grew up hearing stories about James Dickey, our "authentic" Georgian, and I went to a number of his poetry readings when I was still in high school. I remember one time my father pulled me out of school so I could attend a literary panel of some kind at Georgia State with Dickey and Bottoms and others. And Dickey was in his "difficult" mode at the time, and he took over the panel and answered every question! It was a bit of a fiasco, but a fascinating fiasco, and I remember that I asked him a stupid question, and he pretty much told me that it was a stupid question. But not that politely. I suppose it was probably a smart-alecky question from a little high school student. Years later, when I was in a poetry group with mostly older men in Atlanta, they would sometimes tell James

A.E. STALLINGS

Dickey stories about his drinking and his unfortunate behavior at parties, and my friend Tony Harrington would always say, "But for 'The Heaven of Animals,' St. Peter will forgive him everything." And I think he will.

I hope so. He was always great to me, but he certainly had his demons. Now let's turn more specifically to your own work. Since your first collection, Archaic Smile, *was published in 1999, you've published two subsequent collections,* Hapax *in 2006 and* Olives *in 2012. I'd like to discuss a number of your poems and certain recurring themes, starting with your celebrated use of Greek and Roman mythology. Your early poem, "Hades Welcomes His Bride" is a masterful dramatic monologue in blank verse in which the Lord of the Underworld takes his wary new bride on a tour of their living quarters. Hades speaks with both enthusiasm and irony as he leads his young wife to the bridal chamber:*

> What? That stark shape crouching in the corner?
> Sweet, that is to be our bed. Our bed.
> Ah! Your hand is trembling! I fear
> There is, as yet, too much pulse in it.

Could you discuss your obvious comfort with revitalizing the old myths in your work?

A.E. STALLINGS: That poem was actually composed at the Institute of Classical Studies while I was washing teacups and serving tea. As I was working, it was forming itself in the back of my head. For as long as I can remember, I've been fascinated by mythology. In Hop-Pop's library, there were a number of books about Norse mythology, which is especially dark, and the Underworld has always held a special attraction for me.

Why do you feel that contemporary writers can use such myths to their advantage?

A.E. STALLINGS: In the first place, you've already got a set of expectations to play off. People will often know some version of the story, and you can try to find ways to go in and alter the myth for your own purposes. It's also a great place for one's imagination to run free — to imagine something like an Underworld. It's also a lot of fun! But I'm not sure that these are really satisfying answers. Sometimes people will ask me about my "Underworld thing" — "What's your deal with the Underworld?" And for a while I thought maybe it was some kind of obsession with death, but I don't really think that's correct. Then I decided it was because I was living, so often, in basement apartments and was *literally* under the ground. Then I decided that maybe it had something to do with depression, but I don't think that's it either. Maybe I just love the scenes in the *Aeneid* where the Underworld is described — and in Dante too. It's a place, as is all mythology, where you can create a world that's both tangible and metaphorical at the same time. With the Underworld, you can make your own map of a literal subconscious, a subtext, a sub-everything.

Sometimes the language gets very contemporary, as in a more recent poem, "Persephone to Psyche," in which Hades' queen, no longer the frightened girl, remarks:

> This place is dead — a real dive.
> We're past all twists, rewards, and perils.
> But what the hell. We all arrive.

I like this poem, but isn't there a risk in making the language too contemporary?

A.E. STALLINGS: I've written a few poems that have definitely gone too far in that way, and for the most part I've wisely never published them. They run the risk of being a little too jokey — or too glib. On the other hand, there's actually a contemporizing tradition within the classics themselves that begins with Ovid and the *Heroides*, in which mythological women write letters to the mythological lovers who've dumped them. Letters like "Medea to Jason" and so on. So Ovid contemporized a number of the ancient myths, and some of them are pretty glib. But I'm still not sure how far we can go. I don't know if something like "Clytemnestra Goes to Her Shrink" can work. I think a poem has to be more than window dressing and certainly more than just a joke.

A.E. Stallings

If you go too far with it, you start to lose the depth of the original.

A.E. STALLINGS: Yes, and, for me, it only works if the characters seem like real people and the settings seem like real settings. It can't just be an excuse to put an ancient character in a modern setting.

Many of your other poems deal with personal matters: your youth; your parents; your sister, Jocelyn; your husband, John; your two children, Jason and Atalanta; and, especially more recently, the passage of time. You always find interesting ways to deal with this familiar subject, as in "Country Song," "Burned," "Dinosaur Fever," and one of my favorites, "Lovejoy Street," which begins:

> The house where we were happy,
> Perhaps it's standing still

Then the persona speculates:

> Perhaps new people live there
> Who think the street name quaint,

And then the poem ends:

> And maybe they are happy there,
> And do not know they are.

Do you feel that way about your own childhood?

A.E. STALLINGS: Actually, that's not a childhood poem. John and I once lived in a place on Lovejoy Street in Clarkston, which is near Atlanta. It was, I suppose, the "salad days" or our relationship, which you don't realize at the time. We loved the house, and we had lots of friends, and I think we were very content. The poem was actually written later in a more difficult period when we were adjusting to life in Greece, and it was hard to resist writing a poem about a place with a name like that.

When things are going well, it's often hard to appreciate it.

A.E. STALLINGS: Yes, almost impossible. Our move to Greece was hard in a number of ways, but also as a poet. What was I supposed to write about? I didn't want to just write travel/tourist poems about Greece, and it took me a while to realize that I could still write about Atlanta, and that I could still write about all the things that were now possibly enriched by being lost — and were still accessible.

A common motif in your poetry, especially in the last two collections, is "argument," a word that appears in a number of poems dealing with the subtle balance necessary in human relationships, especially between lovers, especially between spouses. Poets have been dealing with the subject for thousands of years, but you manage to find new ways to phrase the difficulties and the challenges:

> *The wind is pacing through the upper floors,*
> *Opening and slamming all the doors,*
> *Like an argument in married love*
> *Repetition will not cure it of. [from "Airing"]*

> *We fall mute, as when two lovers come*
> *To the brink of the apology, and halt,*
> *Each standing on the wrong side of the fault. [from "Aftershocks"]*

> *After the argument, all things were strange.*
> *They stood divided by their eloquence*
> *Which had surprised them after so much silence. [from "The Argument"]*

Are you conscious of this thread in your work?

A.E. STALLINGS: Well, I'm more conscious of it now!

Sorry.

A.E. STALLINGS: I think it's one of those things that poetry is especially good at exploring — differences and arguments. There's also the very useful rhetorical concept of the argument, being a kind of exposition with plot and so forth. I suspect that I've written most of those poems *after* arguments, when I'm in a more poetic mood.

But I don't think I have a really good answer for that question.

I was just curious if you knew it was a common thread in your work. Do you know that you also refer to laundry a lot — and cemeteries?

A.E. STALLINGS: Neither really surprises me! Early on in my career as a Greek housewife, I probably spent more time writing *about* the laundry than actually doing it. John would come home, and say, "Well, I guess the laundry hasn't been put out today," and I'd say, "No, but I wrote a poem about it!" In Greece, nobody owns a clothes dryer, so you put your laundry out on the clothesline, and there's something very thought-provoking — as with Richard Wilbur's famous poem — about seeing these empty, clean human forms hanging on the line. There's something very human about them, as if they're almost alive.

My brothers and I are cemetery-goers, visiting the dead. I hope that doesn't sound too creepy, but you've got a lot of cemeteries in your poems.

A.E. STALLINGS: I like going to cemeteries, and I find them kind of comforting. I don't know why.

I understand.

A.E. STALLINGS: In Athens, we live very close to the oldest cemetery in the city — in a city where land is at a premium. So, oddly enough, like the ancient sites, cemeteries are almost like parks. They're little islands of quiet and greenery in a very noisy, overcrowded, concrete, unplanned city. In fact, a lot of them are essentially little wildlife refuges with rare kinds of butterflies and flowers. We've also attended a lot of funerals; and, in Greece, death is more out in the open, and there's more of a rhythm to the mourning process. Unless you're from a very wealthy family with a mausoleum, at the end of three years, your bones are dug up and sent back to your family in a box — because there just isn't enough space.

Is that just in Athens proper?

A.E. STALLINGS: No, it's common in the islands as well, and in many other places in Greece. After a death, there's a forty-day period of intense mourning, and there are memorial services at nine days, forty days, one year, and three years, which all seems very natural. So it's very different from the States where six weeks after the burial, people are saying, "Snap out of it." Or, sometimes, even less than that — as soon as you've sent back the Pyrex dishes.

Some of my favorite poems are the creepy ones, like "Bad News Blues," "Deus Ex Machina," and "Ghost Ship," which is about a mysterious ship lost at sea:

> *There is no port where she can dock,*
> *She flies no flag,*
>
> *Has no allegiance to a state,*
> *No registry, no harbor berth,*
> *Nowhere to discharge her freight*
> *Upon the earth.*

Do these poems just "come"? Or do you start off in a mischievous mood?

A.E. STALLINGS: I like creepy poems too, although I'm not sure exactly where they come from. "Bad News Blues" and "Ghost Ship" were written not long after the death of my father, written under that shadow. "Ghost Ship" is a very Larkin-influenced poem, and "Bad News Blues" initially went through a whole range of forms, being a bad sonnet, bad quatrains, and so forth. Then I finally hit on the blues idea, and it clicked. Sometimes, oddly enough, people will read those poems and find them rather whimsical, even funny, but I assure them, "No, that's scary. I'm scared of it myself."

Don't worry, they're creepy! I also wanted to ask you about an interesting poem in Hapax *called, "Explaining an Affinity for Bats." Generally you seem to avoid the* ars poetica *poem, but I wonder if the ending of "Bats" relates to a poetic "affinity"?*

> *Who find their way by calling into darkness*

A.E. Stallings

To hear their voice bounce off the shape of things.

A.E. STALLINGS: Yes, I think it's pretty ars poeticky, but I *really* do like bats. At that point in our lives, we were living on the side of Mount Lykabettos in Athens, and every evening the bats would swarm off the mountain. I'm always delighted when I see bats. I suspect the poem is also influenced by the Wilbur poem, "Mind," and I actually went back and re-read the Wilbur poem to make sure I hadn't stolen anything. As for "bounce off the shape of things," I was translating Lucretius at the time, and that's a very Latin type of phrase: "the shape of things."

Cemeteries, the underground, creepy stuff, and bats.

A.E. STALLINGS: You should see my drawings! My parents still have this big box of my drawings from when I was about four years old, and when I looked them over I figured they must have been done around Halloween because they're all vampires, skeletons, bloody skeletons, bats, black cats, and jack-o-lanterns. Then I started looking at the dates and I discovered that was drawing them throughout the year. I can't imagine what my poor preschool teacher thought!

Last year, after you received a MacArthur grant, you said, "The first thing I plan to do is rent an office." Have you done so, and has it affected when and how often you're able to write?

A.E. STALLINGS: I did. During the previous year, there'd been an empty apartment next door to us, and I was always thinking, "I wonder how much that apartment is?" At that point, with our second child, my desk had been moved into the living room, and I really didn't have access to my books because they were in the children's room. I could always go out and work in a café, even with the throbbing music, but it was always such a nuisance to drag all your stuff with you, and then when you get there, you always discover that you'd forgotten something you needed. So the grant has allowed me to rent a place.

A.E. Stallings

The one next door?

A.E. STALLINGS: Yes, right next door. It's a little one-bedroom apartment, with good lighting, and I can pick up Wi-Fi from our house. It's so close that I can hear the children playing in the yard.

Could you discuss your method of composition? I believe that, except for translations, you never set out to write in a particular form or format.

A.E. STALLINGS: That's generally true. But sometimes if I'm stuck, I'll write a sonnet, but not a publishable sonnet, just something to get me going. Most of my published sonnets didn't start out as sonnets. They often start out as longer quatrain poems that I enjoy cutting down to size. But it really varies. Often, I'll have some kind of "entry" into the poem, often the first line, and I usually don't know where I'm headed until about three quarters of the way through. Then I start to see where it might end up, and, generally, I stumble upon the ending.

Are there any forms that you haven't used that you'd like to try?

A.E. STALLINGS: As someone who teaches a lot of forms, I sometimes feel a bit hypocritical, since there are so many that I've never done myself. I've never done a ballade, for example, or a ghazal, or a straight sestina.

How about the traditional ballad? I don't think you've ever done one of those.

A.E. STALLINGS: No, but it might happen sometime. Recently, I've been doing some longer poems in ottava rima.

Your husband, John Psaropoulos, who was the editor of the Athens News *for ten years, is also your first reader. You once said that John is right about "ninety-eight percent of the time." Is he still that accurate?*

A.E. STALLINGS: These days, with the two children, I don't always have my first reader available. But whenever we can make the time, I still like to show him my work, and he's usually a very good barometer of whether something's working or not. And, if not, where the problem lies. He's also very helpful about something that I'm not very confident about, and he'll say, "No, I really like this one." So I'll send it off to a really good journal, and it'll get taken. But sometimes it goes the other way, and he'll be very wary of something, but it'll turn out all right.

Do you revise sometimes if he says something like, "Well, I'm not sure about the ending," or "I'm not sure about this section"?

A.E. STALLINGS: Yes, many times. As poets get older and more experienced, we have the hope that we'll develop more of a sense of ourselves as writers, but I still have my doubts about lots of things.

You once said that, "Rhyme is a method of composition." Could you discuss that a little?

A.E. STALLINGS: Rhyme is often criticized in the mainstream, and often in the reviews of my books, with comments like, "This would be a really good poem if it didn't rhyme." I suspect that there's a belief among writers who don't rhyme themselves that you simply "know" what you're going to say and then you rhyme it. But I feel that rhymes give you the permission to say something shocking or something totally unexpected that you might not have thought of before. It's like stream of consciousness, and I think that's one of the reasons why rhyme seems threatening for some people. In general, people don't get very exercised about meter unless they write meter themselves. Those who don't write in meter simply don't hear it, but rhyme is pretty much in your face, and I think that's why it often provokes an emotional reaction from some people. But I believe it's a very powerful rhetorical device and a very powerful irrational method of persuasion. The advertising world certainly understands its power.

So how do you respond to people who claim that writing metrical poetry is restraining — or even a straightjacket?

A.E. STALLINGS: Again, like rhyme, I feel it's very much the opposite. It's helpful and effective to have some limitations on one's choices and even to "give up" some control over the poem. Which, I suppose, is a little scary for some people. To give up some control to the muse, to outer things. I feel there's almost a sort of Ouija Board feeling about rhyme and meter, where maybe you're in control, and maybe you're not. Or, at least, you're cooperating with some other forces — which I guess brings us back to the creepiness. Maybe it's a negative freedom, something like a negative capability type of freedom.

You've translated Catullus, Lucretius's The Nature of Things, *and you're now working on Hesiod. Do you think that your translating work affects your own poetry in any significant way?*

A.E. STALLINGS: It does. I think it's very useful for a poet to have a translation project underway because you can always get to work whether you're inspired or not. You can hammer out this or that, while using the same kind of muscles. But, again, it's also about giving up one's ego and control since it's not about you. It's also very useful to be trying other voices, other genders, and writing about other periods of time.

You need to be subservient, especially in translation.

A.E. STALLINGS: You do. Some translators are more interested in showing off their language skills as translators, but the best translators try to be of service to the original author and the original poem. In order to do that, you need to have a real chemistry with the person you're translating. I always have to have some sympathy with the poet and the poet's work. In my own case, I've done translations of many long, didactic poems by crotchety, sometimes misogynistic, dead white males. Whom I seem to have a great affinity for! With Hesiod, for example, we know about his background, and his family, and his brother, and where he lived, and how he felt about this and that. So it's a strange communion. A conversation with the dead.

A.E. Stallings

You once said that you felt the classical poets seemed more "contemporary" than much of modern American poetry. Could you discuss that a bit?

A.E. STALLINGS: There's excellent work being produced these days, but many writers seem to be limited to a conversation with the immediate generation preceding them — if that. They're very caught up in the present, and they think they're being very contemporary, but they're really just caught up in the contemporary mannerisms of our time, which will soon seem dated. They seldom seem like the ancient wedding guest who's really trying to buttonhole you and tell you something that's truly urgent. Or even something that's relevant. But when you read some of the Greeks and the Romans, say someone like Catullus, and he's talking about going to a dinner party where someone has stolen a napkin, you really feel like you know this person who's telling you this — like maybe you went to college with him. And he seems much more relevant to our own personal lives, and he does so within very elegant poetic forms.

How about the Fugitives? As a Southerner, do you feel any special affinity?

A.E. STALLINGS: Definitely. By an odd coincidence, when John and I were living in a basement apartment near Emory, our upstairs landlady was a niece of John Crowe Ransom — Julie Ransom — and John Crowe Ransom has always been very important to me.

He's my favorite of the Fugitives, and one of my favorites, period.

A.E. STALLINGS: I've always loved his essays and his poems and certain words and phrases that can't be dissociated from John Crowe Ransom, like "brown study."

And "transmogrified."

A.E. STALLINGS: Yes, "transmogrified." I have a bunch of old friends from college who've become part of this urban chicken movement, where urbanites and suburbanites are raising chickens, and whenever they email me about how one of their chickens died, and their children are distraught, I always tell them about the John Crowe Ransom poem.

"Old chucky."

A.E. STALLINGS: Yes, "old chucky." Ransom is one of those people who's written four or five perfect poems that will last forever, and that's as much as anyone can aim for.

It's now time to ask the inevitable but important question: what advice do you have for aspiring poets?

A.E. STALLINGS: Well, I think it's a good idea not to get too caught up in poetry as a "profession." Which is not to say I'm anti-MFA programs, which I think can work for some people, but I think the "professionalism" of poetry hasn't really helped American poetry very much. I would suggest that young poets read what they like to read, explore whatever they're attracted to, and write the way they want to write. Even if that's not what's in fashion or what's considered "cool." I think I was very fortunate to have gone about things in a very haphazard and amateurish and autodidactical way. I was always determined to be a professional writer, but I followed my own interests. It seemed to me that all the poets I admired had studied classics, so I went that route and found my own way, and I think every young poet, even in an MFA program, should find his or her own way. When I was young poet, I went through a period where I wasn't having much luck getting published, so I did a lot of readings, especially in the Atlanta area, and I was very involved in the spoken word scene, which was quite lively in the mid-'90s. And it was an important epiphany for me to realize that the point of poetry was *not* to be boring — that we shouldn't just write to get published — and that publication will eventually come if you write interesting poems that people enjoy.

I'd like to end our conversation today by reading the lovely ending of the first poem in your first collection, "A Postcard from Greece," about a near-fatal car crash:

A.E. Stallings

> *Somehow we struck an olive tree instead.*
> *Our car stopped on the cliff's brow. Suddenly safe,*
> *We clung together, shade to pagan shade,*
> *Surprised by sunlight, air, this afterlife.*

Thanks, Alicia.

A.E. STALLINGS: Thank you, Bill.

APPENDIX I.
Pound, Flint, Imagism, and Vers Libre

In 1914, Ezra Pound published *Des Imagistes* and initiated English-language Modernism. One of the most significant consequences of *Des Imagistes* was its successful promotion of *vers libre*. In the previous century, two talented metrical poets, Walt Whitman and W.E. Henley, had experimented with nonmetrical verse, but Whitman produced no real followers (and few admirers, excepting Ralph Waldo Emerson), and Henley's nonmetrical verse was obviously substandard and was essentially ignored. In France, some of the later Symbolists (particularly Arthur Rimbaud) had also experimented with *vers libre*, which, as Stéphane Mallarmé pointed out, was supposed to be, at most, a small, experimental "side chapel" in the great "cathedral" of metered poetry.

In 1914, Pound changed all that.

POUND (BRIEFLY)

Born in Hailey, Idaho, in 1885, Pound began college at the age of fifteen at the University of Pennsylvania, and he finished in 1905 at Hamilton College in upstate New York. After a master's degree at Penn, and a trip to France, Italy, and Spain to study the troubadour poets, Pound briefly taught at Wabash College in Indiana, where he was fired as a "Latin-Quarter type" for breaking the curfew rules. Unconcerned, the ambitious, talented, and flamboyant Pound sailed on a cattle boat for Europe, where he passed himself off as a tour guide to wealthy Americans in Spain and Italy, and where he also self-published for eight dollars his first collection of poems, *A Lume Spento* (1908). He was now ready to go to England.

The following year, after the death of George Meredith and Algernon Swinburne, the ever-confident William Butler Yeats declared, "And now I'm king of the cats." Regardless of Yeats's bravado, it was true, and Pound *knew* it was true in 1908 when he arrived in London, where the Irish poet was currently living. At the time, the British capital was the "where it's happening" place for aspiring English-language poets like Pound, and he quickly made alliances with young

British poets, like F.S. Flint and Richard Aldington, and with American expatriates, like Hilda Doolittle (whom he'd known in the States) and William Carlos Williams. Convinced that he needed to revive English verse, which he felt was stuffy, diffuse, and worn-out, Pound (along with Flint) created Imagism. It had three key principles:

1. Direct treatment of the "thing" whether subjective or objective.
2. To use absolutely no word that does not contribute to the presentation.
3. As regarding rhythm: to compose in the sequence of the musical phrase, not in sequence of a metronome.

In 1914, Pound published the first Imagist anthology, *Des Imagistes*. Two years earlier, in Chicago, Harriet Monroe had begun publishing a new poetry journal called *Poetry*, with Pound serving as her foreign correspondent. Thus, Imagism and its practitioners had great influence at the new poetry journal. Nevertheless, within a year of *Des Imagistes*, Pound had abandoned his new movement to another American expatriate, Amy Lowell, and he quickly moved on to create Vorticism, referring disparagingly to Imagism as "Amygism." Certainly, the Imagist emphasis on carefully crafted images did help to revive a visual specificity in English-language poetry. But most of the poems were short, with little substance, and with the unfortunate air of pretentiousness about them. Whatever one's response to the more famous of the Imagist poems, it's hard not to appreciate Howard Nemerov's dismissal of Imagist poems as "costume jewelry."

F.S. FLINT

Since Pound was essentially a medievalist (the troubadour poets), then where did Imagism really come from? Despite some borrowings from T.E. Hulme and the sinologist Ernest Fenollosa, it came mostly from F.S. Flint, who was an expert on French Symbolism, which became (along with Asian poetry) the primary theoretical model for Imagism. In 1908, six years before *Des Imagistes*, Flint had written an article in *The New Age* about the similarities of method between Mallarmé and the Japanese poets. It's quite significant that Frost (who was in London at the time, rejecting Pound's enticements to become an Imagist) and Edward Dahlberg both claimed that Flint was the true "founder" of Imagism.

MORE POUND

Pound, of course, had no interest in abiding by the limitations of his own Imagist constraints, so he quickly moved on to other kinds of verse. In 1920, he would again dramatically alter the history of modern English-language poetry by drastically editing the poetic fragments of his American protégé T.S. Eliot. The resulting poem, *The Waste Land*, was eventually published in *The Criterion* in 1922. It is impossible, of course, to overestimate the impact of both Imagism and *The Waste Land*. But Eliot's poem, unlike most of the little Imagist pieces, was highly literate and intellectual, and its disjunctive construction and its countless literary allusions created immense literary interest, especially among young poets and young professors (always readily attracted to the "new," especially when it has some "theoretical" basis). As a result, nonmetrical verse soon became the currency of the times.

AFTERMATH

The renowned British poet and historian Robert Conquest has discussed the results in his lecture, "But What Good Came of It at Last? An Inquest on Modernism," which he read at the General Meeting of England's Royal Society of Literature in 1979:

> As to free verse, once it had established itself in the 1920s in England it became pervasive. No more than a decade later school magazines of expensive girl's schools—always keener on "creativity" than boy's schools—were full of vague pieces of chopped up prose with vaguely emotional content. This may remind us that one notoriously bad effect of "free" verse is that large numbers of people educated during the last half century no longer understand the structure of real verse.
>
> W. H. Auden was to remark in his later years:
>
> > I cannot settle which is worse,
> > The Anti-Novel or Free Verse ...
>
> The truly astonishing discovery made by free versifier and anti-novelist alike was how much they could get away with. People have taken seriously, in recent times, novels consisting of loose

pages in a box which the reader is invited to shuffle in any order he likes. It was of such things, and the many worse ones which will be familiar to all of you, that Philip Larkin writes, "The adjective 'modern,' when applied to any branch of art, means 'designed to evoke incomprehension, anger, boredom, or laughter'" and defines modernism as "tending towards the silly, the disagreeable, and the frigid."

In a fuller context the same writer tells us:

> I dislike such things not because they are new, but because they are irresponsible exploitations of technique in contradiction of human life as we know it. This is my essential criticism of modernism, whether perpetrated by Parker, Pound, or Picasso: it helps us neither to enjoy nor endure. It will divert us as long as we are prepared to be mystified or outraged, but maintains its hold only by being more mystifying and more outrageous: it has no lasting power.

Certainly Larkin's comments, cited approvingly by Conquest, are rather incendiary. But Larkin (1922-1985), who is often considered the best English poet of the latter half of the twentieth century, raises important questions that need to be seriously considered. Are free verse poems "irresponsible exploitations of technique"? And, is it possible that free verse "has no lasting power"? Regarding the second question, there have been, ever since the publication of *Des Imagistes*, numerous predictions of doom for the free verse poetics. Maybe the most persuasive case was made by A.D. Hope in his 1950 essay entitled "Free Verse: A Post-Mortem." Hope (1907-2000), possibly Australia's most distinguished poet of the twentieth century, predicted that free verse had run its course and would eventually be seen as a historical anomaly. But this was before the Beats, the New York School, the Black Mountain poets, and the many other new groups that developed in the fifties and used free verse for their various purposes and thus encouraged the use of non-metrical verse. This was further encouraged by the development of creative writing programs in American universities, which hired American poets (most of them practitioners of free verse) as teachers. As a result, free verse increased its popularity among university-trained writers and became the dominant poetic mode, the status quo.

Nevertheless, these undeniable facts really don't adequately address Larkin's claim about "lasting power," since he wasn't writing about whether free verse would continue to be written. Larkin was, instead, claiming that free verse poems, because they lacked an underlying beat, would, as a consequence, also lack literary "staying power." This question will, naturally, be best answered several centuries from now, but the fact remains that after nearly a century of free verse domination, almost all of the most highly regarded English-language poets were metricists: Thomas Hardy, Edwin Arlington Robinson, William Butler Yeats, Robert Frost, and W.H. Auden. Pound and Eliot, of course, are special cases, especially since Eliot wrote much of his later work in various meters. A few decades ago, William Carlos Williams was generally regarded as the preeminent free verse poet of the twentieth century, but his reputation has clearly diminished.

Another interesting fact is that some of the most anthologized work by free verse poets is actually metrical. Examples include such indestructible poems as "We Real Cool" by Gwendolyn Brooks and "Traveling Through the Dark" by William Stafford. Stafford's gentle and evocative poetic touch made him the most imitated poet of the 1970s and 1980s, and a virtual free verse icon. Yet, this kindly man's most famous poem is basically blank verse (iambic pentameter). It begins:

> Traveling through the dark I found a deer
> dead on the edge of the Wilson River road.
> It is usually best to roll them into the canyon:
> that road is narrow; to swerve might make more dead.

As for Larkin's other charge—that free verse poems are "irresponsible exploitations of technique"—it might be more useful to ask if such verse is rather a mode that *lacks* a crucial technique. If human beings like rhythm, and if meter offers a species of rhythm that people have enjoyed since Chaucer, is it wise to eliminate it? Frost had no doubts, and he gave the world his famous analogy that free verse is "like playing tennis with the net down." We hear this comment so often that we seldom stop to consider how carefully constructed Frost's analogy actually is. Frost's free verse tennis players still have their racquets; they still have the same court boundaries; they still score in the same way; etc., but they are lacking one particular element of the game that seems fundamental. They have lowered the net. Now it might seem that a better analogy would portray the players competing on the court with the net actually removed, but even here Frost is accurate. If the net is rhythm, then the free verse players can still use various other sonic devices to create certain rhythmic effects. They will also have the natural "ghost" of meter that exists in all English-language writing, given the language's predominance of iambs. So the net is down. The meter is disrupted. And very few people would go to Wimbledon to see such a game of tennis.

POUND AGAIN

In the immediate aftermath of Imagism and Vorticism, Pound became disgusted with the metrical irregularity that he'd done so much to promulgate. He later explained his reactions in a famous essay that appeared in *The Criterion*.

> That is to say, at a particular date in a particular room, two authors, neither engaged in picking the other's pocket, decided that the dilution of *vers libre*, Amygism, Lee Masterism, general floppiness had gone too far and that some counter-current must be set going. Parallel situation centuries ago in China. Remedy prescribed "Emaux et Camées" (or the Bay State Hymn Book). Rhyme and regular strophes.
>
> Results: Poems in Mr. Eliot's *second* volume not contained in his first (*Prufrock*, Egoist, 1917), also "H. S. Mauberley."
>
> Divergence later.

As Pound recollects, he used both rhyme and (rough) meters in much of his famous poem "Hugh Selwyn Mauberley" (1920), which included quatrains that were clearly based on the hymnal measure of the Bay State Hymnal. While Eliot progressed with his own metrical studies, poems, and verse dramas, Pound clearly diverged "later," returning to a free verse of an even wilder construction for his epic poem, the *Cantos*.

In 1920, Pound moved to Paris, eventually migrating south to Rapallo, Italy, in 1925. While living in Italy, Pound not only supported the Fascist regime of Benito Mussolini, but he actually broadcast over Radio Rome a series of rather incomprehensible attacks against the United States, encouraging the American G.I.s to throw down their weapons. Thus, the most influential poet in the world had become a kind of fascist Tokyo Rose.

When the war ended, Pound was arrested for treason and placed in a restraining cage in the city of Pisa, and the following year, after being brought back to America, he was committed "of unsound mind" to St. Elizabeth's mental institution in Washington, D.C. Despite his behavior during the war and his blatant anti-Semitism, countless American poets visited Pound at the hospital, and his influence continued. In 1958, due to the intercession of a number of well-known poets (including Eliot, Archibald MacLeish, and even Frost), Pound was released from St. Elizabeth's, and he set sail for Italy. As soon as he arrived, he gave a fascist salute, called America "an insane asylum," and continued to mistreat his wife and avoid his son.

RECONSIDERATIONS

But, eventually, Pound's guilts—both literary and personal—caught up with him. In 1962, he admitted that he was "wrong, wrong, wrong. I've always been wrong." The following year he claimed, "Everything that I touch, I spoil. I have blundered always." In 1966, he admitted that his "opus," the *Cantos*, "don't make sense," and he dismissed his 803-page poem as "stupidity and ignorance." He called all of his work "a botch," saying, "I picked out this and that thing that interested me, and then jumbled them into a bag. But that's not the way to make a work of art."

And what of F.S. Flint, the co-creator of Imagism? Flint stopped writing poetry after 1920, claiming in a 1932 article for *The Criterion* that his own verse made him feel "physically ill." More importantly, in an interview in the 1950s, Flint claimed that, at the beginning, no one took Imagism "very seriously," admitting that it had been "a joke" started by a bunch of lively young people in London. Pound himself had admitted, back in 1915, that "the whole affair was started not very seriously chiefly to get H.D.'s [Hilda Doolittle's] five poems a hearing without its being necessary for her to publish a whole book."

These comments and later doubts by the founders of Imagism do not, of course, necessarily negate their founding principles, specifically free verse, but they should encourage all aspiring writers to carefully consider their choices. The fact remains that the founders of Imagism came to disavow their methods. This is a true story that, unfortunately, is not often told to young aspiring writers. Certainly, serious poetic artists need to experiment, but not all experiments are necessarily useful or permanent. Even in the seventeenth century, Milton, on rare occasions, experimented with a looser metric, as did later poets like Blake, Dryden (surprisingly), and Christopher Smart. Nevertheless, Smart's contemporary, Samuel Johnson, in his famous dictionary, still defined poetry as "metered language," and prose as "unmetered language." Oddly enough, even now, after nearly a hundred years of *vers libre*, the current *Random*

House Webster's still defines poetry as "literary work in metrical form" and prose as "the ordinary form of spoken or written language, without metrical structure, as distinguished from poetry or verse." Johnson, like most poets in the great tradition, believed that meter was "indispensably necessary to a poet." As he explained:

> However minute the employment may appear, of analysing lines into syllables, and whatever ridicule may be incurred by a solemn deliberation upon accents and pauses, it is certain, that without this petty knowledge no man can be a poet; and that from the proper disposition of single sounds results that harmony that adds force to reason, and gives grace to sublimity; that shackles attention, and governs passion.

Tennis, anyone?

APPENDIX II.
The Formalist Revival

A BRIEF HISTORICAL NOTE

For many decades, American poetry has been dominated by free verse. It fills the literary journals; it's taught in the classrooms; and it's the most common form of poetic expression. Yet, at the present time, there's a sizable and active Formalist community within the larger world of American poetry. Although various people have claimed credit for this revival, it was essentially a logical reaction against the limitations of free verse that affected disparate members of the baby boom generation. These poets realized that the contemporary poetry of the sixties and seventies had abandoned something of great value—meter—which had powerfully enhanced the great poetic works of the past.

THE FIFTIES, SIXTIES, AND SEVENTIES

Despite the fact that a number of distinguished poets—like Howard Nemerov, Richard Wilbur, Anthony Hecht, and James Merrill—continued to write and publish formal poetry, the dominant trend in the late 1950s, the 1960s, and the 1970s was for short, free verse lyrics, often autobiographical. The emergence of various groups like the Beats, the Black Mountain poets, the New York School, the Deep Imagists, and others encouraged this trend, as did the fact that free verse quickly became the lingua franca of the newly forming creative writing programs in the American universities. With the exception of some metrical poetry written by established senior poets, by the 1970s, very little formal verse was being published in the literary journals, and both meter and rhyme were considered, at best, an outdated aspect of the literary past, or, much worse, a debilitated form of bourgeois or capitalist control. Occasionally, these attacks, at their worst and most shrill, even descended into fantastic charges that formal poetry was actually "fascist" (as William Carlos Williams once delineated the sonnet), in spite of the fact that most of the best poets of the twentieth century had used poetic forms, and that even leftists like

Federico García Lorca and Pablo Neruda (a Communist) had also written in traditional forms.

In 1972, X.J. Kennedy and his wife Dorothy initiated a short-lived journal called *Counter/Measures*, and they received an "enormous volume" of interested mail. Kennedy, born in 1929, was a member of the generation between the senior poets (like Nemerov) and the baby boomers. Kennedy, along with other established poets like Miller Williams, Lewis Turco, James Whitehead, and Dick Allen, had chosen not to abandon poetic forms despite a sometimes hostile environment.

Despite that environment, various younger poets of the baby boom generation, often in isolation, began writing in meter, forms, and rhymes. The influence of Yvor Winters at Stanford led Timothy Steele to attend graduate school at Brandeis, where he studied with Winters' former student, J.V. Cunningham. Similarly, at Louisiana State University, another of Winters' former students, Donald E. Stanford, had an important influence on a number of young poets, including Wyatt Prunty, David Middleton, and John Finlay. At Harvard, the influence of Robert Fitzgerald and several other professors encouraged poets like Rachel Hadas, Dana Gioia, Brad Leithauser, and Mary Jo Salter. Nevertheless, there was no true center for the gradually reviving Formalism, as many isolated young poets in various parts of the country began experimenting with meter and rhyme.

So where did the revival begin? People can debate this endlessly, but it's certainly significant that Rachel Hadas's first chapbook, *Starting From Troy*, was published by Godine in 1975; Charles Martin's first book, *Room for Error*, was published in 1978; and Timothy Steele's first collection, *Uncertainties at Rest*, appeared the following year.

THE EIGHTIES

The 1980s were the decade of formation for the Formalist revival. Many of the new metrical poets published their first books in this decade, and others wrote articles and essays defending the practice of formal poetry. From 1979–1982, Frederick Turner and Ronald Sharp served as the editors of the newly revived *The Kenyon Review*, in which they published both poems and literary essays by the new generation of poets. At the same time, Brad Leithauser was writing several excellent essays for *The New Criterion*, particularly "Metrical Illiteracy," which appeared in January 1983. Two years later, Frederick Turner and Ernst Pöppel published their seminal and award-winning essay, "The Neural Lyre:

Poetic Meter, the Brain, and Time," in *Poetry Magazine*. This in-depth essay discussed new scientific evidence for the neurological foundations of the human pleasure response to regular rhythm.

Thus, gradually, the larger literary world began to take notice of the new metrical poets, who were dubbed "the New Formalists" in a negative article entitled "The Yuppie Poet" written by Ariel Dawson for the *AWP Newsletter* (May 1985). Nevertheless, a number of the mainstream literary journals began to include metrical poetry within their pages, including *The Southern Review*, *Poetry Magazine*, and *The Hudson Review*. Later in the decade, two valuable anthologies appeared that highlighted contemporary formal poetry by writers of all generations: *Strong Measures: Contemporary American Poetry in Traditional Forms* (1986), edited by Philip Dacey and David Jauss; and *The Direction of Poetry: An Anthology of Rhymed and Metered Verse Written in the English Language Since 1975* (1988), edited by Robert Richman.

Also particularly significant at mid-decade was the creation of Story Line Press by Robert McDowell in 1985. In subsequent years, McDowell would publish several of the new voices in the Formalist revival, especially through the press's annual Nicholas Roerich Poetry Prize (now called the Frederick Morgan Poetry Prize in honor of the late founding editor of *The Hudson Review*). McDowell was also the co-editor, with Mark Jarman, of *The Reaper* (1981–1989), a journal of narrative poetry that further expanded contemporary poetic possibilities beyond the free verse lyric. At the end of the decade, the poet Wyatt Prunty, a professor at the University of the South in Sewanee, Tennessee, became the founding director of the extremely influential Sewanee Writers' Conference. The intensive poetry workshops at this annual summer gathering were taught by senior faculty members (like Howard Nemerov, Mona Van Duyn, Donald Justice, or Anthony Hecht) along with a member of the Formalist revival (such as Charles Martin, Rachel Hadas, Andrew Hudgins, or Mary Jo Salter).

THE NINETIES

The year 1990 saw the publication of the first issue of *The Formalist: A Journal of Metrical Poetry* (which I edited); the publication of Timothy Steele's masterful critical study, *Missing Measures: Modern Poetry and the Revolt Against Meter*; and the initial issue of *Hellas: A Journal of Poetry and the Humanities*, edited by Gerald Harnett. In 1994, *Sparrow*, edited by Felix Stefanile, rededicated itself entirely to the sonnet, and several other formalist-friendly journals were initiated: *The Edge City Review* (1994); *The Dark Horse* (1995); the revived *Pivot* (1995); *The Tennessee Quarterly* (1995), and *Janus* (1996).

The early nineties also saw the publication of important critical works by two of the leading figures in the Formalist revival: Wyatt Prunty's *"Fallen From the Symboled World": Precedents for the New Formalism* (1990) and Dana Gioia's *Can Poetry Matter?: Essays on Poetry and American Culture* (1992). Four years later, Story Line Press published *Rebel Angels: 25 Poets of the New Formalism*, an anthology edited by Mark Jarman and David Mason; and, in 1998, the University of Evansville Press initiated the Richard Wilbur Poetry Award, an annual book competition that has created further publishing possibilities for Formalist poets.

At mid-decade, Dana Gioia and co-director Michael Peich initiated another extremely important writers' conference. The Exploring Form and Narrative Poetry Conference began in the summer of 1995 at West Chester University in Pennsylvania, and it provided, among other features, specialty writing workshops conducted by such revivalist poets as Timothy Steele, Emily Grosholz, and R.S. Gwynn. Within a few years, the annual West Chester gathering was the largest summer poetry conference in America.

THE TWENTY-FIRST CENTURY

At the present time, the Formalist revival is ever-expanding and as vibrant as ever. The pleasures, challenges, and rewards of writing metrical poetry are constantly attracting serious poets from the younger generations. Despite some residual complaints from the free verse orthodoxy, formal poetry is generally accepted as a viable poetic option, and the anathematizing attacks of the previous decades are fewer in number and essentially insignificant.

In the meantime, two new journals have stepped forward to replace those that have been discontinued: *Iambs & Trochees* (2001) and *Measure* (2006). In 2000, Kevin Walzer founded Word Press in Cincinnati, which has published many books by poets associated with the Formalist revival. Also, several new and exciting poetry prizes that include book publication have been initiated: the Donald Justice Poetry Award, directed by Michael Peich at West Chester University; the Anthony Hecht Poetry Prize, directed by Philip Hoy at England's Waywiser Press; and the Anita Dorn Poetry Prize, directed by Alfred Dorn of New York City.

In retrospect, the current Formalist revival has many similarities with the great Romantic revival of the early nineteenth century. Both revivals breathed new and passionate life into the traditional poetic forms while simultaneously emphasizing the contemporary idiom. While it's certainly true that contemporary Formalism is still a literary subset of the overall poetry world, it proudly traces its roots back to Chaucer (and to Homer as well), seeing itself as the natural extension of the great tradition of English-language poetry.

Index

A

A Lume Spento, 323
Abba Abba, 150
Aeneid, The, 32, 111, 306, 307, 311
Aerialist, 21
Aldington, Richard, 324
Allen, Dick, 133, 332
Amahl and the Night Visitors, 229
American Arts Quarterly, 183
American Poetry Review, 49
American Scholar, The, 1, 100, 277
Amherst College, 107
Anderson, Daniel, 7, 22
Anderson, Hans Christian, 300
Anderson, Sherwood, 235
Antaeus, 166
Aquinas, Thomas, 244
Aristotle, 76, 244
Armstrong, John, 188
Aspects of the Novel, 97
Athens News, 317
Atlanta Review, 299
Atlantic Monthly, The, 47, 205, 211-212, 229
Auden, W.H., x, 5, 31, 40, 41, 47, 60, 70, 81, 208, 266, 271-272, 303, 325, 327
Aurelius, Marcus, 72
Avery, Peter, 257
AWP, 133
AWP Newsletter, x, 49, 333

B

Baez, Joan, 2, 230
Baldwin, James, 64
Balzac, Honoré de, 69
Barber, Charles, 96
Baron, John, 305
Barth, R.L., 242, 245
Baudelaire, Charles, 34, 40, 102
Bawer, Bruce, 177
Bayley, John, 188
Beach Boys, The, 51-52
Beat Poets, 39, 40, 190, 326, 331
Beethoven, Ludwig van, 2
Belli, G.G., 155-156
Bellow, Saul, 35
Beloit Poetry Journal, 308
Bennett, Bruce, 115
Berry, Wendell, 240
Berryman, John, 113
Best American Poetry, 308
Bible, The, 141, 217, 228, 230, 238, 295
Biographia Literaria, 73
Bishop, Elizabeth, x, 6, 21, 33, 34, 40, 41, 110-111, 113, 115, 145, 155, 209-210, 224
Black Mountain Poets, 40, 326, 331
Blake, William, 244, 254, 301-302, 329
Blass, Bill, 169
Bleak House, 69
Bogan, Louise, 70
Bone, Paul, xi
Borges, J.L., 127
Borzoi Reader Online, The, 219
Boston University, ix
Bosworth, Edmund, 257
Bottoms, David, 309
Bowers, Neal, 179
Bowers, Edgar, 52, 70, 71, 231, 258, 259, 263, 266, 272

Index

Brache, Rafael, 277
Brame, Gloria Glickstein, 95
Brandeis University, 63, 67, 69, 332
Bread Loaf School of English, 86
Bread Loaf Writers' Conference, 7, 86
Bridgford, Kim, xi
Brodsky, Joseph, 205
Brontë, Branwell, 243
Brooks, Gwendolyn, 327
Brosman, Catharine Savage, 227
Brown, Clarence, 92
Browning, Robert, 74, 163
Buchan, John, 185
Bunyan, John, 23
Burgess, Anthony, 35
Burke, Edmund, 201
Burns, Robert, 88, 152
Byrd, William, 246
Byron, Lord, 118, 180

C

Calder, Norman, 257
California State University, Los Angeles, 63, 81
Cambridge University, 205, 211, 212, 251, 252, 253, 254, 255, 257, 260
Campion, Thomas, 2
Canterbury Tales, The, 272
Canto, 26
Cantos, The, 32, 328, 329
Carroll, Lewis, 207
Carver, Raymond, 172
Cassity, Turner, 71, 309
Cat Magazine, 302
Catholicism, 30, 32, 33, 34, 43, 142, 281
Catullus, 137, 147-148, 319, 320
Cavafy, Constantine, 35, 42, 93
Cecil, David, 188
Cedar Rock, 166
Chandler, Raymond, 69, 255
Chaplin, Charlie, 170
Chappell, Fred, 242-243
Chaucer, Geoffrey, 81, 151, 211, 272, 327, 335
Child's Garden of Verses, A, 64

Chronicles of Narnia, The, 185
Cicero, 98
Clampitt, Amy, 222
Cleary, Meghan, 224, 226
Close, Ann, 222
CNN, 307
Coleman, Eliot, 4
Coleridge, Samuel Taylor, 50, 71
Collins, Wilkie, 69
Columbia University, 85, 86, 87
Confessional Poetry, 39, 40, 43, 49, 179
Conquest, Robert, 76, 255, 325
Cooper, Gary, 216
Cope, Wendy, 173
Core, George, 236
Corn, Alfred, 222
Coulette, Henri, 71
Counter/Measures, 26, 332
Cowper, William, 147
Creeley, Robert, 138, 190
Criterion, The, 325, 328, 329
Culture of Narcissism, The, 166
Cummings, E. E., 40, 64, 88, 135, 136, 146, 229
Cunningham, J. V., 6, 63, 67, 75, 231, 254, 272, 332
Curtis, Michael, 212

D

Dacey, Philip, 333
Dahlberg, Edward, 324
Dale, Peter, 211
Dante, x, 23, 32, 45, 247, 248, 271, 311
Darbandi, Afkham, 256, 257, 262, 266, 267, 268
Dark Horse, The, 334
Darling, Robert, 116
Davenport, Guy, 154
Davidson, Donald, 236-237
Davie, Donald, 67, 255
Davis, Dick, 26, 71
  Works: "A Bit of Paternity," 266; "A Christmas Poem," 265; "Afkham," 266; *A Kind of Love: New and Selected Poems*, 251; *A Trick of Sunlight*, 251, 269; "Aubade," 264; "Author, Translator . . .," 269; "A World Dies . . .," 262-263; *Belonging*, 251;

Borrowed Ware: Medieval Persian Epigrams, 251, 268; "Déjà Lu," 267; "Exiles," 263; "Farewell to the Mentors," 266; "Guides for the Soul," 264; "Growing Up," 265; *In the Distance,* 251, 259, 260; "In the Gallery," 263; "Maximilian Kolbe," 265; "Memories of Cochin," 267; "Monophyme for the Shower," 266; "Out of Time," 259; "Political Asylum," 263; "Preferences," 267; "Rembrandt's Return of the Prodigal Son," 265; "Secrets," 260; *Seeing the World,* 251; *Selected Writings of Thomas Traherne,* 251; "Shadows," 266; "6 A.M. Thoughts," 274; *The Conference of Birds,* 251, 257, 268; *The Rubaiyat of Omar Khayyam,* 251, 268-269; *The Shahnameh: The Persian Book of Kings,* 251, 268; "There," 265; "To the Memory of My Brother," 259; *Touchwood: Poems 1991-1995,* 251, 260; "Touring a Past," 262; *Vis and Ramin,* 251, 271; "West South West," 261; *Wisdom and Wilderness: The Achievement of Yvor Winters,* 251, 259

Davison, Peter, 212
Dawson, Ariel, x, 49, 333
de Rachewiltz, Mary, 32
Deep Imagist Poets, 40, 104, 165, 169, 331
Defoe, Daniel, 145
DeMille, Cecil B., 52
Des Imagistes, 323, 324, 326
Dickens, Charles, 69, 185, 188
Dickey, James, 15, 178, 299, 309-310
Dickinson, Emily, 15, 70, 93, 179, 219, 224, 254, 297
Dillon, Wentworth, 270
Dinosaur Dilemma, The, 108
Direction of Poetry, The, 333
Divine Comedy, The, 32, 45
Don Juan, 118
Donahue, Charles, 136
Donne, John, 21, 163, 272
Donovan, 230
Doolittle, Hilda, 324, 329
Dorn, Alfred, 334
Dos Passos, John, 64
Dostoyevsky, Fyodor, 24
Doyle, Arthur Conan, 185
Drabble, Margaret, 308
Drummond, William, 74

Dry Sun, Dry Wind, 112
Dryden, John, 50, 151, 165, 274, 329
Duncan, Harry, 35, 36
Duncan, Robert, 190
Dyer's Hand, The, 70
Dylan, Bob, 2, 230

E

Earle, Robert, 164
Eddington, Arthur, 197
Edge City Review, The, 334
Edwards, George, 85, 94-95, 105
El Corte Massacre, 277-278
Eliot, T. S., 23, 40, 60, 64, 74, 75, 76, 83, 188, 229, 232, 238, 282, 303, 304, 325, 327, 328, 329
Emerson, Ralph Waldo, 11, 323
Emory University, 320
Empson, William, 142
England, Eugene, 66
Engle, Monroe, 110
Erikson, Eric, 90
Espaillat, Rhina P., xi
  Works: *Agua de do rios/Water from Two Rivers,* 277; "Almost," 290-291; "Bilingual/Bilingüe," 280; "Contingencies," 290; *El olor de la memoria: cuentos/The Scent of Memory: Short Stories,* 277; "Evan Breathing," 287-288; "For the Lady in the Black Raincoat Who Slept through an Entire Poetry Reading," 288; *Her Place in These Designs,* 277, 291, 293; "If There Had Been," 290; "January '41," 291-292; *Lapsing to Grace,* 277, 286; "Nativity," 297-298; "On the Impossibility of Translation," 294; *Playing at Stillness,* 277; "Poetry Reading," 289-290; "Prosody," 288; *Rehearsing Absence,* 277, 286; "The Ballad of San Isidro," 294; *The Shadow I Dress In,* 277; "Translation," 294; "Triptych," 291; "Warning:," 289; *Where Horizons Go,* 277, 286; "Workshop," 286-287, 288

Espy, John, 76
Esquire, 38, 47
Exploring Form and Narrative Poetry Conference, xi, 29, 50, 57-58, 82, 85, 159,

251, 272, 277, 299, 334

F

Fairchild, B.H., 170
Faulkner, William, 12, 235
Feldman, Irving, 138
Fenollosa, Ernest, 324
Ferguson, Margaret, 223
Ferlinghetti, Lawrence, 190
Field, Eugene, 30, 64
Fields, Kenneth, 67
Finlay, John, 5, 26, 230, 231-233, 248, 259, 332
First Things, 277
Fitzgerald, Edward, 257, 266, 268-269
Fitzgerald, Robert, 32, 33, 34, 41, 58, 88-89, 91, 110, 111-112, 196, 209, 210, 332
Flaubert, Gustave, 34
Flint, F.S., xi, 323, 324-325, 329
Foote, Horton, 18, 21
Ford, Ford Maddox, 76
Fordham University, 133, 136, 137
Formalist, The, ix, x, 19, 143, 180, 333
Forster, E.M., 97, 257
Foucault, Michel, 34
Fourteen on Form: Conversations with the Poets, x
Fraser, J.T., 193
Fresh Meadow Poetry Workshop, 284
Frost, Robert, 2, 5, 26, 40, 42, 49, 50, 64-65, 70, 73, 74, 77, 81, 86-87, 93, 99, 102, 126, 163, 208, 218, 229-230, 239, 240, 296, 297, 327-328, 329
Fry, Christopher, 60
Fugitives, The, 25, 236-237, 320
Fussell, Paul, 58

G

Gardner, Helen, 188
Garton, Charles, 147
Galileo, 218
Gasset, Ortega y, 73
Georgia State University, 300, 307
Georgians, The, 309
Gibson, John, 253-254

Ginsberg, Allen, 91, 190
Gioia, Dana, x, xi, 29-62, 70, 82, 88, 104, 159, 171, 178, 179, 202, 332, 334

Works: *The Barrier of a Common Language*, 61; "Beware of Things in Duplicate...," 45; "Can Poetry Matter?," 47; *Can Poetry Matter?: Essays on Poetry and American Culture*, 29, 47, 61, 334; "The Corner Table," 41; "Counting the Children," 43-45; "Cruising with the Beach Boys," 41, 51, 52; *Daily Horoscope*, 29, 36, 39, 40, 41, 54, 61; "Do Not Expect...," 61; "The End of the World," 46; *The Gods of Winter*, 29, 54; "Guide to the Other Gallery," 45; "Insomnia," 42; *Interrogations at Noon*, 29, 41, 54, 56; "Interrogations at Noon," 42; *An Introduction to Fiction*, 29; *Literature: An Introduction to Fiction, Poetry, and Drama*, 29; *An Introduction to Poetry*, 29; "The Litany," 56; "The Memory," 41; *Nosferatu: An Opera Libretto*, 29, 59; "Prayer," 46; "Speaking of Love," 41; "Summer Storm," 41; "Thanks for Remembering Us," 45; "Time Travel," 45; "The Letter," 45-46; *Tony Caruso's Final Broadcast*, 60

Goethe, 199
Goldsmith, Oliver, 151
Gonne, Maud, 80
Grant, Cary, 215
Graves, Robert, 309
Greenblatt, Stephen, 202
Gregory, Horace, 149
Griffith, Rob, xi
Grimaldi, William, 137
Grimm, The Brothers, 300
Grosholz, Emily, 94, 98, 104, 334
Gross, John, 107
Gullens, Charles, 71
Gunn, Thom, 70, 71, 254, 255
Gwynn, R.S., 159-181, 334

Works: "Among Philistines," 167-168, 171, 174; "At Rose's Range," 167, 178; "At the Center," 171; *Bearing and Distance*, 159, 165, 166; "Before Prostate Surgery," 171; "Body Bags," 167; "Bone Scan," 171; "Cléante to Elmire," 175, 176; *Contemporary American Poetry*, 159; "Dogwatch," 161, 174,

176; "Horatio's Philosophy," 169; *New Expansive Poetry: Theory, Criticism, History,* 159; "1969," 181; *No Word of Farewell: Selected Poems,* 159, 167, 168, 171, 181; *Poetry: A Pocket Anthology,* 159; "Randolph Field, 1938," 161; *The Advocates of Poetry: A Reader of American Poet-Critics of the Modern Era,* 159, 177, 178; "The Ballad of Burton and Bobby and Bill," 167, 168; "The Classroom at the Mall," 168; "The Dark Place," 169; "The Denouement," 168; *The Drive-in,* 159, 160, 167; "The Great Fear," 168, 171; *The Narcissiad,* 159, 165, 166, 180; "The Professor's Lot," 168; "The Slave Ship," 176-177; "Untitled," 170

H

Hacker, Marilyn, 71, 210
Hadas, Moses, 85-86, 97, 98
Hadas, Rachel, x, 332, 333

> Works: "Alternatives," 101; *A Son from Sleep,* 94; "Benefit Night, New York City," 99; "Flying Home," 104; *Halfway Down the Hall: New and Selected Poems,* 85; *Helen* (Euripides), 85; *Incredible,* 85; "In the Grove," 97; *Merrill, Cavafy, Poems, and Dreams,* 85; "Moments of Summer," 97; *Other Worlds Than This: Translations,* 85; *Pass It On,* 98; "Roadblock," 96; *Slow Transparency,* 92; *Starting from Troy,* 91, 332; "The Blue Bead," 92; "The Compact," 100; *The Empty Bed,* 85; "The Red Hat," 94-95, 99; "Water and Fire," 92, 105

Haggard, Rider, 184
Hall, Donald, 41, 50
Halpern, Daniel, 166
Hamilton College, 323
Hamlet, 169
Hammond, Mac, 138
Hardy, Thomas, x, 54, 70, 74, 81, 93, 171-172, 220, 239, 282, 287, 297, 303, 327
Harnett, Gerald, 333
Harrington, Tony, 310
Harris, Robert, 304
Harrison, Bill, 165
Harvard Advocate, The, 209
Harvard University, ix, 18, 29, 32, 33, 34, 85, 88, 91, 93, 107, 110, 112, 113, 205, 208-211, 306, 332
Hass, Robert, 147
Heaney, Seamus, 309
Heart's Needle, 112
Hecht, Anthony, x, 21, 26, 48, 49, 50, 70, 110, 112, 113, 128, 150, 154, 177, 212, 214, 222, 331, 333
Heidegger, Martin, 11
Heine, Heinrich, 176-177
Hellas, 333
Hemingway, Ernest, 64
Henderson, Alva, 59-60
Henley, W.E., 323
Henry, Marguerite, 65
Herbert, George, 21, 23, 74, 120, 163, 211, 217, 238, 272
Hernandez, Miguel, 294
Heroides, 311
Herrick, Robert, 21, 23
Hersch, Fred, 225
Hesiod, 319
Hiawatha, 120, 302
Hill, Geoffrey, 232
Hilliard, Asa, 307-308
Hine, Daryl, 139
Hitler, Adolf, 200
Hopkins, Gerard Manley, 93, 189, 197, 272
Hollander, John, 49, 87, 89, 91, 139, 155
Hollins College, 163
Hollins Critic, The, 178
Homage to Catalonia, 64
Homer, x, 32, 52, 247, 248, 295, 335
Hop on Pop, 301
Hope, A.D., 326
Hope Abandoned, 210
Hope Against Hope, 210
Horace, 102, 137, 215
Horse Illustrated, 302
Housman, A.E., 266, 282, 303-304
Howard, Richard, 87
Howe, Tina, 18
Hoy, Philip, 334

Index

Huckleberry Finn, 68
Hudgins, Andrew, 333
Hudson Review, The, 70, 277, 333
Hulme, T.E., 324
Hunter College, 277, 282, 291

I

Iambs & Trochees, 334
Idylls of the King, 94
Iliad, The, 70
Imagism, 99, 149, 323-325, 328, 329
Institute of Classical Studies, The, 304-305, 310
Irwin, John, 7, 20

J

Jacobs, Catherine Haydon, 281
James, Henry, 212
James, William, 72, 83
Janus, 334
Jarman, Mark, 333, 334
Jarrell, Randall, 16, 115, 127-128, 163, 177
Jauss, David, 333
Jeffers, Robinson, 49, 50
Jefferson, Thomas, 218
Jenkyns, Richard, 305-306
Jerome, Judson, 166
John of the Cross, 289, 294
Johns Hopkins University, The, 1, 4, 7, 8, 14, 17, 85, 91, 92, 133, 152, 154, 155, 205
Johnson, Samuel, 238, 244-245, 329-330
Jonson, Ben, 2, 70, 74, 232
Joyce, James, 83, 156
Jungle Book, The, 185
Justice, Donald, 6, 7, 15, 16, 17, 21, 48, 49, 50, 112, 169, 333
Justin Morgan Had a Horse, 65

K

Kael, Pauline, 162-163
Kant, Immanuel, 11
Keats, John, 64, 70, 81, 93, 102, 156, 189
Kees, Weldon, 37, 40, 42, 169
Keller, Johanna, 153

Kelly, Robert, 135
Kennedy, Dorothy, 332
Kennedy, X.J., 59, 63, 70, 71, 133, 173, 251, 286, 332
Kenner, Hugh, 154
Kenyon College, 183, 190-191
Kenyon Review, The, ix, 6, 183, 191-192, 332
Keys, Frances, 65
Khayyam, Omar, 251, 268-269
Kierkegaard, Søren, 11
Kim, 185
Kipling, Rudyard, 30, 184, 189
Kirchman, Rose, 284
Kirsch, Adam, 177
Kizer, Carolyn, 150, 219
Kondylis, Stavros, 89-91
Korwin, Yala, 284
Kumin, Maxine, x, 50
Kunitz, Stanley, 297

L

Ladies' Home Journal, The, 281-282
LaFleur, Rick, 304
Lamar University, 159, 165
Larkin, Philip, x, 6, 7, 21, 40, 41, 70, 71, 116, 154, 155, 241, 255, 315, 326-327
Lasch, Christopher, 166
Last of the Thorntons, The, 21
Lattimore, Richmond, 70, 82
Lawrence, D.H., 70, 77, 254
Lear, Edward, 64, 87
Lee's Lieutenants: A Study in Command, 12, 235
Leithauser, Brad, x, 49, 70, 88, 107-131, 205, 207, 209-210, 212, 216, 221, 225, 332

  Works: *A Few Corrections*, 122; "An Eighteenth-Century Microscope," 131; "A Science Fiction Writer of the Fifties," 117; "At Greg's," 123; *Cats of the Temple*, 116, 123; *Darlington's Fall: A Novel in Verse*, 107, 117-118, 121-122, 123; *Equal Distance*, 107, 122, 123; *Hence*, 122; *Hundreds of Fireflies*, 107, 115; "Metrical Illiteracy," 125-126, 127; "Old Bachelor Brother," 119, 123; "Old Hat," 116; *Penchants & Places*, 107, 127, 129-130; *Seaward*, 107, 122, 130; "The Confinement of Free Verse," 127; *The*

Friends of Freeland, 107, 122; "The Ghost of a Ghost," 130; *The Last Odd Thing She Did*, 107, 116, 118; "The Last Odd Thing She Did," 118; *The Norton Book of Ghost Stories*, 129; "Trauma," 119; "Two Summer Jobs," 110, 114, 116

Lem, Stanislaw, 118
Levin, Phyllis, 92
Lewis, C.S., 185, 238, 303
Lewis, Janet, 66, 70, 259
Lind, Michael, 183
Lindner, April, 47
Logan, John, 138
Logan, William, 177
London Times, The, 271, 308
Longfellow, Henry Wadsworth, 64, 121, 148
Lorca, Federico García, 289, 332
Lord of the Rings, The, 185
Louisiana State University, 1, 5, 7, 11, 14, 26, 227, 230, 232, 233, 234, 245, 259, 332
Louisiana Tech, 227, 230, 236
Lovecraft, H.P., 46
Lowell, Amy, 324, 328
Lowell, Robert, 6, 21, 50, 88, 89, 110, 111, 128, 177
Loy, Myrna, 215
Lyrical Ballads, The, 72
Lytle, Andrew, 3, 163, 235

M

MacDonald, Cynthia, 91
MacDonald, George, 87
Macdonald, Ross, 69
MacDowell Colony, The, 220-221
Mackail, J.W.H., 150
MacLeish, Archibald, 329
Madame Bovary, 253
Maio, Samuel, 277
Mallarmé, Stéphane, 323, 324
Mandelstam, Osip, 142, 210
Mantle, Mickey, 170
Martial, 140
Martin, Charles, x, 18, 26, 71, 103, 133-157, 332, 333

Works: "A Burial at Shanidar," 156; "After," 144; "A Night at the Opera," 141-142; "At Home with Psych and Eros," 141; "A Walk in the Hills above the Artists' House," 143-144, 144, 151, 152; *Catullus*, 133, 155; "Complaint of the Watchman," 141; "Death Will Do Nothing," 142, 144; "Deconstructing the Zebra," 139, 154; "Easter Sunday, 1985," 151; "Even as We Sleep," 142; "Four for Theodore Roethke," 140; "Just a Smack at Larkin," 140, 146; "Lot's Wife Looks Back," 145; *Ovid: Metamorphoses*, 133, 148-150, 152, 155; "Passages for Friday," 141, 145, 151; "Poison," 144; "Prufrock Balena," 140; "Reflections after a Dry Spell," 146; *Room for Error*, 133, 139, 332; *Starting from Sleep: New and Selected Poems*, 133, 139, 144, 153; *Steal the Bacon*, 133, 139; "The Fissure," 151; *The Poems of Catullus*, 133, 146-148; "The Two of Them," 143; "To a Reviewer," 154; *What the Darkness Proposes*, 133, 139, 143

Mason, David, 247, 334
Master of Ballantrae, The, 184
Masters, Edgar Lee, 328
Maytag, Missy, 190
McDowell, Robert, 333
McPhillips, Robert, 29
Measure: A Review of Formal Poetry, xi, 277
Mecom, Mary, 303
Mehigan, Joshua, 180, 272
Melville, Herman, 24
Mendelson, Edward, 109
Menotti, Gian Carlo, 229
Merchant, Preston, 22
Meredith, George, 323
Meredith, William, 86
Merker, Kim, 35, 36
Merrill, James, 89, 90, 91, 92-93, 96, 97, 100-101, 105, 113, 118, 166, 331
Mezey, Robert, 277
Middlebury College, 66
Middleton, David, 5, 26, 227-249, 259, 332

Works: *As Far As Light Remains*, 227; "A Quiet Reply," 239; "Azaleas in Epiphany," 244; *Beyond the Chandeleurs*, 227, 237; "Blue Essences: The 1890s," 243; *Bonfires on the Levee*, 227; "Farmyard in Winter,"

241; "For John Finlay (1941-1991)," 248; "Final Prayer," 244; "From the Journal of Branwell Brontë," 243; "Night Fears: A Lullaby," 237; "Oak Alley," 240; "On Recovering the Use of His Eyes," 245; "On the Suicide of the Chairman of the Math Department," 243, 244; *Reliquiae*, 227; *The Burning Fields*, 227, 237; "The Fiddler of Driskill Hill," 248; *The Fiddler of Driskill Hill: Poems of Louisiana North and South*, 248; *The Habitual Peacefulness of Gruchy: Poems After Pictures by Jean-François Millet*, 227, 237, 241-243; *The Language of the Heart*, 227; "The Maker in Lent," 237-238; "The Old Bank in Saline," 229; "The South," 239-240; *The Undivided Realm*, 227; *Under the Linden Tree*, 227

Middleton, Francine, 233, 234, 235, 236, 238-239
Millay, Edna St. Vincent, 281
Miller, Arthur, 18
Millet, Jean-François, 241-243
Milton, John, 78, 110, 189, 197, 218, 245, 247, 253, 271, 329
Miscellany, The, 163
Mitchell, Joni, 230
Montale, Eugenio, 35
Moore, Demi, 169
Moore, Marianne, 120
Moore, Merrill, 156
Moore, Richard, 146
Moskowitz, Alfred, 277, 282-283, 284, 285, 291, 294
Mother Goose, 64
Mount Holyoke College, 107, 128, 205, 210, 218, 225
Movie-Going, 87
Mozart, Wolfgang Amadeus, 2
Murdoch, Iris, 188
Mussolini, Benito, 328

N
Nabokov, Vladimir, 35
Nemerov, Howard, x, 5, 6, 7, 15, 20, 21, 24, 26, 48, 112, 146, 324, 331, 332, 333
Neruda, Pablo, 332
New Age, The, 324
New Criterion, The, 332

New Critics, The, 177
New Republic, The, 133
New York Review of Books, The, 115, 127
New York School Poets, The, 40, 326, 331
New York Times, The, 107, 115
New Yorker, The, 1
Newman, John Cardinal, 137
Nicholls State University, 227, 233-234, 235
Nims, John Frederick, 86, 247
Notre Dame College of Staten Island, 133, 138

O
O'Brien, Tim, 18
O'Connor, Flannery, 38
O'Connor, Frank, 83
Odyssey, The, 32, 189, 196
Ohio State University, 251, 272
Oldtown Folks, 68
Olson, Charles, 138
On Music, 274
Ortiz, Theodore, 30
Orwell, George, 64
O.S.S., 88
Othello, 67
Out of the South, 179
Ovid, 311
Owen, Wilfred, 126
Oxford Book of Sonnets, The, 127
Oxford Companion to Twentieth-Century Poetry, The, 94
Oxford University, 183, 188, 189, 190, 195, 299, 305-306, 308
Ozsváth, Zsuzsanna, 200-201

P
Paradise Lost, 78, 81, 218, 253
Parker, Dorothy, 326
Peacock, Molly, 91
Peich, Michael, xi, 29, 35, 36, 57-58, 82, 334
Percy, Walker, 5, 11, 14, 16
Perspective, 26
Peters, Cheri, 19
Petrarch, 266

Phillips, Anne, 66
Picasso, Pablo, 326
Pinkerton, Helen, 71
Pivot, 334
Ploughshares, 1
Poe, Edgar Allan, 30, 46, 69, 303
Poetry Magazine, 74, 277, 324, 333
Pope, Alexander, 67, 170
Pöppel, Ernst, 192, 332
Porter, Cole, 129
Pound, Ezra, xi, 26, 31, 32, 40, 67, 75-76, 135, 142, 149-150, 154, 232, 247, 323-325, 326, 327, 328-329
Powow River Poets, The, 277, 285-286
PR Review, 26
Prelude, The, 94, 100, 253
Presentation Piece, 71
Pride and Prejudice, 87
Princess and the Goblin, The, 87
Princeton University, 85, 92
Prisoner of Zenda, The, 51
Prunty, Wyatt, xi, 1-28, 70, 71, 82, 232, 259, 332, 333, 334

> Works: "A Baseball Team of Unknown Navy Pilots, Pacific Theater, 1945," 11; "A Child's Christmas in Georgia, 1953," 11; "A Note of Thanks," 14; *Balance as Belief*, 8; "Balloons," 8; "Elderly Lady Crossing on Green," 14; "Extravagant Love," 6; "Falling through the Ice," 10, 11; "Haying," 10; "Husband," 11; "Late Fall, Late Light," 28; "Learning the Bicycle," 8, 9, 10; "March," 10; "New Territory," 10; "Oh General, Oh Spy, Oh Bureaucrat," 11; "Reading Before We Read, Horoscope and Weather," 10; *Run of the House*, 1; *Since the Noon Mail Stopped*, 1; *Sewanee Writers on Writing*, 1; "The Actuarial Wife," 14; "The Kite," 8; *The Time Between*, 8; *Unarmed and Dangerous: New and Selected Poems*, 1, 8; *"Fallen from the Symboled World": Precedents for the New Formalism*, 1, 7, 23, 26, 334; "Water," 8

Psaropoulos, John, 299, 307, 312, 318-319, 320

Q

Queens College, 283
Queensboro College, 133, 138, 154
Quinn, Alice, 95

R

Radnóti, Miklós, 200-201
Ransom, John Crowe, 3, 5, 6, 25, 171, 178, 236, 237, 299, 320
Ransom, Julie, 320
Reaper, The, 333
Rebel Angels, 334
Reign of Wonder, The, 254
Return of the Native, The, 171
Rexroth, Kenneth, 190
Rhodes, Eugene Manlove, 68
Rhyme's Reason, 103
Richards, I. A., 83
Richman, Robert, 333
Ricks, Christopher, 211
Riley, James Whitcomb, 30
Rilke, Rainer Maria, 92
Rimbaud, Arthur, 323
Roach, Susan, 236
Roberts, Kenneth, 69
Robinson, Edwin Arlington, x, 3, 5, 26, 49, 50, 70, 72, 74, 83, 163, 171, 327
Rodrigo, Joaquin, 289
Roethke, Theodore, 6, 40, 112
Rossetti, Dante Gabriel, 271
Rowling, J.K., 223
Rubaiyat, The, 257, 268-269
Rummonds, Gabriel, 36
Rutgers University, Newark, 85, 103

S

Said, Edward, 34
Sale, Arthur, 211
Salerni, Paul, 60
Salter, Mary Jo, 88, 107, 114, 128, 205-226, 332, 333

> Works: "A Benediction," 214, 215; "Advent," 216; *A Kiss in Space*, 205, 219, 222; "Another Session," 213; *A Phone Call to*

the Future, 205; *Are You Sleeping Yet?*, 223; "Argument," 214; *Falling Bodies*, 205, 218; "For an Italian Cousin," 219-220; "Frost at Midnight," 218-219; *Henry Purcell in Japan*, 205, 212, 217, 219; "June: The Gianicolo," 226; "Marco Polo," 213; "Night Thoughts," 217; *Open Shutters*, 205, 212-213, 222; *Rooms of Light*, 225; *Sunday Skaters*, 205, 213, 218, 222; "Tanker," 217; "The Age of Reason," 216; "The Hand of Thomas Jefferson," 218-219; *The Moon Comes Home*, 205, 223; *The Norton Anthology of Poetry*, 205, 224; "The Twelfth Year," 214; "The Upper Story," 224; "Trompe l'Oeil," 212-213; "Unfinished Business," 223; *Unfinished Painting*, 205, 206, 219; "Video Blues," 215, 222

Sandburg, Carl, 64, 162
Sappho, 143, 148, 149, 150
Sayles, John, 69
Schmitt, Richard, 21
Schoerke, Meg, 61
Schopenhauer, Arthur, 11
Schuett, Stacey, 223
Schulman, Grace, 85
Seneca, 60, 72
Sequoia, 31, 37
Serling, Rod, 130
Seth, Vikram, 49, 70
Sewanee Review, The, 3, 4, 26, 163, 236
Sewanee Writers' Conference, xi, 1, 8, 18, 19, 82, 107, 146, 205, 333
Sewanee Writers Series, 20
Shakespeare, William, x, 2, 10, 21, 22, 52, 65, 70, 78, 81, 93, 102, 103, 162, 169, 185, 188, 189, 203, 207, 211, 247, 248, 254
Sharp, Ron, 191, 332
Shaw, Robert, 32, 71, 88
Shelley, Percy Bysshe, 64
Siam, 21
Sidney, Philip, 70, 78
Simon and Garfunkel, 230
Simpson, Lewis P., 231
Simpson, Louis, 103
Sissman, L.E., 118
Smart, Christopher, 329

Smith, Adam, 201
Smith, William Jay, 37, 155
Snodgrass, W.D., 71, 112
Sondheim, Stephen, 129
Sor Juana Inés de la Cruz, 289, 294
Sound and Sense, 103
Southern Literary Festival, 234-235
Southern Review, The, 1, 5, 26, 32, 69, 230-231, 232, 333
Southwest Review, The, 144
Southwest Texas State University, 159, 165, 166
Sparrow, 333
Spender, Stephen, 210
Spenser, Edmund, 23, 78
Spielberg, Steven, 38
Stafford, William, 327
Stall, Lindon, 230, 232
Stallings, A. E., xi, 101, 180, 299-322
  Works: "A Postcard from Greece," 321-322; *Archaic Smile*, 299, 307, 310; "Bad News Blues," 315; "Burned," 312; "Country Song," 312; "Crazy to Hear the Tale Again," 307; *De Rerum Natura (The Nature of Things)*, 299, 316, 319; "Deus Ex Machina," 315; "Dinosaur Fever," 312; "Explaining an Affinity for Bats," 315; "Ghost Ship," 315; "Hades Welcomes His Bride," 310; *Hapax*, 299, 310, 315; "Lovejoy Street," 312; *Olives*, 299, 310; "Persephone to Psyche," 311; "The Argument," 313-314

Stallworthy, Jon, 223
Stanford, Donald, 5, 230-231, 233, 236, 259, 332
Stanford University, 29, 31, 32, 34, 35, 36, 37, 46, 63, 66, 67, 69, 189, 332
State University of New York, Buffalo, 133, 137-138, 149
Stefanile, Felix, 333
Steele, Robert, 112
Steele, Timothy, x, 23, 32, 46, 63-84, 231, 246-247, 259, 332, 333, 334
  Works: *All the Fun's in How You Say a Thing: An Explanation of Meter and Versification*, 63, 77, 80, 83; "An Aubade," 71; "Baker Beach at Sunset," 72; *The Color Wheel*, 63, 71; "1816," 72; "Eros,"

71; "Golden Age," 69; "Home is Here," 69; "Janet," 79-80; "Last Night As You Slept," 71; "Learning to Skate," 72; "Love Poem," 71; Messenger," 69, 72; *Missing Measures: Modern Poetry and the Revolt against Meter,* 63, 73, 75, 77, 81, 83, 246-247, 333; "Old Letters," 84; "The Poems of J. V. Cunningham," 63; "Sapphics Against Anger," 72; *Sapphics against Anger and Other Poems,* 63, 69, 71, 84; *Sapphics and Uncertainties: Poems, 1970-1986,* 63; "The Skimming Stone," 79; "Snapshots for Posterity," 69; *Uncertainties and Rest,* 63, 69, 70, 71, 332

Steinbeck, John, 64
Steiner, George, 150, 211
Stephens, Phil, 7, 19, 22
Stevens, Wallace, 40, 41, 42, 47, 54, 70, 78, 92, 96
Stevenson, Anne, 92
Stevenson, Robert Louis, 64, 184
Stewart, Jimmy, 216
Sting, 169
Stokesbury, Leon, 169
Stone, Robert, 18
Stoppard, Tom, 226
Stowe, Harriet Beecher, 68
Strand, Mark, 15
Stravinsky, Igor, 274
Strong Measures, 333
Swenson, May, 112
Swift, Jonathan, 111
Swinburne, Algernon, 323
Swiss Family Robinson, The, 185
Symbolists, The, 323, 324

T

Tallis, Thomas, 246
Tanner, Tony, 254
Tartuffe, 208
Tate, Allen, 3, 6, 15, 17, 25, 231, 236, 237
Taylor, Henry, 216
Taylor, Peter, 2, 14, 28
Teasdale, Sara, 281
Tehran University, 255
Tennessee Quarterly, The, 334

Tennyson, Alfred Lord, 64, 93-94, 109, 303
Thomas, Dylan, 12, 207, 229, 232, 233
Tibullus, 102
Time, 127
Times Literary Supplement, 92
Todd, Richard, 212
Tolkien, J.R.R., 88, 303
Treasure Island, 184
Trimpi, Wesley, 67
Troilus and Criseyde, 272
Trollope, Anthony, 69
Trujillo, Rafael, 277, 278
Tuck, Lily, 21
Tufariello, Catherine, 180, 272
Turco, Lew, 173, 178, 332
Turner, Frederick, xi, 183-204, 332
  Works: *April Wind and Other Poems,* 183; *Beauty: The Value of Values,* 183; *Foamy Sky: The Major Poems of Miklós Radnóti,* 183, 200-201; *Genesis,* 195, 196; "Habits," 196-197; *Hadean Eclogues,* 183; "In the Villa Adriana," 204; *Natural Classicism: Essays on Literature and Science,* 183; "O Ancient Prisons," 200; *Paradise: Selected Poems,* 183; *Shakespeare and the Nature of Time,* 183, 188, 192; *The Culture of Hope: A New Birth of the Classical Spirit,* 183; *The Garden,* 183, 191; "The Kite," 197; "The Mei Lin Effect," 195; "The Neural Lyre: Poetic Meter, the Brain, and Time," 192-195, 332-333; *The New World,* 183, 195, 196; *The Prayers of Dallas,* 198; "To All My Friends," 196; *Shakespeare's Twenty-first Century Economics: The Morality of Love and Money,* 183

Twichell, Chase, 44
Twilight Zone, The, 45-46, 130

U

Uncle Remus, 301
University of Alabama, Tuscaloosa, 44, 232
University of Arkansas, 159, 164, 176
University of California, Berkeley, 206
University of California, Los Angleles, 63
University of California, Santa Barbara, 63, 183, 190, 251, 258, 259, 264, 272

Index

University of Evansville, 227, 334
University of Georgia, 1, 299, 304, 305, 306
University of Iceland, 107
University of Manchester, 251, 257-258
University of Pennsylvania, 323
University of Texas, Austin, 305
University of Texas, Dallas, 183
University of the South, The, 1, 3, 4, 8, 21, 22, 333
University of Vermont, 63, 65
Untermeyer, Louis, 135, 282
Updike, John, 107, 120

V

Valéry, Paul, 92
Van Duyn, Mona, 6, 18, 21, 48, 333
Vendler, Helen, 115
Verse, 29
Villon, François, 163
Virgil, 32, 189, 295, 305
Virginia Polytechnic Institute, 1, 7
Vorticism, 324, 328

W

Wabash College, 323
Wagoner, David, 112
Walcott, Derek, ix, x, 18, 50, 197, 220
Walker, Ted, 112
Walzer, Kevin, 202, 334
Warren, Robert Penn, 15, 25, 235, 236, 237
Waste Land, The, 75-76, 136, 325
Watkins, Ed, 191
Weekly World News, 179
West Chester University, 29, 334
Western Wind, 247
Whigham, Peter, 150
Whitehead, Jim, 165, 332
Whitman, Walt, 15, 224, 247, 323
Wilbur, Richard, x, 6, 15, 16, 21, 26, 48, 49, 50, 51, 58, 70, 71, 81, 112, 128, 154, 159, 163, 173, 177, 208, 210-211, 214, 223, 296-297, 298, 309, 314, 316, 331, 334
Wilde, Oscar, 142
Williams, Miller, 165, 176, 332

Williams, Sonny, 202
Williams, Tennessee, 8, 18
Williams, William Carlos, 70, 76, 324, 327, 331
Williamson, Greg, 7, 20, 22
Wilmer, Clive, 235-236
Winters, Yvor, 5, 66, 67, 135, 230, 231, 232, 237, 254, 259, 332
Wittgenstein, Ludwig, 263
Wordsworth, William, 56, 73, 94, 146
Writer's Digest, 167
Writing Metrical Poetry, xi
Wyatt, Sir Thomas, 2, 254

Y

Yale Review, The, 1, 299
Yates, David, 166
Yeats, William Butler, x, 23, 40, 43, 60, 76, 80, 81, 93, 109, 111, 189, 228, 323, 327
Yost, Chryss, 61

Z

Zodiac, The, 178

www.ingramcontent.com/pod-product-compliance
Lightning Source LLC
Chambersburg PA
CBHW021149230426
43667CB00006B/312